AYURVEDA

AYURVEDA

A WAY OF LIFE

Dr. Vinod Verma

SAMUEL WEISER, INC.

York Beach, Maine

First published in 1995 by
Samuel Weiser, Inc.
Box 612
York Beach, Maine 03910–0612

Library of Congress Cataloging-in-Publication Data
Verma, Vinod.
    [Ayurveda. English]
    Ayurveda : a way of life / by Dr. Vinod Verma.
       p.   cm.
    Includes bibliographical references and index.
    1. Health. 2. Medicine, Ayurvedic. 3. Self-care, Health.
I. Title.
RA776.5.V4613 1995   95-15228
615.5'3—dc20   CIP

ISBN 0-87728-822-4
MV

Typeset in 11 point Baskerville

Printed in the United States of America

02 01 00 99 98
10 9 8 7 6 5 4 3

This book is dedicated to
my Ayurveda Guru

Acharya Priya Vrat Sharma

Without his guidance and his tremendous work
on Ayurveda—specifically on the pharmacological properties of Ayurvedic products—it would
not have been possible to write this book.

TABLE OF CONTENTS

Philosophical aspects, Sāṃkhya and Yoga, concept
of Karma, Karma and Ayurveda, the body—a microcosm, Tridoṣa—or the Three Humors, the evolution
of Ayurveda.

Understanding the humor theory, the Three Humors, humoral patterns, the environment and the
humors, Ayurvedic terms.

Health in relation to color, form, sensation, and
smell. Examination of stool, urine, sweat, breath,
body temperature, pulse, general appearance, eyes.

Cleansing: mouth, teeth, tongue, nasal passages,
eyes, skin, hands and feet, head, hair, vagina, internal
purifications, unction or fat cures, fomentation or
sweating treatments, emetics, enemas, purging.

FOREWORD

Ayurveda deals with life in its totality. It concerns not only the body but the mind and the soul. The body, mind, and soul are the three limbs upon which the three-dimensional therapy of Ayurveda–the physical, mental, and spiritual–stands. Ayurveda has a holistic view of life and health care practices. Perfect health can only be achieved when body, mind, and soul are in harmony with each other and with the cosmic surroundings.

The second dimension in this holistic view of Ayurveda is the social level. It not only pays attention to the personal wellbeing of an individual, but also tells us the ways and means of establishing harmony with and in society. The life of any individual at the social level can be good or bad, and at the personal level it can be happy or unhappy. A good life is beneficial for the wellbeing of the society and a bad life is the opposite. A healthy person is happy and a sick person is unhappy.

The three-humor theory of Ayurveda is based upon the law of the uniformity of Nature; e.g., the same laws apply to the human body as to the rest of the cosmos. The three humors, or vital forces, of the body are not only responsible for physiological functions, but also for mental activities and human behavior. In fact, there is an interaction between the body humors and mental qualities (*guṇas*). Therefore, in Ayurveda, therapy is determined by considering body and mind in their totality, and not by dividing the body in terms of its parts.

Ayurveda lays special emphasis on the individual constitution, which varies from person to person. Thus, the analysis of health and the therapeutic method is decided according to the person's basic constitution. In fact, Ayurvedic methods of health care are devised to help nature take its course to restore physical and mental balance. Mental equilibrium is sought by bringing in harmony the three qualities of the mind—the *sattva, rajas,* and *tamas.* In Ayurveda, the cure does not mean suppressing the symptoms of an ailment, but actually restoring harmony to the body.

Ayurveda believes that the state of health is a normal condition and therapy should be based upon reestablishing this natural state through appropriate nutrition, drugs, exercise, etc. That is why the therapy in Ayurveda is also called *prakrtisthapan* (reestablishing nature), meaning that therapy is used to restore the normal state.

Ayurveda is an integral part of Indian culture. Indian cooking is based on Ayurvedic principles. It dominates the routine of everyday life and plays a part in customs and rituals. Even leisure time and holidays are planned so people do not fall sick with the stress and strain of time.

Dr. Vinod Verma has understood the soul of Ayurveda, and with extensive study and practical experience, she has enlarged her horizon of wisdom. Her research has led her to add two more purification practices, diuresis and blood-purifying, to the classical five—the *Panchakarma*—and thereby it may be named *Saptakarma* (the seven practices).

Dr. Verma provides an understanding of the true message of Ayurveda and its holistic approach to health. This book is an excellent example of her contribution to this field. Through her lucid writing, she has made it possible to use Ayurvedic wisdom in modern lives.

I congratulate her for this great achievement and it is my desire that in the sacred *yajna* of Ayurveda, her sacrificial offerings may always burn to enlighten the world with wisdom so we can maintain and achieve perfect health.

—Priya Vrat Sharma

NOTE TO READER

The information provided in this book is not intended to re-place the service of a physician. The material is presented for educational purposes and for self-help. The author and the publishers are in no way responsible for any medical claims re-garding the material presented.

To use herbal or other remedial formulas described in this book for commercial purposes requires permission from the author. Write to the author in care of the publisher for more informa-tion.

PREFACE

There is a lot of new interest in the Indian wisdom—Ayurveda (the science of life). This body of knowledge—usually considered exclusively to be a medical discipline—is even discussed in the media in Western countries. The renewal of this interest coincides with a general transition taking place in the world. The shift in our value system is evident from the number of health and ecological movements, and in the modern search for spiritual consciousness.

Ayurveda is a stream of knowledge like the other Vedas[1] and it is said that its existence is as old as we are. It is considered to be eternal as no one knows when it was not there. Ayurveda does not deal only with disease and its cure, but with life in general, so that people can have a better quality of life as well as longevity. According to *Caraka Saṃhitā*, the most well-known and complete treatise on this discipline, Ayurveda is defined as "that which deals with good-bad, happy-unhappy [aspects of] life, promoters and non-promoters [of life] and their nature and measurements."[2] *Ayus* is further defined as the conjunction of body, sense organs, mind, and soul. When this conjunction ends, life finishes. Thus, the word *ayus* means life.

Ayurveda is a science of life. If you wish to know about Ayurveda and want to follow this path, you must begin with the

---

[1]Vedas are the books of wisdom of ancient India. There are four principal Vedas, namely: *Ṛg Veda, Yajur Veda, Sām Veda, Atharva Veda.*
[2]*Caraka Saṃhitā, Sūtrasthana,* I, 41. Translations from ancient texts are mine.

understanding that this science of life is based upon sound philosophical concepts about our being and our relationship to this
universe. Here, you are not dealing with a set of rules and do's
and don'ts to be followed: therefore it is essential to understand
the principles which form the basis of Ayurvedic practices.

While using any system of medicine, your main concern
should be to search for life-promoting methods, preventive
measures to ward off diseases and, in case of an ailment, the use
of correct medication (which cures and also spares the individual from side-effects), and other curative aids. We should not be
fanatic about any system of medicine, nor should we reject totally any prevailing system. Many effective methods from various systems of medicine can be complementary to each other.

Modern medicine is concerned primarily about disease and
is not concerned about health. Medical research is directed toward finding cures for diseases, but there is little talk about finding methods to maintain good health and adopting preventive
measures to avoid various ailments. Healthy living and preventive
measures are not a part of the medical education. In Ayurveda,
the principal focus is on maintaining good health and adopting a
healthy way of living. The second important drawback in our
modern system of Western medicine is that it treats all human beings the same way. Individual differences and individual constitutions are not taken into consideration. We differ as much inwardly
in our reactions and responses to a given treatment as we vary in
our external appearance and personality traits. In Ayurveda, individual variations are taken into consideration and health care and
treatment are based upon the individual constitution.

Before beginning to use this book, it is important to realize
that Ayurveda's concept of body is different from the concepts
prevalent in modern medicine. Ayurveda does not dichotomize
body and mind, and neither is the body viewed as a machine
that can be analyzed in terms of its parts. In fact, when one
speaks of the body in Ayurveda, it also includes mind, because
this word is used to denote our physical, destructible self, differ-
entiated from soul. Soul is indestructible, without substance, a
form of energy. Mind is considered as a sixth sense. Body, mind,
and soul form a living being. Soul is the real "self" of an individual and is the cause of consciousness. Body and mind form
the physical part of a being and cannot exist without soul. This

energy or soul is, in turn, linked to the universal soul, or cosmic energy. In Ayurveda, the living body (a person) is not considered as an independent entity. Biological, mental, spiritual, and cosmic activities are interdependent and interrelated. Therefore, in Ayurveda, ailments and malfunctions are treated in the context of an individual's social, cultural, and spiritual environment and cosmic link. For example, the primary human constitution depends upon the relative proportion of the three humors which maintain the integrity of the body and are responsible for all physical and mental functions. These three humors are derived from the five fundamental or material elements (ether, air, fire, water, earth) which form the material reality of this universe. You will see, during the course of this book, that principles which govern the cosmos are also applicable at the biological level. Thus, the approach to health care in Ayurveda is very different from modern allopathic medicine.

In Ayurveda physical or chemical intervention is not enough for curing an ailment. Health is harmony within oneself and with one's environment. Treatment is based upon these principles. To cure is to re-establish this harmony, and it necessitates several other steps in addition to the administration of drugs. You will see that in this book there are many more health instructions than drug recipes. In fact, you will find that both are integrated in various chapters. The formulas or recipes for making various medicines are not meant to be used independently without following the general health instructions.

Ayurveda is an extensive and vast source of knowledge. This book is only an introductory guide to the Ayurvedic way of life. I describe day-to-day practices and what we can do for ourselves in order to keep good health and bring harmony in our lives. Various methods for developing sensitivity to the body and its surroundings, for self-diagnosis, for curing minor ailments through simple measures, for preventing disease, for making simple herbal medicines, and for inner and outer cleaning of the body are discussed here. Every practical detail is explained and information about the availability of various products is provided. Ayurvedic medicines are not limited to the herbs that grow in India (especially in the Himalayas) where the original literature of Ayurveda was compiled. Identification of the herbs according to taste and other properties of the drugs are explained in detail. The drugs in Ayurveda are not time- and space-bound. As Ayurveda traveled to South India and Sri Lanka, many local herbs and minerals were added. Similarly, many drugs were added in Ayurvedic literature from Greece and the Middle East.

This book is written to help people become conscious of their health—to make them aware that a little care can save them from minor health problems, as well as from long-term health hazards. With the increasing number of ailments and a universal rise in health care costs, it has become more and more essential for each individual to make a personal effort to maintain good health. The old wisdom of *rsis* (sages) teaches us the use of preventive measures and mild medicine for maintaining good health instead of waiting until body and mind are exhausted and there are major disorders in the organism.

The purpose of this book is not only to reveal the knowledge of Ayurveda, for that has been done in many books recently published on the subject. My principal effort is to present methods people can use to improve the quality of life. For this, it is essential to begin from a new beginning. First of all, we have to see where our modern civilization has brought us in terms of our mental state and our way of living. We live our lives in bits and pieces, fragmented in time, space, body, and mind. Therefore, to adapt Ayurveda in our lives, we just cannot start the application of its principles on our disintegrated beings. What I mean by a new beginning is that first we need to see and feel ourselves as "whole," as a "unit," and an "integrity" and then we can realize our oneness with the cosmos. Holistic medicine is not possible without a holistic way of life. This book is presented in a way that will make us self-aware so we can realize our integrity as body, mind, and soul.

This book is written for general readers who may not have any background of Ayurveda or medicine in general. A special effort has been made to explain the technical terms in an easy-to-understand manner. Comments and suggestions from readers are welcomed.

—Dr. V. Verma
The New Way Health Organization (NOW)
A–130, Sector 26,
Noida 201301, UP, India

ACKNOWLEDGMENTS

This book has required many years of research and extensive traveling in various parts of India. I am grateful to all those who assisted me in this endeavor. This wide array of people includes professors in various Ayurvedic colleges, physicians, and villagers who gave me a warm welcome and generously shared their wisdom of Ayurveda with me. I especially extend my warm thanks to the late Mr. J. P. Kundalia of Ranari and his family, and the summer inhabitants of Gangotri in Gharwal, Himalayas, for assisting me in every possible way.

This work was written during the time when the Delhi Center of NOW (The New Way Health Organization) in Noida was under construction, and I am particularly grateful to my generous friend, Naresh Jhanji, and my two brothers, Rajesh and Kuldeep, who helped me with the ordeals of construction and let me devote my time to writing.

I am indebted to Dr. Kapila Vatsyayan who has been extremely generous with her immense knowledge of all aspects of Indian tradition and medicine, and who has been a constant guide.

My warmest thanks to Eckhard Biermann and Andrea Wolff-Biermann, who provided me with a home in Freiburg, and to Nancy Meyerson-Hess in Munich. Without their assistance, it would not have been possible to write this book. Financial assistance from Dietlind Sieker is also gratefully acknowledged.

I graciously thank Dr. Elmar R. Gruber for helping me in every way during the course of researching this book; Mahendra Kulshrestha and Catherine Singh for generously devoting their time to editing and giving valuable suggestions.

I am thankful to my nephew and niece, Abhinav and Gayatri, for all their help with the photographs of the yogāsanas.

The German edition appeared in 1992, and Spanish, Italian, French and Hindi editions have followed. I am grateful to all my students in Europe for giving me encouragment and feedback on this theme. This has led me to make some additions in this American edition, especially regarding the humor theory which is difficult for the Western mind to understand.

I am grateful to my American publisher for bringing out this English edition which will help spread the message of health care in the English-speaking world. There has been a great demand for this edition in my own country, and besides, I write in the English language, so the English edition is close to my heart.

PRONUNCIATION OF SANSKRIT

There are different ways to pronounce Sanskrit words, and here we will list the alphabet, the vowels and the consonants. The accents that have been carried in this text indicate the special ways that this phonetic language is pronounced.

The Alphabet

a ā, i ī, u ū, ṛ r̄, ḷ, e ai, o au
k kh g gh ṅ
c ch j jh ñ
ṭ ṭh ḍ ḍh ṇ
t th d dh n
p ph b bh m
y r l v
ś ṣ s
h
ṃ
ḥ

Vowels

a—a in America or o in come
ā—a in far or in father
i—i in pit or in pin
ī—ee in feel or i in machine
u—u in put or pull

ū—u in rule
ṛ—properly *ur*, but by modern Hindus as *ri* in river or in writ.
Ṛta (*Rita*), *Ṛg Veda* (*Rig Veda*), *Prakṛti* (*Prakriti*), *Kṛṣṇa* (*Krishna*).
e—ay in say or a in made
ai—i in rite or ai in aisle
o—o in go
au—ou in loud

Consonants

Consonants are pronounced approximately as in English, except for the following:

g—g in gun or in get (always "hard")
c—ch in church
sh (ś, ṣ)—sh in sheet or in shun

When *h* is combined with another consonant (e.g., th, bh), it is aspirated: *th* as in boathouse; *ph* as in uphill, etc. The palatal ñ is like the Spanish señor (jña, however, is pronounced most often by modern Hindus as "gyah," with a hard g).

As a city manager is cautious in the duties of the city, and a charioteer in those of the chariot, a wise person should be cautious in duties relating to the body. An axle fitted in a vehicle endowed with essential qualities carries on and perishes in time by depreciation of its normal limit; similarly, the lifespan of the body of a human being gets its end after the normal limit. Such a death is known as timely. Just as the same axle gets destroyed on the way due to an overload, uneven road, want of a road, breaking of the wheels, defects in the vehicle or driver, separation of a bolt, lack of lubrication or being thrown, similarly, the lifespan of a human comes to end in the middle due to over-exertion, a diet not in accordance to one's nature, irregular meals, complicated body postures, over-indulgence in sexual intercourse, the company of ignoble persons, suppression of impelled urges, non-suppression of suppressible urges, infliction by an organism, poisonous winds and fire, injury, or the avoidance of food and medicaments.

—Caraka, Sixth century B.C.

1

INTRODUCTION TO
AYURVEDIC CONCEPTS

THE FIRST HISTORICAL documents concerning Ayurveda are found in the *Ṛg Veda* and *Atharva Veda*, two of the four principal Vedas (or books of wisdom) of ancient India. The word "*veda*" literally means knowledge. There are diverse opinions about the period when the four Vedas—namely *Ṛg*, *Yajur*, *Sām* and *Atharva*—were written. Some historians believe that the Vedas were written by the Āryans who arrived in India about 2000 B.C. from Eastern Europe and Central Asia and conquered the people of the Indus civilization.[1] On the other hand, it is argued that the Āryans were pastoral people and could not have acquired a mastery over language to write in such a sophisticated style and on diverse subjects shortly after conquering the Indus people. In fact, before the ruins of the Indus civilization were discovered (only about seventy years ago), it was believed that the Āryans encountered only tribal people when they invaded India. However, the recent researches on the Indus civilization have shown that not only was this civilization highly advanced but a cultural continuity exists from those days to present-day India.[2] Therefore, it is difficult to assert whether the Vedic knowledge was a continuity from the Indus civilization or the Vedas were written later. In the former case, we may assume that they are 3500 to 5000 years old.

Ṛg Veda makes various references to the medicinal and healing arts, whereas *Atharva Veda* is a source-book of Ayurveda

---

[1] A. L. Basham, *The Wonder that was India* (London: Fontana Books, 1967), p. 29.
[2] Mircea Eliade, *Yoga: Immortality and Freedom*, translated by Willard R. Trask, Bollingen Series LVI (Princeton, N.J.: Princeton University Press, 1958, 1969), pp. 353–358.

which was *later* written as a separate Veda. "Atharvan" means fire (also light–the sun god). *Atharva Veda* gives instructions to counteract disease and calamities. It is not exclusively a treatise on medicine as it also deals with other aspects of life, such as the material, social, political aspects, etc. It deals with the following aspects of health care: 1) food and digestion; 2) ways to increase intellect; 3) ways to get rid of ailments and knowledge about medicinal plants; 4) ways of maintaining good health and longevity; 5) instructions for getting rid of bad character and acquiring a pleasant character and personality. It is worth mentioning that the system of health care described in the *Atharva Veda* is very strongly oriented toward using the power of "self" (*ātmaśakti*) and using it for autosuggestion and healing. In ancient times, the *ṛṣis* (sages) believed very strongly in using inner power, along with precautionary measures and remedies, to cure oneself.

While looking at the treatise on medicine, which was written several thousands of years ago, we must be considerate in our judgment as this was written to suit the lifestyle of the people who lived at that time. There are instructions for saving oneself from enemies, ghosts, and maladies, and various ways of fighting back with these are described. In fact, the shift from one of these to another is so sudden that one tends to think that a malady was treated like an enemy or vice versa. Probably, there were frequent fights between various tribal groups during those days and such instructions were very important. Let us now examine some of the aspects concerning health care described in this Veda. There are some strongly suggestive methods that are apparently meant to cure a patient by altering his/her psychological state.

> . . . I destroy your ailments linked to the urinary system. May the held up urine in you come out! . . . Oh suffering human, I take away your ailments. May the held up urine come out from your body. . . . Your stopped urine may come out making noise. That urine which is held up in your bladder covered with urinary tubes, may that come out soon making a sound. The way one paves the way to bring out water from a river, similarly I pave the way for bringing out your urine. May all your accumulated urine come out. To take out water from a sea, lake or a pond, a way is made. Similarly, I have opened a doorway of your bladder in order to let your held up urine out. May all your urine come out making noise. The

way an arrow goes toward its target after being left from the bow, similarly, all your held up urine may come out making a sound.[3]

Atharva Veda is the first written document on the concept of three humors. Later, this theory took a very sophisticated form through constant experience and experimentations. During vedic times, the medical descriptions were associated with prayers to the forces of nature.

> Oh Sun, let us be free from the diseases born out of three humors (*tridoṣa*). . . . Oh Sun, let this individual be free from headache and diseases related to *kapha* which has penetrated each part of the body (of the individual). Let this individual be free from *kapha* born out of rain and water; *vāta*, born from air; and fevers, etc. caused due to deformation of *pitta*. May these groups of maladies leave the individual and go to forests and lonely mountains.[4]

There are mantras for a smooth delivery which are addressed to the god *Pusa*–the god of delivery. "Oh *Pusa* god, let the womb be free from placenta. We also open the way to the womb for a smooth delivery. Oh god of delivery, be kind and let the joints of a pregnant woman loose. Oh *Sutī*, the god of wind, let the mouth of the uterus be downward to inspire it (the uterus). Oh delivering woman, this placenta will not make you healthy. This placenta is not related to your flesh, bones, skin, etc.; it is only worth throwing. . . . Oh pregnant woman, I widen your womb's outlet for letting the baby out. . . . The way wind and mind go with fast speed, the way birds move around swiftly in the sky without any restriction, similarly, oh ten months wombed baby, you come out with the placenta and let this placenta fall out."[5]

In the context of curing fevers, it is further added that pain-giving fevers that render life difficult are born out of fire. By sprinkling hot water on the sacrificial fire, the fevers are requested to go back to their place of origin–the fire. There is a description of different types of fevers including malaria. These fevers are all requested to go out from the body of the sick and

---

[3] *Atharva Veda*, I, 3.
[4] *Atharva Veda* I, 12.
[5] *Atharva Veda* I, 11.

are saluted in farewell. Perhaps all these mantras were accompanied by complicated ceremonies performed during those days by Ayurvedic physicians cum priests (vaidyas and pandits).

We see that maladies were treated with respect, and were requested to go out of the body. Drugs were given the status of gods in *Atharva Veda*.[6] It must be remembered that the word "god" in ancient India is used to describe the different forces of nature. Anything which is powerful, effective, friendly, and which helps could get the designation of a god. For example, all the five elements of the *Prakṛti* (cosmic substance)—earth, fire, water, air, and space were gods, and so were the stars, planets, trees, and rivers. Later in evolution, these gods acquired human forms or sometimes merged with animals. Animals and plants, rivers, lakes and seas, mountains and stones, sun, moon, stars, planets, etc., were all integrated into human life. They were properly gratified through prayers. Many of these practices are still followed, although modernization has altered the consciousness about nature's gratitude. In fact, the millions of gods known from this still-surviving ancient Hindu culture denote various forms of energy in nature. Humans form a relationship of harmony, respect, and gratitude toward them. It is a way of expressing gratitude to nature for all it gives while at the same time respecting its strength and integrity.

In *Atharva Veda*, the medicinal plants are described in detail with their characteristics and specific roles in a cure. "Full of vitality, oh *Haridre*! (Curcuma), you are the best of all medicines, like the sun and the moon during the day and night respectively."[7] Further, there is a grouping of the medicinal plants which cure various skin diseases (I, 24). There are descriptions of diseases like hepatitis, malaria, typhoid, tuberculosis, epilepsy, etc., and also anatomical details of the human body are described (II, 33). We will not go into the details of these descriptions as they are primarily of historical interest for us now. The most important aspect of this Veda is the dynamism and force of the language used in suggestive and ceremonial healing. I cite below what I call the antibiotic mantras of *Atharva Veda*.

---

[6]*Atharva Veda*, I, 30.
[7]*Atharva Veda*, VI, 29.

The mill made out of that stone of Indra which destroys all the krmis (harmful bacteria and other parasites), I crush all the krimis like the grains are crushed (with a mill). I destroy all the visible and invisible krimis which are attacking the body. I destroy all those krmis which are like networks, they poison blood and flesh. I destroy those krmis with mantras and medicines. May all these krmis dry and die. I finish all these krmis with the power of this mantra. The worms of the intestines, head, muscles and all other kinds (of parasites) we destroy with the power of mantras. All the krmis originating from the forests, mountains, vegetation, animals, etc., and which have invaded the body through food or water, or through wounds, I stop them from flourishing, and destroy them.[8]

Thus, we see that vedic people had detailed knowledge about external parasitic attacks on the body, their dispersion and toxicity in the body, their source of origin, and their ways to enter the body. There are also antibiotic mantras for animals which I have not mentioned here.

The idea of health means more than keeping the body free of disease. In ancient times, human beings considered health to be the fulfillment of the totality of personality, and this included the achievement of inner peace. They were also well aware of the importance of man-woman relationships and all the problems these relationships generate. An ancient document on medicine and health contains this amusing quotation:

Oh lady! Just like a small straw which whirls around with wind, I stir your mind so that you begin to desire me and may not stay away from me. . . . May this woman come to me with a desire for a husband. Desiring her, I may also completely give myself to her. I have come to her with wealth, just like a best horse goes to his female counterpart.[9]

During vedic times, human beings attained knowledge about the plant world by their friendly association with nature. . . . They were aided in their search (for drugs) by animals. They began to use those plants which animals used for themselves, and in this way it was possible to do research on these plant products to establish them (as medicines). Although during those days, there were no advanced technical instruments like today but nevertheless they (vedic people) successfully provided the scientific validity (of the

---

[8]*Atharva Veda* II, 31.
[9]*Atharva Veda* II, 30.

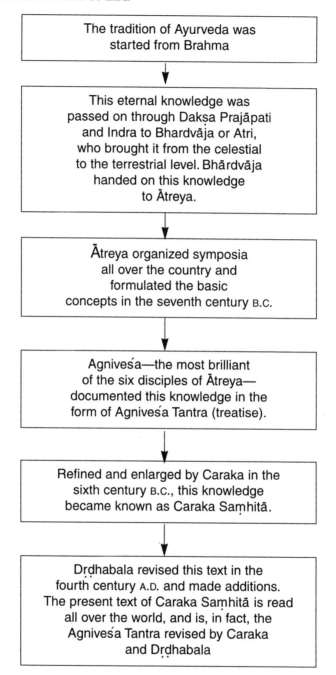

Figure 1. A summary of the Ayurvedic tradition according to the Caraka Saṃhitā.

drugs) because of their fine observations and divine vision. Due to the participation of animals in the accumulation of this (medical) knowledge, many drugs are named after birds and other animals.[10]

The most complete and detailed text we possess on Ayurveda is *Caraka Saṃhitā*, which was written at least a thousand years later than the *Atharva* Veda. Ayurveda is closely linked to the *Atharva* Veda. It is said that the basic concepts of *Caraka Saṃhitā* were originally formulated by the sage Ātreya. It is believed that the knowledge of Ayurveda came to Ātreya from the gods (see Figure 1). The tradition of Ayurveda was started by Brahmā with the creation itself. This knowledge was then passed to Dakṣa Prajāpati, who passed it to Indra. The sage Bhārdvāja was asked by other sages to go to the god Indra to attain this knowledge for the good of mankind. He brought it to the terrestrial level. It was Bhardvāja who imparted this knowledge to Ātreya. Sage Ātreya discussed the topics of medicine with the scholars and sages in different symposia organized in various parts of the country. Most brilliant of his disciples was Agnivesa, who documented these in a treatise—Agnivesa's treatise. Afterward, this text was refined and enlarged by Caraka and became known as *Caraka Saṃhitā*. A Kashmiri scholar called Dṛḍhabala rewrote the text and this more modern text is what we use today. According to an historical analysis by Professor Priya Vrat Sharma, Ātreya existed around the seventh century B.C.[11]

Caraka's text is important and revolutionary because it "got rid of" the blind beliefs and superstitions of olden days in respect to the cause and cure of disorders and developed a rational attitude toward these problems. Caraka emphasizes working according to *yukti* (rationale). He advises us to move always with knowledge. . . . Caraka has emphasized the process of investigation which is essential for arriving at scientific truths."[12] We will be using the *Caraka Saṃhitā* throughout this book to illustrate various concepts of Ayurveda as well as to demonstrate the

---

[10]Sharma, P. V. *Dravyaguna-Vijñāna*, Part IV, Vedic Plants and History of Dravyaguna (Hindi), Chaukhambha Sanskrit Sansthan, Varanasi, 1977, p. 2.
[11]Sharma, P. V. *Caraka Saṃhitā* (text with English translation), Chaukhambha Orientalia, Varanasi, 1981, Introduction, p. xi.
[12]*Caraka Saṃhitā* p. xxvii.

practical importance of various preventive and curative methods in daily living.

At the time of Ātreya, another important school was that of Sage Dhanvantrī, and this was exclusively a surgical school. The Ātreya school referred cases to Dhanvantrī school, but there is no mention of cases being referred from the surgical school to Ātreya. It shows that surgical intervention was made only when all other methods of treatment failed.

There are numerous texts on Ayurveda which are of great importance and value. *Suśruta Saṃhitā* was written by Suśruta, who probably was a contemporary of Caraka. This book is of tremendous value because in addition to medicine, it contains descriptions of techniques of surgery, rhinoplasty and describes surgical instruments. The third major work in Ayurvedic medicine is the *Aṣṭanga Saṃgraha* of Vagbhata. Vagbhata worked in the medical school of Nalanda University (near present day Patna). He summarized the views of Caraka and Suśruta, and added original scientific data concerning the treatment of diseases.

This was a golden era for the development of Ayurvedic medicine. In addition to the principles of general medicine and surgery, the ancient Ayurvedic literature describes eight different specialities:

1) Internal medicine;
2) Pediatrics;
3) Diseases relating to eye, ear, nose and throat;
4) Psychiatry;
5) Surgery and rhinoplasty;
6) Toxicology;
7) Rejuvenation and longevity;
8) Virilization.

During the medieval period, although extensive commentaries were written on previous works, there were few new additions. For the sake of brevity, we will not go into an historical account of this period. However, it is worth mentioning that in spite of being an ancient discipline, Ayurveda has never been static in its evolution. There was and still is a constant enrichment of this knowledge because new material is added. For example, during Alexander's visit to India in the third century B.C., many new plants and methods of treatment were incorporated into this timeless knowledge. In fact, some Greco-Arabic ancient methods of treatment have survived in India whereas they are lost in their countries of origin. Similarly, during the last two hundred years, modern scientific research has helped us provide the chemical composition of medicinal plants and the rationale behind Ayurvedic therapies in terms of modern science. Many readers may not be aware that some very important chemical drugs are derived from the Ayurvedic pool of knowledge. Two most famous examples are the plants *Rauwolfia serpentina* and *Ephedra gerardiana*. *Rauwolfia serpentina* has been used in India since antiquity for lowering blood pressure. However, it was introduced in Europe in 1703 by French botanist Plumier, and its Latin name comes from a physician named Rauwolf. "Sarpa" means snake, thus "serpantina" is retained from its Sanskrit name *sarpagandha* in its Latin name. In 1931, two Indian scientists succeeded in separating the active compounds reserpine and rescinamine from this plant.[13] Later, in 1945, research on this plant was carried on by a Swiss pharmaceutical company called Ciba Pharma, Bombay, and this company was credited for making the first allopathic drug to cure hypertension. Similarly, the plant *Ephedra gerardiana*, which grows high in the Himalayan mountains, is an ancient medicine for curing bad coughs and asthma. The principle active compound in this plant is *ephedrine* and it is now used worldwide for curing asthma.

PHILOSOPHICAL ASPECTS

For making Ayurveda a way of life, we have to learn to live with the cosmic rhythm. It is not possible to adopt this holistic system of medicine without leading a wholesome life, as everything in this universe is interconnected and interrelated. To

---

[13]*Caraka Saṃhitā* 10, p. 249.

understand this cosmic unity, we must consider the conceptual and philosophical thinking that is the very foundation of Ayurveda.

Sāṃkhya and Yoga

Sāṃkhya and *Yoga* are closely related, and are two of the six schools of thought from ancient India. *Sāṃkhya* forms the philosophical basis of *Yoga. Yoga*, however, shows us the techniques to achieve the goal laid down by *Sāṃkhya*. According to *Sāṃkhya* (the literal meaning is number), the reality of the cosmos is divided into twenty-five components, or *tattva. Puruṣa*, the Universal Soul, and *Prakṛti*, the Cosmic Substance, are the two principle components.[14] (See figures 2 and 3, pp. 11-12.) *Prakṛti* has three constituent qualities or guṇas: *sattva* (quality of truth, virtue, beauty and equilibrium), *rajas* (quality of force and impetus) and *tamas* (quality that restrains, obstructs, and resists motion). The *Prakṛti* has no urge to action because it is inanimate. The *Puruṣa* is the animating principle of *Prakṛti* and it is without any qualities or *guṇas*. It is *Puruṣa* which breathes life into matter. It is only by the combination of the *Puruṣa* and the *Prakṛti* that all existence manifests. By this combination, the next three components arise. They are intellect, the individuating principle, and the mind; thus, individual identity. Through these three arise five subtle elements: sound, touch, appearance, flavor and odor. The subtle elements have corresponding material or fundamental elements: ether, air, fire, water, and earth. Relating to these last five are the five organs of sense (hearing, feeling, seeing, tasting, smelling) and the five organs of action (expression, grasping, moving, excreting and procreating).

Before the manifestation of the objective world, that is, before the association of the *Puruṣa* and the *Prakṛti*, the three qualities of the *Prakṛti* are in a state of perfect balance. After the manifestation of existence, this balance is constantly changed by action (*karma*). *Karma* is the inherent nature of the combination of *Puruṣa* and *Prakṛti*. We, as beings, are the microcosm of the

---

[14]These tables are from my book *A Scientific Exposition of Patanjali's Yogasutra* (New Delhi: Patanjali Yogadarshana Society).

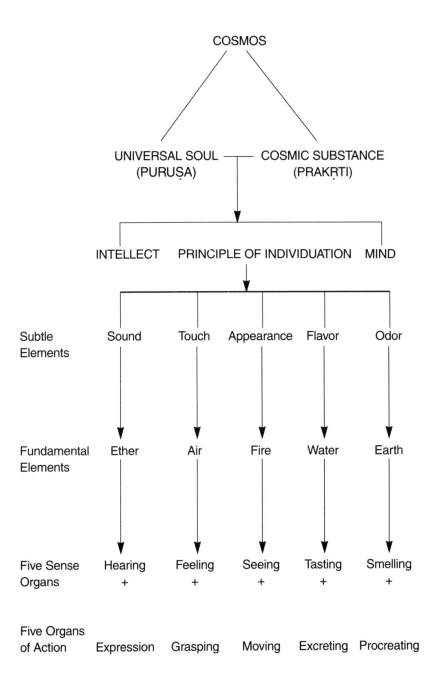

Figure 2.   The various elements of the cosmos according to Sāṃkhya.

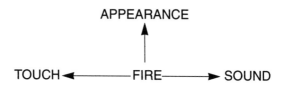

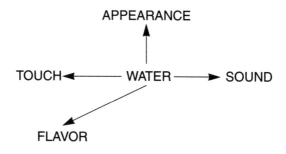

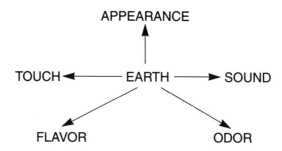

Figure 3.   The relationship between the five fundamental elements.

macrocosm described above. Our souls are a part of *Puruṣa* within us. The combination of the soul with the Cosmic Substance first gives rise to intellect, the individuating principle, and the mind. All this combined is our individual identity, which also includes the five subtle elements. We perceive material elements through these subtle elements.

The material elements give rise to the organs of sense and action. It is our inherent nature to perform action or *karma*. Individual souls undergo a cycle of birth and death called *saṃsāra*. From the *karma* of one life, fruits in terms of birth, pain, and pleasure are decided for the next. This cycle continues from one life to the next, and freedom from this pain of birth and death is sought. According to both *Sāṃkhya* and *Yoga*, the freedom lies in following the path of immortality. This is done by realizing the two ultimate realities of the universe through knowledge. The ultimate aim is to get rid of *saṃsāra* and to become one with the Universal Soul—or *Puruṣa* or *Brahman* as called in Vedic literature.

Why is *saṃsāra* painful, and why do we seek freedom from it? We look at time in terms of our lifespan. On a larger time scale of several lives, each time we come to this world, we learn and build, becoming involved and attached to it as if we will remain here forever. However, one day we have to leave behind everything we have built, loved, and accumulated. The body with which we identify ourselves decays and the true self—the soul (the essence of *Puruṣa* in us) goes away from the body and is reborn. The great Hindu *ṛsis* (seers), who could perceive time in its eternity, sought to stop this "coming" and "going" from this mortal world to find immortality and freedom.

To grasp the idea of pain expressed in *saṃsāra* (the cycle of life and death), let us take an example of the time in one day. Imagine that you are told to sit in a room the whole day and that you are repeatedly called to the next room for a few minutes at a time. You are then told to go back to your original room to wait for the next call. You go back and are called to the other room again. This process goes on for one whole day. You will certainly find it irritating, boring, and tiring. You will try your best to find a way to stop this "coming" and "going."

The Concept of Karma

To benefit from the discipline of the science of life, you must understand the concept of karma. The process of karmic evolution is widely misunderstood and misinterpreted. The results of previous karma are taken into account rigidly, and a deterministic attitude is made for the present life. The status and quality of life in this birth is dependent upon our accumulated karma from previous lives. The fruits of some of our actions are experienced in the same life and whatever balance is left accounts for the quality of the next life.

Previous *karma* can be understood in terms of time and space, and can be best illustrated with an example. Imagine that you want to have an orchard. First you will choose a piece of land according to the climatic conditions suitable for the trees you want to grow. Then you begin to plant all the possible varieties which grow under these climatic conditions. Imagine that you grow bananas, mangos, leechis, oranges, lemons, pomegranates and guavas. Each of these trees will bear fruit in different time periods. Lemons, oranges, pomegranates, guavas, and bananas may yield fruits between two and five years. Leechis might take ten years to bear fruit, whereas the mangos from the trees you planted may be destined for your children. You could not have grown apple, cherry, or plum trees in this garden, as they need a colder climate than the trees we described earlier. Similarly, with the given *saṃsāra* from the results of the *karma* of past lives, you are already in a specific situation, and thus are limited just as you were in the choice of trees in the above example. As various trees give fruits in different time periods, similarly, your *karma* of past lives and of this life fructify at an appropriate situation. Let us imagine that you have hurt someone, or that you did not return borrowed money in one of your previous lives. Circumstances may not allow an encounter with that specific person again in this life or even in several lives) as contact also depends upon this person's previous *karma* and its unfolding. However, in strange circumstances and peculiar conditions the encounters are made and previous give-and-take is constantly balanced. Nature has its perfected system. Just as a fruit tree gives ripened fruits when the time comes, and a mango tree will not give oranges, similarly, the universe has a perfectly organized system which coordinates the events and the results of the *karma* nature at a specific time. Freedom lies in our power of discretion and will. We can do good *karma* to lessen the effect of the past bad *karma* and to improve the future for this life and for the next lives. In the example of the fruit trees, we are just like gardeners, who, by effort and hard work, can create right conditions for a better quality of fruit or by whose neglect the fruit is poor quality.

As the gardener, or the maker of our own destiny, we should not grumble about the terrain or our *karmabhūmi*, the circumstances we already have. Instead, we should make maximum effort to do our best on a given terrain. By our effort, will, and hard work, we can make a desert green and by lack of initiative, enthusiasm, and by laziness, we can make ourselves miserable even in a blooming garden. We must understand that if we are suffering, it is our own doing; and if we are enjoying worldly pleasures with good health and plenty of resources, then we are also reaping the fruits of our own harvest. What we do now is a preparation for the next harvest. Good deeds, like kindness, compassion, friendship, etc., are never wasted; they work as fertilizer for the soil and make the ground of action (*karmabhūmi*) fertile for a good harvest. Similarly, bad deeds, like hurting, killing, stealing, etc., make the ground of action infertile and pave the way for future hardship.

It is through our intellect and power of discretion that we are supposed to discriminate between good and bad karma. By doing good karma in this life, we can lighten the effect of past bad karma. While enjoying the results of past good karma, we must remember that it is like a bag of money; if we spend it indiscriminately, we will finish it. However, if we invest this money wisely, we will reap the harvest. If we are privileged because of past karma, we should not become vain, cruel, selfish, careless, or insensitive. Instead, we should be modest, generous, kind, and disciplined. These good qualities should be retained even when going through rough periods. We should make the best effort to lighten the effect of previous karma. This statement will be considered in reference to Ayurveda as well.

Karma and Ayurveda

According to Ayurveda, longevity and the quality of life depends upon two factors—*daiva* and *purusakara*. *Daiva* are deeds (or *karma*) done in a previous life or lives.[15] *Purusakara* is what we do now in this life. It is said that coordination between *daiva* and *purusakara* leads to a healthy, happy, and long life. For example, if someone is condemned to have stomach problems because of bad karma in a past life (*daiva*), this person could take care of the stomach, and could do everything possible to prevent or cure this chronic ailment (*purusakara*). By so doing, this person is making the ailment mild and is, thus, making a better and longer life for himself or herself. However, if care is not taken (i.e., there is a lack of coordination between the results of past deeds and that of the present), the stomach ailment may result in ulcers, cancer, etc., leading to an unhappy or short life. I mention this example to show that although we account for past karma, this does not mean that everything is predestined. If life was predetermined and suffering from disease was preordained, then I would not be writing this book, nor would you be reading it to learn how to change your life. This view is very well expressed by Caraka himself.

> If there be a determined lifespan for all, there would not be any necessity to apply mantras, medicines, gems, auspicious rites, offerings, gifts, oblations, observance of rules, expiations, fasting, blessings, bowing, visits to temples, etc., with a desire for longevity; nor any need to avoid excited, fierce, and moving cows, elephants, camels, asses, horses, buffalos and terrific winds, etc. Likewise, one would not abstain from waterfalls, mountains, uneven and difficult places, strong water currents, or from careless, insane, excited, fierce, and unstable persons, from those inflicted with confusion and greed; from enemies, from furious fire, from various poisonous reptiles, serpents etc., from over-exertion, from behavior unsuited to place and time, or from the king's wrath. These and other similar factors should not be destructive because of the determined life span.[16]

Thus, we see that Ayurveda emphasizes making a personal effort to keep good health in order to have a pleasant and long

---

[15] *Caraka Saṃhitā, Vimānasthānam,* III, pp. 29–32.
[16] *Caraka Saṃhitā, Vimānasthānam,* III, 36.

life. We are all born with different constitutions and have different physical and mental capacities due to past *karma*. To fight the ill effects of our past *karma* is up to each of us, for our efforts can diminish weaknesses and can improve the quality of our lives. This, however, does not mean that people blessed with good physical and mental health (due to their past karma) should become careless and take liberties with themselves. They have an equal responsibility to maintain health so that they continue to feel energetic until their last days and enjoy a long life. Such people may boast or play with fate by eating in excess. They say things like this, "My stomach is very strong, it can even digest stones," or, "I have a great capacity to drink and do not get hangovers," or, "I can work without getting much sleep for months," etc. Such people overtax their energies and capacities and one day will pay for this misuse. People of this category don't need to worry about health as those with inherent health problems do, but all of us should do what we can to keep ourselves free from disease. We are all well aware that intellectual, spiritual, and economic progress is only possible for those who have stamina. It is our first and foremost duty to make the effort to create balance and harmony within ourselves so we can use our energies to help ourselves as well as for the well-being of this universe.

THE BODY: A MICROCOSM

We go back to the *Sāṃkhya* definition to look at our microcosm. (See figure 2 on page 11.) The five material elements (ether, air, fire [or light], water, and earth) are the basic eternal substances and they are believed to be the ultimate constituents from which the physical world is derived. These five basic elements are intermixed in a special and specific way to form diversity in the physical world. The principle of life and the manifest world have been discussed previously in the description of *Sāṃkhya*. We humans represent the cosmos in its microform. The *jīva* or *ātman* within us is the animating principle and a part of the cosmic immensity, *Puruṣa*. The physical self is constituted of the five basic elements (ether, air, fire, water, and earth). *Jīva* is the indestructible and unchangeable self, whereas the physical form undergoes constant transformation. The various creatures of the universe are different from each other because of their external organization—the five basic elements which provide them with physical form. The *jīva*, or the living essence which renders life to this physical form, is the same in an ant, an elephant, or a human being. At death, the life-giving force, *jīva*, departs from the physical self. The physical self returns to the five elements. In due course of time, the *jīva* may acquire a different form of another living creature. Previous karmic conditions will decide the type and form of the rebirth. According to Caraka, "The embryo is produced from the self—*jīva* (source of life)—which is devoid of illness, old age, death and decay. . . . he entering into uterus and combining with sperm and ovum produces himself in the form of an embryo. The birth of that self is not possible due to its beginninglessness. . . . The same foetus . . . attains the stages of childhood, youth, and old age. During the stage in which he exists, he is called "born" (or become) while during the preceding stage, he was "would be born or become." . . . In fact, birth is only a transformation in respect to age and conditions. . . . The embryo, while being born, cannot be produced by factors other than the self, as a sprout cannot grow from non-seed."[17]

It is important to understand that in this holistic system, the physical form of the entire cosmos is fundamentally built using the five basic elements, and these are further divided into invisible elements. The five elements are different forms of energy which organize, and reorganize, and constantly transform or change. There is a fundamental unity between all living creatures in the universe and *all* that exists. Therefore, everything around us affects us in one way or another, and we affect our surroundings as well. In order to have cosmic equilibrium and harmony, it is also essential to have harmony between the five subtle elements. Everything in our cosmos is interconnected and interrelated, and the fundamentals of Ayurveda are based on maintaining harmony between various forces of nature.

---

[17] *Caraka Saṃhitā, Śariasthānam,* III, 8–9.

TRIDOṢA: THE THREE HUMORS

All physical and mental functions of the body are governed by three humors or *tridoṣa—vāta, pitta* and *kapha*. These three humors maintain the integrity of the whole body and govern the physical structure and the mental processes. A coordinated and balanced functioning of the three humors sustains life and helps keep good health. Humoral imbalances cause decay in the body and problems in the personality. Human variability in physical form, personality traits, as well as in biological reactions, are due to the predominance of one or more of these humors. However, an extreme predominance of any of the three humors causes inner disorders and makes people vulnerable to external attacks. The variability of the humors is responsible for our basic constitution, and describes our suceptibility to various diseases, the pattern of their presentation, the body's general immunity, responses to given therapies, and even determines personality traits. In Ayurveda, the human constitution is a psychosomatic entity. The *tridoṣa* theory is, in fact, a further biological application of the five elements that constitute this universe. *Vāta* is derived from ether and air, *pitta* comes from fire, whereas *kapha* is from earth and water (see figure 4 on page 21). The three humors not only govern the totality of an individual but also relate the individual to the cosmos. Some people may not understand that the body is a single unity and that it relates to the cosmos. According to modern medicine, different organs of the body, like the brain, liver, stomach, kidneys, lungs, etc., have diverse functions and are considered like different parts of a machine. When an organ malfunctions, the defect is specifically attributed to this organ of the body and cured precisely there. However, in a holistic system of medicine like Ayurveda, all the organs are a part of the whole. Thus, when a malfunction occurs, Ayurveda resolves it in terms of the humors. A cure comes from eliminating the factors that cause the ailment.

Modern medicine is also called allopathy. Allopathy is a system of medical practice that combats disease by treatment that produces effects different than those produced by the disease. This treatment totally depends upon diagnosing the symptoms of an ailment and treating to suppress those symptoms. For ex-

Table 1.   Reductionist and holistic approaches to medicine.

Reductionist	Holistic
The human body is compared to a machine which can be analyzed in terms of its parts.	An individual is considered as a non-divisible unity, an integrated whole which cannot be reduced in terms of its parts, nor can the individual be separated from the social, cultural and spiritual environments and the cosmic link.
An illness is seen as the malfunctioning of its (body-machine) parts.	An illness is viewed as the consequence of disharmony within the cosmic order. It is not limited in space and time.
The various mechanisms of the body are understood at biological and molecular levels, and malfunctions are treated by physical and/or chemical intervention. Thus, for the purpose of treatment, body and mind are considered as separate entities.	Malfunctions are understood and treated in the context of the social, cultural, and spiritual environment. For the purpose of treatment, body, mind, and soul are considered integral.
Chance plays an important role in phenomena causing disease.	The universe is a perfectly organized whole where nothing happens without reason or fortuitously and everything is moving toward a definite goal. It is not a meaningless combination and separation of chemicals occurring by chance that causes disease.
Both time and matter are reduced to smaller units.	Matter is interlinked, interconnected, dynamic. It is constantly changing and it is this transformation that denotes time. Time is eternal.

Figure 4. *The physical and mental functions of the body are governed by three humors, which, in turn, are derived from five material or fundamental elements.*

ample, in case of pain, a pain killer is given; to cure acidity, antiacids are given; to cure menstrual disorders, hormones are administered; to cure an allergy, antihistamines are given. The allopathic system is not holistic, for in Ayurveda, the whole body, along with the entire spectrum of an individual's activities, is taken into consideration to cure an ailment.

Modern medicine has a reductionist approach to disease. It compares the body to a machine and believes that the body can be analyzed in terms of its parts. Ayurveda uses a holistic approach for preserving and restoring health, and is based upon the idea that an individual is an integral whole which cannot be reduced in terms of its parts and that people cannot be separated from their social, cultural, and spiritual environments, or their link with the cosmos. Table 1 shows various points of comparison between the reductionist and holistic approaches to health.

The term "holistic" has been used a great deal in the West during recent years. This term is very loosely employed to designate all diverse methods of health care which are alternative to allopathic medicine. However, using individual techniques from these traditions does not really mean a holistic approach to medicine. If you take an Ayurvedic medicine or some other herbal cure, or try accupuncture therapy, etc., this does not really mean that you are using holistic health care methods. "Holistic" means that we consider the body as a single unity, but it also includes our social, cultural, and spiritual environment. Using an holistic approach to preserving and restoring health comprises a holistic way of living.

According to the Ayurveda, various health problems are caused by an imbalance in one of the three humors. The first step toward a cure means that all factors causing this imbalance are researched. Then various cures are recommended and these

Table 2. *Tridoṣa* (the three humors) and the five elements.

Three Humors or *tridoṣa*	Related Fundamental Elements	Physical Characteristics	Physical Functions
Vāta	Ether and Air	Light, dry, mobile, all-pervasive, abundant, swift, cold, rough.	Blood circulation, breathing, excretion, brain functions, anxiety, grief, enthusiasm, move-ment, activity.
Pitta	Fire	Hot, pungent, sour, mobile.	Vision, body heat, hunger, thirst, softness and luster of the body, cheerfulness, intellect.
Kapha	Earth and Water	Heavy, cold, soft, unctuous, sweet, slimy, immobile.	Constitutes entire solid structure of the body, firmness, heaviness, potency, strength, forebear-ance, restraint.

usually include preventive methods, a specific diet, various exercises, and herbal treatments. The combination of treatments are used to re-establish the humor-balance in the body.

The basic properties of the three humors are similar to the subtle elements from which they derive, and their activities in the body correspond to the nature of the subsequent subtle elements. For example, *vāta* is derived from ether and air, and characteristics of *vāta* are related to these two elements. *Vāta* is all pervasive, rough, light, dry, mobile, abundant, swift, and cold. Functions of *vāta* happen according to these properties—the physiological and psychological functions that involve motion, are swift, and involve all parts of the body. *Vāta* is responsible for blood circulation, brain functions, as well as functions of peripheral nerves, excretion, body movements, breathing, anxiety, grief, enthusiasm, etc.

The subtle element of *pitta* is fire, and, thus, it is hot in nature. *Pitta* is also characteristic in being sharp, pungent, sour, and mobile. It is responsible for vision, digestion, maintaining body heat, hunger and thirst, softness and luster in the body, cheerfulness and intellect.

Kapha is heavy, cold, soft, unctuous, sweet, immobile, and slimy. It constitutes the entire solid structure of the body. The other functions of *kapha* are binding, firmness, heaviness, strength, potency, forbearance and restraint.

The characters and functions of the three humors are outlined in Table 2.

The diminution of any of these three humors causes a deficiency in normal functions; whereas their aggravation gives rise to abnormal functioning, vulnerability to disease, and other related defects. For good physical and mental health, it is absolutely essential to maintain balance. We will discuss this balance in the following chapter.

The basic human constitution is determined in terms of three humors. The variations of expression of these humors accounts for the different variety of physiological and psychological types. A humor that dominates, or has a mere tendency to dominate, gives a particular nature, personality, and physiological type. However, this does not mean that there are only three types of people. It is the permutations and combinations of the humors that gives rise to the large variety, and this will be demonstrated in the next chapter.

External factors—weather, climate, nutrition, the emotional state, relationships, social circumstances, age, time of day—constantly alter humoral composition. Ayurveda provides practical ways to maintain a balance within, and these ways should be adapted according to our basic constitution and other life circumstances. In Ayurveda, all people are not treated the same, and it is not assumed that all people can stay healthy with the same instructions for life style, the same food, the same set of rules or the same medicines.

THE EVOLUTION OF AYURVEDA

It is interesting to look at the diverse directions in which this most ancient science of life is evolving. In present-day India, where people tend more and more to adopt the Western medical system (allopathy), Ayurveda still has a strong hold in familial traditions, especially in the rural areas. In the cities, where this old tradition was getting lost, a revival of alternative health care methods is now taking place. Older people are particularly conscious of their basic constitution and are careful in their choice of foods and medicines. These people only eat certain foods at certain times of the day or during certain seasons. I was struck by this fact when I was shopping at a traditional Ayurvedic nutrition and medicine shop in my home town. It was July and a customer asked for a bottle of Brahmi sharbat (a sweet syrup with Brahmi and other herbs in it). The shop owner replied that he did not stock it at this time, for during monsoons people did not take sharbats. Ayurvedic texts forbid the consumption of sweet cold drinks during the rainy season.

The people who have kept the Ayurvedic tradition of natural medicine most alive are the tribal people in India. They are remarkably healthy and untouched by the influence of strong chemical drugs.

In traditional families, the kitchen provides an apothecary which is usually run by the mother, grandparents or some other wise person. They know what foods to combine in order to prepare a wholesome diet—a spoon of this and that to prevent small ailments. There are also effective methods for dealing with stress and shock. For example, when someone dies, and family members do not cry, various forceful methods are used to make people cry. After death, thirteen days of intensive ceremonies are carried on to bring conscious realization to the minds of the family and loved ones that the person is really dead.

A few days before a wedding ceremony, both bride and groom are given an unguent to apply. This is a special paste made from chickpea flour, mustard oil, curcuma (turmeric), sandalwood oil, etc., which has cleansing, perfuming, and antiseptic effect. It makes the skin smooth. This ceremony is done to prepare the couple for intimacy and physical sharing. On the one hand, it makes them more relaxed, and on the other hand it makes their bodies more clean, infection-free, lustrous and smooth.

Coming to the religious aspect and our cosmic connection with respect to the holistic tradition of Ayurveda, the five fundamental elements are worshipped in the forms of various gods who manifest the link between the biological and cosmic aspects of life. Fasting, in the Hindu tradition, is very important to learn to exercise self-control and to clean the body. However, a complete fasting is forbidden in Ayurveda as it increases *vāta* in the body. Therefore, most of the fasts done are semi-fasts. These semi-fasts are associated with various gods and these gods in turn are different forms of cosmic energy. For example, Tuesday is the fast day for the god Hanuman in certain parts of India. Hanuman is the god born from wind and is thus associated with *vāta*. During this fast, no salt is eaten. Grain food is eaten only once a day. Fruits, milk, etc., may be taken at other times. You will learn during the course of this book that all these measures are taken to keep vāta in balance.

Thursday, is the fast day for the goddess of learning, whereas Friday is for the goddess of satisfaction. Again it is interesting to note that for the Friday fast, one can eat salt but sour is not allowed. One is supposed to take a single meal a day. The sour enhances *pitta* and therefore this fast will keep this humor in equilibrium. *Pitta* gives hunger and therefore, symbolically, the goddess of satisfaction also represents a balance in the intake of food.

There are also monthly fasts for the beginning of the moon month (new moon) or for the full moon. During the time of eclipse, it is forbidden even to drink water. All this is observed to bring a cosmic consciousness in human beings. Imagine the executives of our times, who work in big, closed, air-conditioned buildings, who hardly look at the sky or realize the pulse of time by looking at the increasing and decreasing moon. Ayurvedic tradition requires that we notice the world.

The other two fasts that are important from the Ayurvedic point of view are the continuous seven-day fasts that are observed twice a year. They fall at the end of winter (around March) and after the monsoons (around September). These fasts are associated with various gods and ceremonies, and they also serve a very important function for inner cleansing. This inner cleansing is recommended by Ayurvedic tradition at the change of two major seasons. These fasts serve a cleansing purpose because one is not allowed to eat any grain for seven days.

Due to rapid urbanization, ancient health-guarding principles and traditions are rapidly getting lost in the big cities of India. With the breaking up of families, the traditions that were once passed on from generation to generation are not being taught. Modernization, increasing stress, the use of pesticides on crops, and increasing air pollution due to industrial and vehicular smoke have caused tremendous health problems in recent years. Hypertension, cardiac ailments, allergies and cancer are becoming more and more common. Because many people are aware of these industrial changes and how they affect our heath, people are going back to the old tradition. Interest in Ayurvedic medicine on a commercial level gives rise to many Ayurvedic pharmaceutical companies all over India. However, in order to make quick money, the products available on the market are not always genuine.

In India, and elsewhere in the world, many research institutions are doing active research in ancient methods of Ayurveda. Some of this research is aimed at proving the validity of Ayurvedic methods. It is a pity that medicines that have worked successfully for many thousands of years on human beings should be put to test on poor laboratory animals.

Another important aspect of modern Ayurvedic research undertaken by pharmaceutical companies is the chemical analysis of Ayurvedic products in order to find active compounds. The aim is to synthesize the active compound in order to eliminate the complicated process of making drugs from plants or other natural materials. In Ayurveda, the emphasis is on the entirety and wholesomeness of the medicinal health care products. An intake of separated active compounds to suppress an ailment disturbs the body's equilibrium and causes side-effects. This kind of treatment does not let the body's immunity develop and acts rapidly by suppressing only the symptoms.

In fact, the Ayurvedic preparations, the seasonal variations while gathering plant material, the methods of drying (sun or shade), the process of grinding, or other instructions, should be strictly followed. Drugs prepared with modern equipment such as drying the plants in ovens, grinding them in high speed electric grinders which produce heat, and using other similar drastic treatments make the medicines ineffective. The ineffectiveness is caused by chemical alterations caused by the production of heat or excessive grinding and the subsequent evaporation of volatile (etheric) substances from the medicines. I mention this to make you aware of the many diversions from the original Ayurvedic system, and to make you realize that commercialization on a large industrial scale does not do justice to Ayurvedic medicines.

In conclusion, an Ayurvedic way of life is comprised first of all of a thorough comprehension of its principles. After this, we proceed to an understanding of ourselves in this light. Then we learn to coordinate our nutrition according to our constitution, environment, climate and weather. This will lead us to an awareness of ourselves and an understanding of our health problems. To provide balance to our bodies and minds, the Ayurvedic way of life teaches us to activate and vitalize all the physical organs and mind processes through yogic exercises. This vitality increases our immunity and gives us a storehouse of energy that can be used to cure chronic ailments and minor health problems, aided, of course, by the use of Ayurvedic mild medicines. We will learn about herbs and minerals, their combination, preparation, and their use in promoting health in the next chapters.

2

THE PRACTICAL
BASIS OF AYURVEDA

T HE FIRST PRIORITY according to Ayurveda should be the
"desire to live."[1] One maintains good health by living a sensible lifestyle and alleviating disorders and malfunctions promptly.
This path helps to maintain the vital power and achieve long life.
The second priority is to have enough money to keep oneself
comfortable in order to promote longevity. After fulfilling the first
two priorities, one should follow the spiritual path in order to experience the reality beyond sensory perception.

Unfortunately, for a large number of people, the first two
priorities are sometimes reversed or confused. There is no
doubt that the desire to live is a basic and innate quality in all
living beings. Even a smallest unicellular animal has means to
save itself from life-threatening attacks. But human beings often
live a paradoxical existence. In spite of having a desire to live,
people lead lives that are largely anti-life, i.e., our lifestyle is unhealthy.

I will give you example to show how—for many people—the
first priority of Ayurveda is actually a second priority in their
practical lives. My way of working with people in holistic medicine demands full participation. Frequently, I meet people who
tell me that it is not possible to devote so much time to curing
themselves. Although I assure them that with their willful participation they will certainly be cured, and even when they have
seen examples of other people who maintain health using holistic methods of preventive and mild medicine, they just do not
participate in curing themselves. Why? Because they are "too
busy," or they "just don't have time." They spend most of their

---
[1]*Caraka Saṃhitā, Sūtrasthāna,* XI, 3–6.

time searching for more money or fame or comfort, etc. They do not give themselves time to realize that the comforts of the whole world, or being a boss of a big company, or any material achievement will have little meaning if their vitality lowers, or they become prey to a disease, or their life ends. Worldly pleasures are only worth something if we can enjoy them. When life ends, pleasures, comforts, and material goods also end.

Most people have a lot of energy when they are young, and they lead a success-oriented and health-ignoring life. After about two decades of such a hectic life, they begin to realize that their vital power is diminishing. Some are alarmed by other negative signs, like hypertension, high cholesterol, insomnia, migraines, shoulder pain, backaches, etc. At the middle stage of their lives, many people are completely involved in a stressful and busy routine, and find it difficult to take time for themselves in order to revitalize their energy through rest, relaxation, and other preventive measures. They get used to taking sophisticated medical tests, swallowing pills, and are trapped in a vicious cycle of over-medication and its side effects.

Another category of people react to the above-described attitude and make the third priority of Ayurveda their first priority. As young people, they leave home in search of God or other supernatural powers without bothering to educate themselves so they can earn a living. This outlook on life is also condemnable because people in this category tend to live in terrible conditions. They are not accepted socially and ultimately they have problems caused by the fact that their spiritual search is not well-rounded.

The Ayurvedic way of life begins by taking the first step. That first step involves getting to know oneself to learn about one's basic constitution. The basic constitution is based upon the humoral composition. However, before discussing the humoral composition we will take a quick look at the classification of disorders. This will help us to relate better to the humoral composition and will also make clear that there are two other important aspects of health care.

According to Ayurveda, diseases are of three types—innate, exogenous, and psychic (see figure 5).[2] Innate are those which

---

[2]*Caraka Saṃhitā, Sūtrasthāna,* XI, 45–46.

arise due to imbalance in three humors—*vāta, pitta* and *kapha.* Exogenous disorders arise due to external factors, such as poison, polluted air, parasites, bacteria, viruses, etc. The third type of disorder is psychic in origin. These are caused by unfulfillment of desires or facing the undesired.

We will see during the course of this book that these three kinds of disorders are interlinked. The imbalance of humors which cause innate disorders also make one vulnerable to the exogenous disorders, because a body with disequilibrium of its functions is not strong enough to fight external attacks. Similarly, exogenous disorders throw the body out of balance and vitiate humors. In every case, the primary cause of a disorder should be traced before it is treated. The third kind of disorder (psychic) also vitiates humors and causes, subsequently, the innate disorders. The innate disorders, on the other hand, have tremendous effect on one's state of mind and can, in some cases, become the cause of psychic disorders. We will discuss the pychic disorders in the next chapter.

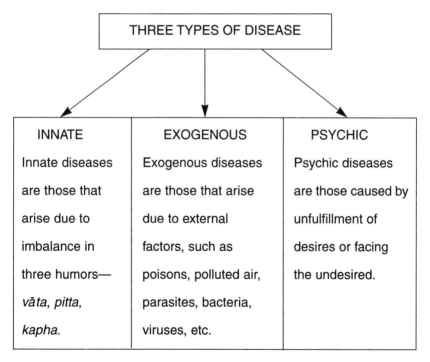

Figure 5. The Ayurvedic classification of diseases.

UNDERSTANDING THE HUMOR THEORY

You know that the three humors responsible for all physical and mental functions are derived from the five basic elements that make up the universe. These three humors are responsible for the physiological functions as well as the personality type. Each humor has its basic functional attributes, and these are similar in character to the element/elements it is derived from. For example, *vāta* is derived from air and ether. Air and ether are dry, light, rough, all-pervasive, and mobile. Therefore *vāta* has a similar character and is responsible for movement, blood circulation, breathing, sensation, etc.

Balance in these humors assures good health and happiness. An imbalance of humors will cause disease. In Ayurveda, to ensure good health, one must maintain balance. Every person has some form of dominance, or a tendency of dominance in one or two of these humors. The dominance determines the basic psychosomatic character or the fundamental nature or *prakṛti* of the person. The difference in the degree of this dominance accounts for the variation in physical and psychosomatic attributes of the individual. The second factor to consider is the various aspects of living that constantly change these humors. Food, weather, climate, different seasons, different times of the day, social circumstances, the way of working, sleeping, etc., alter the humor balance. Taking in consideration the basic nature of the individual, the aim should be to live a life that keeps the three humors in balance.

Let's learn how the humoral composition accounts for people's fundamental nature. There are people who have different physical outlooks, stamina, intelligence and other abilities. For a moment, forget about these qualities and try to look at the people around you from their humoral attributes. Let us symbolically represent the three humors by various figures.

Vāta is represented by △, pitta by ○ and kapha by □. Imagine a person with ideal health and intellect (it probably does not exist!). Hypothetically, we'll represent this person using all three of the above-described signs (see figure 6). However, there may be other people who are also healthy, and who have equilibrium in their humors, but their stamina and intellect is lower than that of the ideal one. But, nevertheless, they have equal proportion of humors (see figure 6B and C).

To continue with our figurative description of humoral theory, we say that some people are generally healthy and have merely a tendency to domination, in varying degrees, of one humor over the other. These people are sensitive in respect to this humor, but with the slightest neglect of the body, this particular humor vitiates and becomes the cause of ill health. Figure 7 (page 34) shows the variations in this category. The humors with a dominating tendency are indicated by shades of color. The reader should multiply the probabilities of figure 6 to figure 7 in order to understand the humoral variations.

Until now, we were only talking about people who have a tendency for the domination of a humor. These people can manage to stay healthy by being somewhat concerned about health. The next category comprises people who have one or

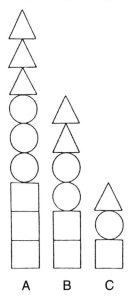

A   B   C

Figure 6.   Triangle, circle, and square represent *vāta, pitta* and *kapha,* respectively. A represents a combination of three signs for each of the three humors, showing an imaginary person with ideal health and intellect. B also shows the three humors in equal proportions, thus representing healthy people, who have less stamina and intelligence when compared to A. C represents an even lower degree of the three humors, but the balance is maintained because it is in equal proportion.

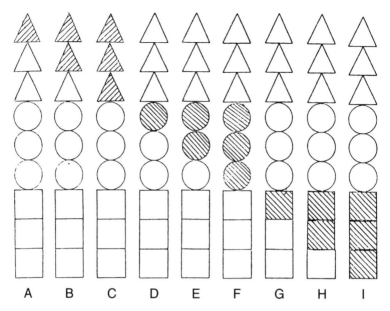

Figure 7. Various kinds of humoral domination. A, B, and C show a tendency of domination of vāta *in varying degree. Similarly, D, E, and F show the dominating tendency of* pitta *in three different degrees. G, H, and I represent the* kapha-*dominating tendency in diverse proportions.*

two humors dominating. They are frequently prey to innate disorders born out of an imbalnce of the humors. Figure 8 represents some of the examples of this category. A, B and C are *vāta-*, *pitta-*, and *kapha-*dominating people respectively. D, E, and F show still a greater degree of dominance of these three humors in the same order.

If we apply the proportions of figure 8 to figure 6, we get still more variety in the humor composition. This way, we can imagine that there are many permutations and combinations in relation to the totality of the humors as well as their varying degrees. Some people have a predominance of two humors, either simultaneously or at different times of the year, month, day, etc. The degree of vitiation is related to lifestyle, nutrition, and the other factors mentioned above.

The next category consists of people with tremendous vitiation of one or more humors. Such people really need to take care of themselves. They are usually complaining of one or the other innate disorders. If they take care of themselves properly,

Figure 8.   A, B, and C show dominating vāta, pitta *and* kapha, *respectively. Domination of a humor is more than the tendency to dominate, as shown in figure 7. D, E, and F show a higher degree of domination of the three humors when compared to A, B, or C.*

they can improve health and bring themselves to a state of equilibrium. If they do not pay attention to the maintainance of an order within themselves, their situation becomes worse due to their negligence and they end up with serious disorders. It is not uncommon to hear that some people suffer from a number of ailments simultaneously; we frequently hear of hypertension, diabetes, migraine, insomnia, and chronic backache. If these people do not take care of themselves, they make themselves vulnerable to exogenous attacks as well. Troubled perpetually with many ailments, they become irritable, disagreeable, short-tempered and may also develop psychic disorders. However, if people suffering from severe humoral disequilibrium try to re-establish physical harmony by making a special effort, adapting the lifestyle, paying attention to nutrition, keeping control over emotions and other allied factors, they remain relatively healthy, and enjoy a long life. This description should clarify the meaning of *daiva* and *purusakara* described in the previous chapter, for a coordination between these two leads to a healthy and long life. When there is a lack of coordination between *daiva* and *purusakara*, the humors go on vitiating further, leading to various states, and pathogenic decay in the body, senses, and mind. Let us look at some figurative examples of extreme cases. Figure 9 shows an extreme vitiation of a particular humor. There can be many combinations like this.

Until now we have seen that the variations of humors give rise to many biological types. When I am talking of humors and our effort to create an equilibrium between the humors, we need to consider what can alter this equilibrium. You are reminded that the humors are derived from the five subtle elements. The universe is a dynamic whole in which changes are constantly occurring; nothing is static. Time is transformation and this continual transformation makes us perceive the succession of one moment after another. Since everything in this universe is a part of the whole, nothing can change without affecting the rest. Therefore, humor equilibrium can be changed by *everything*—climate, weather, season, geographical location, time of the day, age, food, social behavior, thought process, human interaction, air, water, and all other factors of our existence. These external factors either increase or decrease one, two, or all three humors to varying degrees.

The Ayurvedic methods of working with oneself can be outlined in three steps:

1) Knowing about yourself and your fundamental constitution.

2) Knowing about the fundamental nature of different nutrients, the humoral effect of your psychological behavior, and the climatic, environmental, and other aspects you interact with.

3) Learning to coordinate the second step with the first so you are able to create a harmony within yourself and with your environment.

With these basic concepts, you will see that in this holistic system, *everything* can be a medicine, or *everything* can be dangerous, poisonous, or cause ill effect on your health. Some ailments can be cured merely with water, salt, or exercise. Similarly, you

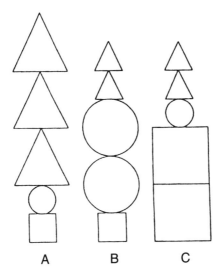

Figure 9.   A, B, and C show extreme vitiation of vāta, pitta, *and* kapha. *The vitiation is shown by exaggerated size of the humor involved.*

can become prey to disorders from insignificant things that do not coordinate with your basic nature.

Consider nutrients for a moment, in order to comprehend their relationship to your body's humors. Figure 10 (page 38) shows five such illustrations (A to E). Figure 9A shows a *vāta*-alleviating, pitta- and kapha-enhancing nutrient; B is a terribly *vāta*-promoting and *pitta*-alleviating nutrient, but it does not effect *kapha*; C is a *vāta*- and *pitta*-alleviating nutrient, and it enhances *kapha*; D promotes both *vāta* and *pitta*; E is very effectively *vāta*-suppressing but increases *pitta*. These are only a few illustrations, but you can imagine thousands of such combinations with varying degrees of humor-promoting or alleviating qualities.

Let's look at the relationship between a person's humor and the nutrients consumed. Figure 11 (page 39) illustrates an example of a person who has largely vitiated *vāta*. With the use of something which alleviates *vāta*, the exaggerated *vāta* is targeted and this person attains equilibrium again.

Imagine a situation contrary to this. A person with vitiated *vāta* (as in figure 8, p. 35), eats some nutrients which increases *vāta*. This will make the condition of this person worse and will give rise to numerous disorders of vitiated *vāta*. If this vitiation stays for a very long time, it gives rise to serious diseases. We will study this in detail soon.

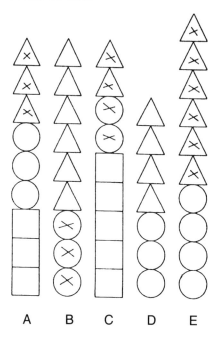

Figure 10.   *Illustrations of the nutrients with respect to variations in their capacity to alleviate and enhance a particular humor. This humor-alleviating factor is shown by a cross in the humor symbol. For example, A alleviates* vāta, *but enhances* pitta *and* kapha. *B alleviates* pitta, *enhances* vata *but does not change* kapha. *C alleviates* vāta *and* pitta, *but increases* kapha. *D increases both* vāta *and* pitta. *E alleviates* vāta, *but increases pitta.*

This system of increase and decrease relating to humors is not as simple as I show you in these easy-to-understand illustrations. Actually, to bring all this in practice, you need training in "knowing" yourself, and you need sensitivity to the effect of your surroundings on your physical type. You also need to learn to create an equilibrium between your state and your nutrients. To achieve this, you may have to get rid of pre-established norms and notions of things or foods being either good or bad. Remember always that you are unique. What may be good for your mother, or your husband or wife, may be harmful to you. Do not blindly follow the media or any instructions that give you standard "do's and don'ts."

It is essential to learn Ayurvedic equilibrium and harmony in its totality, as otherwise, in the process of curing one vitiated humor, you may end up in vitiating another humor. I have seen

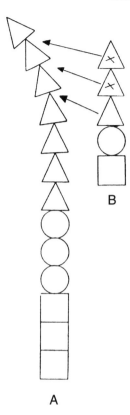

B

A

Figure 11.   A represents a person with vitiated vāta. *By taking an appropriate* vāta-*alleviating diet (B), the excessive* vāta *is targeted, and humoral balance is established.*

this happen to people who suddenly become enthusiastic about alternative and herbal medicine. They gather information from here and there and start to take some herbal treatments. They think that everything herbal and natural can only be useful and has no harmful side-effects. They end up making their systems imbalanced and also fail to relate this imbalance to the herbal home remedies. A famous example is the use of garlic. Lately, garlic has been much advertised as a wonder medicine. There is no doubt that fresh garlic, grown in the proper soil and climatic conditions, works wonderfully to cure many ailments. In some Ayurvedic texts, it is mentioned that garlic is a medicine for thousands of ailments. However, the indiscriminate use of garlic is strictly forbidden. Garlic cures *vāta* vitiation and its allied disorders. However, garlic increases *pitta*. Therefore, the use of garlic as medicine should be done very carefully, and should be accompanied by nutrients that decrease *pitta*. The people with a dominating *pitta* should take garlic in low dose.

At this stage, all this might sound complicated, but once you adapt to the Ayurvedic way of life, this sensitivity becomes part of your nature. Then you cease to see your physical self and the cosmos as two separate entities. This universe is constituted of a series of actions and reactions, and health is nothing else but a harmonious flow of these energies.

THE THREE HUMORS

Let us now study the details of the humors, their functions, the disorders their vitiation can cause, the factors which affect them, and learn to know our basic nature (*prakṛti*). This last part will be discussed after the detailed description of the three humors because the detailed knowledge of the humors will facilitate the understanding of your basic constitution.

Vāta

As you know, *vāta* is from the element ether and air. Ether is light and air is dry. Like these two elements, *vāta* is subtle, light, mobile, dry, cold, rough and all-pervasive. It governs all movement, and activities of body and mind. It is responsible for inspiration and expiration as well as for excretion. *Vāta* is responsible for the information system of the brain; it gives direction to the thought process, and is responsible for speech, sensation, touch, hearing, and smelling. It regulates the psychosomatic functions of the body. Feelings like fear, anxiety, grief, enthusiasm, inspiration, courage, etc., are controlled by *vāta*. *Vāta* regulates natural urges, ensures proper circulation of the blood, and is responsible for sexual vigor and formation of the fetus.

Thus, we see that the functions of *vāta* are related to its formative elements. For example, blood circulation, the thought process, and sensation involve swift movement, like air. The blood invades all parts of the body, like ether which is all-pervasive. Similarly, the natural urges have a force like air. Speech, sensation, touch, and hearing involve rapid communication between the peripheral and central nervous system. The medium for speech and hearing is space. Breathing involves movement and, of course, it directly involves air.

Extending the above-described characteristics to personality, people with *vāta* as the dominating character are agile, quick, and unsteady in their movements, swift in taking action, and quick in *vātika* characteristics, such as anger, fear, irritation, etc. Due to the cold character of air and ether, *vātika* people are intolerant to cold and shiver easily. The coarse character of air is shown in the hair and nails. *Vātika* people have prominent blood vessels.

Let us now learn about all the factors which increase *vāta* and subsequently discuss the precautionary measures and care to bring back equilibrium to this humor. The factors which increase *vāta* are: 1) fasting; 2) excessive physical exercise; 3) exposure to cold; 4) laziness; 5) staying awake at night; 6) the rainy season; 7) old age; 8) evening and the last part of the night; 9) eating over-ripened, dry, and cooked well in advance (bāsā)[3] food and astringent substances; 10) injury; 11) excessive blood letting; 12) excessive indulgence in sexual intercourse; 13) anxiety; 14) uneven body postures; 15) suppression of natural urges; 16) feelings of regret and guilt.

We see from the above factors that time, in every respect, is very important in humor theory. Time in terms of a single day, season, as well as one's age, all have an important significance. Similarly, behavioral and emotional aspects are of equal impor-

---

[3]*Bāsā* is a word for cooked or prepared food left over from one meal and served for the next meal. There is no equivalent for this word in English or other European languages. Traditional Indian people are very fussy about eating *bāsā* food or any form of preserved food, even if it is kept with modern techniques. In fact, referigerators brought problems in Indian homes. Older, traditional people did not want to eat *bāsā* in any condition, whereas younger people thought this was a primitive idea because low temperatures keep everything fresh for a few days. However, this does not mean that there are no traditional methods of preserving food in Ayurveda. In Ayurveda, food can be preserved by using various spices and herbal mixtures in order to keep the wholesome character of the food.

Vāta is light, subtle, mobile, dry, cold, rough, and all-pervasive, like the basic elements (Air and Ether) from which it derives.

Vāta is responsible for body movement and mind activity, blood circulation, respiration, excretion, speech, sensation, touch, hearing, feelings (like fear, anxiety, grief, enthusiasm, etc.), natural urges, the formation of the fetus, the sexual act, and retention.

Vāta-dominating People	Factors which increase Vāta	Signs of Vitiated Vāta	Treatment of Vitiated Vāta
• Agile; • Quick and unrestricted in their movements; • Swift in action; • Quick in fear, and other emotions; • Gets easily irritated; • Intolerant to cold and shivers easily; • Coarse hairs and nails; • Prominent blood vessels.	• Fasting; • Excessive physical exercise; • Exposure to cold; • Laziness; • Staying awake late at night; • Rainy season; • Old age; • Evening and last part of the night; • Eating over-ripened, dry food which is kept a long time after cooking; • Injury; • Blood loss; • Excessive sexual intercourse; • Anxiety; • Uneven posture; • Suppression of natural urges; • Guilt.	• General stiffness and pain in the body; • Bad taste and dryness in the mouth; • Lack of appetite; • Stomachache; • Dry skin; • Fatigue; • Dark colored stool; • Insomnia; • Pain in temporal region; • Giddiness; • Tremors; • Yawning; • Hiccups; • Malaise; • Delirium; • Dull complexion; • Withdrawn and timid behavior.	• Sweet, sour and hot therapeutic measures; • Enema; • Vāta-decreasing diet; • Massage; • Anointing; • Appropriate rest, relaxation and sleep; • Peaceful atmosphere; • Cheerful mental state.

Figure 12. The origin, function, and characteristics of vāta.

tance. For no other reason than keeping awake until late at night and having guilt feelings, one may make oneself prone to *vāta* disorders. Maintaining good health does not only involve one's physical efforts but also control over the emotions. This does not mean a suppression of the emotions. We will discuss this issue elsewhere in this book. What is important to understand here is that one should learn to act in an appropriate way at the right time and direct one's efforts toward not letting a humor vitiate. Let us see what the symptoms are of vitiated *vāta* so that you are able to diagnose and relate it to the above factors.

Vitiated *vāta* gives a general stiffness and pain in the body, bad taste and dryness in the mouth, stomachache, dry skin, fatigue and dark colored stool. It gives pain in jaws, pain in the eyes, contraction in the eyelids, pain in the temporal region, a feeling of darkness before the eyes, giddiness, tremors, yawning, hiccups, malaise, delirium, dull complexion, withdrawn and timid behavior. Caraka described eighty different disorders of *vāta* and said that "these are eighty prominent disorders among the innumerable disorders of *vāta*."[4] Many of the eighty disorders are different types of pain, and for brevity I have given the principle disorders caused by the vitiated *vāta*.

The first step is to understand oneself in relation to a humor in order to prevent an imbalance. The second step is to learn to cure malaise or ailments occurring due to a vitiated humor by re-establishing equilibrium. Therefore, let us see what can be done for calming down the vitiated *vāta* to recreate the balance.

Vāta should be, first of all, treated by clearing the bowels. and then by an appropriate diet. An appropriate diet in this case will be food that includes substances which will pacify the enhanced *vāta*. The details of nutrition will be discussed later. As for other factors, one is advised to keep warm, eat sweet, sour, and salted foods, have massage, take warm baths and get appropriate rest or sleep. Peaceful environments and a cheerful mental state are also required to cure vitiated *vāta*.

To cure the vitiated *vāta*, we must know what promotes this humor. As soon as we realize the symptoms of enhanced *vāta*, we should immediately take measures to cut down all the *vāta*-promoting factors. Also we should learn to act wisely (in time) in

---

[4]*Caraka Saṃhitā, Sūtrasthāna*, XX, 11.

certain situations. For example, the rainy season and humid weather increases *vāta*. During this season, we should avoid eating or doing all actions that enhance *vāta*. We should adopt that way of life which diminishes *vāta* so that we do not have this humor vitiated due to the effect of the weather. The more the *vāta*-enhancing factors combine, the worse will be the effect. For example, if we are age 55–60, the weather is humid, we stay awake until late at night, we worry a lot and tend to eat *vāta*-promoting foods (like potatoes, rice, cauliflower, etc.), we are sure to suffer from *vātika* disorders. Similarly, people suffering from injuries tend to have enhanced *vāta* and should avoid all *vāta*-promoting factors and should do everything to keep the enhanced *vāta* in control. Figure 12 on page 42 briefs the *vāta* characteristics, the factors which increase this humor, and signs of vitiation and treatment.

Now that we are talking about vitiated *vāta*, I am especially addressing people who have this humor dominating, or with a tendency to dominate. That means the people who have *vātika* constitution. These people are more vulnerable to *vāta* vitiation and therefore should pay special attention to ward off the *vāta*-promoting foods and lifestyle. Don't think that we may be deprived of some of our favorite foods. We simply have to eat *vāta*-promoting foods in combination with *vāta*-diminishing nutrients. Our favorite potato dish should be followed by a tomato salad which contains some garlic. This combination will establish a natural balance. If *vātika* people do not take care, they will be

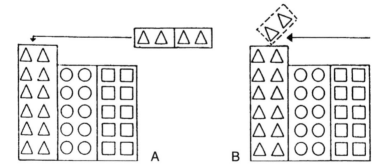

Figure 13. A) A vāta-*dominating person who may vitiate this humor by adding up* vāta-*promoting factors. B) Shows how the same person manages to establish a humoral equilibrium by the use of* vāta-*alleviating factors.*

perpetually complaining of aches and pains and will look older than their age. Figure 13 illustrates how, with a little dominating *vāta*, we can either go on adding to it and vitiate it (A) or with the *vāta*-diminishing factors, we can keep reducing it (B) to maintain the balance between the three humors.

In our age of chemical fertilizers, pesticides, and the use of all sorts of preservatives to increase the shelf life of food, there are general signs of enhanced *vāta*, especially in the West. This accounts for respiratory and blood-related diseases, arthritis, obesity, serious stomach problems, insomnia, and mental disorders. Keeping this in mind, we all should pay special attention to save ourselves from the vitiation of this humor and from becoming prey to the related diseases.

Pitta

Pitta is derived from the fundamental element Fire, and therefore it is hot in nature. It is also characterized as being sharp, sour, pungent and with a fleshy smell. It is responsible for vision, hunger, thirst, digestion, the regulation of heat in the body, softness and luster in the complexion, cheerfulness, intellect and sexual vigor. All these functions are related to the element *pitta* derives from. This ancient wisdom has also influenced our language, for it is not without reason that we use such words as "brilliant," "bright," "shining," etc. to appreciate someone's intellectual capacities and power of assimilation. Similarly, we use words like "radiant," "lustrous," "glowing," "beaming," etc. to describe someone's complexion. With subdued *pitta*, even an intelligent person may lack the power of assimilation and intellect. A beautiful person may look dull without the luster of *pitta*. We also know that the digestion of food is directly related to the production of energy and its assimilation. It is this energy which is responsible for the heat in the body. In fact, the power of digestion is called *agni* in Ayurveda, which means fire.

People having a predominance of *pitta* are intolerant to heat, have usually hot faces, delicate organs, lustrous complexions, and a tendency to have moles, freckles, and pimples. They have excessive hunger and thirst; they eat frequently and take plenty of food and drink. They also may develop wrinkles, graying hair and they may lose hair at an early age. They tend to

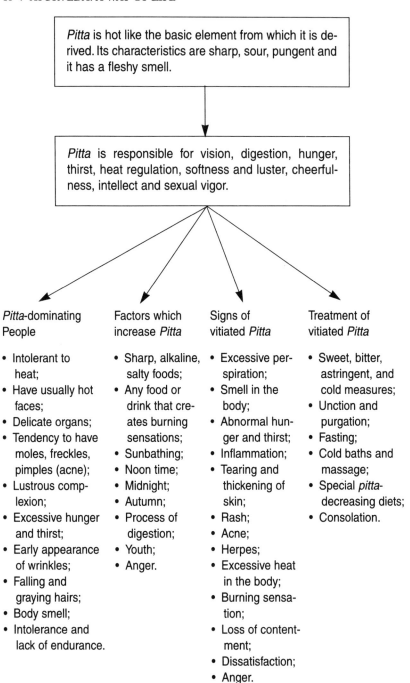

Pitta is hot like the basic element from which it is derived. Its characteristics are sharp, sour, pungent and it has a fleshy smell.

Pitta is responsible for vision, digestion, hunger, thirst, heat regulation, softness and luster, cheerfulness, intellect and sexual vigor.

Pitta-dominating People	Factors which increase *Pitta*	Signs of vitiated *Pitta*	Treatment of vitiated *Pitta*
• Intolerant to heat; • Have usually hot faces; • Delicate organs; • Tendency to have moles, freckles, pimples (acne); • Lustrous complexion; • Excessive hunger and thirst; • Early appearance of wrinkles; • Falling and graying hairs; • Body smell; • Intolerance and lack of endurance.	• Sharp, alkaline, salty foods; • Any food or drink that creates burning sensations; • Sunbathing; • Noon time; • Midnight; • Autumn; • Process of digestion; • Youth; • Anger.	• Excessive perspiration; • Smell in the body; • Abnormal hunger and thirst; • Inflammation; • Tearing and thickening of skin; • Rash; • Acne; • Herpes; • Excessive heat in the body; • Burning sensation; • Loss of contentment; • Dissatisfaction; • Anger.	• Sweet, bitter, astringent, and cold measures; • Unction and purgation; • Fasting; • Cold baths and massage; • Special *pitta*-decreasing diets; • Consolation.

Figure 14. The origin, function, and characteristics of pitta.

have axilla, mouth and body odor. *Pitta*-dominating people are intolerant and lack endurance. Readers are once again reminded not to forget the large variety of people which varying degrees of permutations and combinations of humors make. Therefore, the above description should not be interpreted rigidly or in a stereotyped manner.

Foods which are alkaline, salty, and sharp increase *pitta*. Intake of food or drink that gives a burning sensation will increase *pitta*. Staying in the sun also enhances *pitta*. Noon, midnight, autumn, and the process of digestion are other factors related to an increase in *pitta*. Anger also increases *pitta*.

The principle signs of vitiated *pitta* are excessive perspiration, burning sensations, fainting feelings, abnormal thirst, pale eyes and skin, and dark yellow urine. Caraka has described forty of the "innumerable" disorders of *pitta* (*Sutrasthan*, XX, 14). He has described burning sensations in some specific parts of the body, a foul smell, tearing of body parts, burning sensations on the skin, moistening of the skin, rashes, etc. Among the other disorders of *pitta* are herpes, jaundice, inflammations of the throat, eyes, anus, and penis, stomatitis (inflammation of the mucous membrane of the mouth). Vitiated *pitta* gives rise to feelings of dissatisfaction and loss of contentment.

The vitiated *pitta* should be cured by sweet, bitter, astringent and cold measures. Unctions and purges should be applied. Massage, fasting, cold baths, as well as drinking cold water will

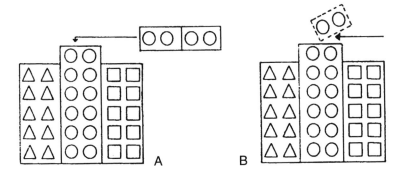

Figure 15.   A is a pitta-*dominating person who may vitiate this humor by the repeated use of* pitta-*promoting factors. B shows how the same person can avoid health hazards caused by vitiated* pitta *by using the appropriate* pitta-*alleviating measures to bring the humors into balance.*

also help alleviate *pitta*. People with the tendency to predominating *pitta* should be cautious and not let this humor vitiate by using various measures to counteract its effect. *Pitta* people should avoid oily and heavy diets. They should eat plenty of fresh vegetables and fruits. They are especially recommended to drink a lot of cold, fresh water so that *pitta* does not accumulate in the body and is excreted out.

Pitta is derived from the element fire (which is hot) and therefore vitiation of *pitta* means an excess of heat in the body. However, we should not confuse this heat with fevers. This heat or fire (*agni*) is a form of excessive subtle energy which erupts out in different pathological forms, such as the tearing of the skin, acne, rashes, herpes, inflammations, etc. This is a hidden and latent form of heat which cannot be measured with instruments. *Pitta*-promoting foods also have this hidden "heat." In the Ayurvedic language, it is common to designate different foods as hot or cold, and this actually means *pitta*-promoting or -diminishing respectively.

Figure 14 on page 46 summarizes the characteristics of *pitta*, the signs of vitiated humor, as well as its treatment. It is important to learn to act wisely according to the time, place, and situation. For example, youth, autumn, and sunbathing increase *pitta*. Many young people take their holidays in autumn and lie in sun on the beach for a long time everyday. It is not uncommon to find skin problems in this age group. If we add factors that enhance a particular humor, we end up creating an imbalance in the body and therefore bring on various health hazards. Alleviating an enhanced humor in time saves us from problems in later life. See figure 15 on page 47.

Kapha

Kapha is also called *slesma*, and is derived from the fundamental elements earth and water. It is smooth, solid, dull, sweet, rigid, cold and heavy. The characteristics of *kapha* are related to the two elements from which it is derived.

Kapha constitutes the entire solid structure of the body. The functions of *kapha* are unctuousness, binding, firmness, heaviness, sexual potency, strength, forbearance, restraint and the absence of greed. People with a predominance of *kapha* have compact and stable bodies with well-developed organs. Due to the sweet quality of this humor, *kapha* people have an abundance of sexual secretions and potency. Due to the dull character of this humor, *kapha*-dominated people are rather dull in their activities, diet and speech. Due to the rigidity of this humor, *kapha* people have delayed initiations. *Kapha* people may be sloppy. They are stable in their movements and have well-united and strong ligaments. Due to the cold character of this humor, *kapha* people have little hunger or thirst and moderate excretions from their bodies. Due to the clear character of this humor, *kapha* people have clear eyes, faces, and complexions.

Kapha increases with the intake of excessive sweet, salty, and alkaline foods, or food that is heavy, oily or fatty nutrients, a sedentary life, the lack of exercise, daydreaming, childhood, morning time, the spring season, and the early part of the evening.

Vitiated *kapha* causes drowsiness, excessive sleep, a sweet taste in the mouth, cold sensations, nausea, itchy feelings in the throat, excessive salivation, heaviness in the body, whiteness in eyes, urine and feces, malformation of body organs, mental and physical weariness, lassitude, inertness and depression.

Kapha should be treated with pungent, bitter, astringent, sharp, hot and rough measures. Fomentation (wet heat), emesis (vomiting), and exercise help alleviate *kapha* disorders very quickly. People suffering from *kapha* disorders should be en-

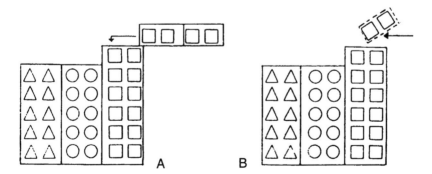

Figure 16.   A illustrates a kapha-*dominating person who, by using* kapha-*promoting measures, may vitiate this humor. B shows that the use of* kapha-*alleviating measures will establish humoral equilibrium.*

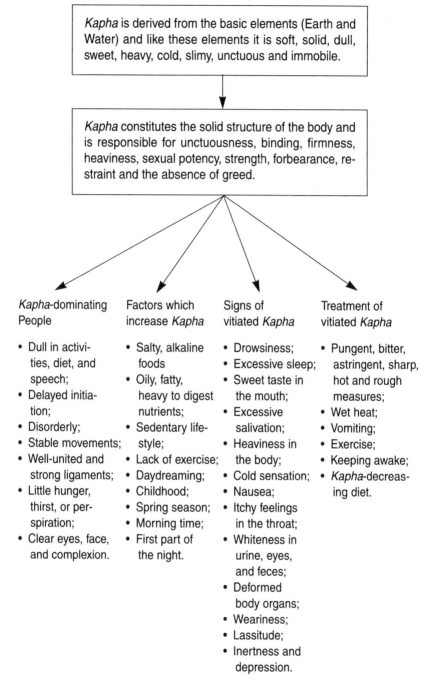

Kapha is derived from the basic elements (Earth and Water) and like these elements it is soft, solid, dull, sweet, heavy, cold, slimy, unctuous and immobile.

Kapha constitutes the solid structure of the body and is responsible for unctuousness, binding, firmness, heaviness, sexual potency, strength, forbearance, restraint and the absence of greed.

Kapha-dominating People

- Dull in activities, diet, and speech;
- Delayed initiation;
- Disorderly;
- Stable movements;
- Well-united and strong ligaments;
- Little hunger, thirst, or perspiration;
- Clear eyes, face, and complexion.

Factors which increase Kapha

- Salty, alkaline foods
- Oily, fatty, heavy to digest nutrients;
- Sedentary lifestyle;
- Lack of exercise;
- Daydreaming;
- Childhood;
- Spring season;
- Morning time;
- First part of the night.

Signs of vitiated Kapha

- Drowsiness;
- Excessive sleep;
- Sweet taste in the mouth;
- Excessive salivation;
- Heaviness in the body;
- Cold sensation;
- Nausea;
- Itchy feelings in the throat;
- Whiteness in urine, eyes, and feces;
- Deformed body organs;
- Weariness;
- Lassitude;
- Inertness and depression.

Treatment of vitiated Kapha

- Pungent, bitter, astringent, sharp, hot and rough measures;
- Wet heat;
- Vomiting;
- Exercise;
- Keeping awake;
- *Kapha*-decreasing diet.

Figure 17. *The origin, function, and characteristics of* kapha.

couraged to become physically active and sleep less. Sleep further aggrevates *kapha* disorders. Therefore, keeping awake is also beneficial to cure *kapha* disorders. Figure 16 (page 49) illustrates that a timely handling of increased *kapha* by alleviating measures keeps the humor in equilibrium, whereas *kapha*-promoting measures will very soon increase it more and one will suffer from *kapha* disorders.

Sometimes it becomes a vicious cycle when people suffer from *kapha*. Since they feel unwell or drowsy, they sleep or stay in bed more. This in turn generates more depression and still more *kapha* disorders. We need a tremendous personal effort or a physician's help to break such a cycle and to become active in order to alleviate *kapha*. As with any other vitiated humor, we should take measures to counteract the vitiation in an appropriate way and according to the time and place. There should be an equilibrium in the various methods applied. Using diet to diminish vitiated *kapha* may not be sufficient. An increase in activity, limited sleep, and physical exercise should accompany any nutrition therapy. Figure 17 summarizes the characteristics of *kapha*, the reasons for its increase, the disorders it causes and their treatment.

HUMORAL PATTERNS

The humors are derived from the five basic elements that form the material reality of this universe. Humors perform their characteristic functions in the body and these are related to the qualities and functions of the five elements in nature. Just as the five elements are life-supporting in their normal state and life-destructive when in an abnormal state, so are the humors. The *Caraka Saṃhitā* says: "The normal air moving about in nature performs the functions of holding up the Earth, kindling the Fire, disposing continuous movements of the Sun, the Moon, and groups of stars and planets, cloud-making and rain, initiation of streams, producing flowers and fruits, sprouting seeds, growth of plants, strengthening trees, ... the demarcation of seasons, removing excessive moisture, absorbing and transformation. However, when the air moves about in nature in vitiated conditions, it shows the following (negative) effects: churning of the tops of the mountains, churning of trees, producing high tides in oceans, overflowing lakes, counter-currents in rivers, earthquakes, loud-sounding clouds, the showering of dew . . . . the derangement of six seasons, the non-compactness of crops, replacing positive factors with negative ones, the release of clouds, Sun, fire and wind, which brings about the end of the four ages."[5]

Thus, we see that vitiation occurs in nature and brings about the negative effects in the same manner as the humors bring about upheaval in the body when they are vitiated. Why does a humor vitiate? The vitiation of a humor occurs due to a prolonged use of measures having similar qualities. Some people eat very selective things and do not realize the long-term effect on their health. They do not vary their nutrition in quality and quantity according to the season and their age. People are suddenly caught by a wave of doing something or eating something which is advertised by the media as "good for the health"; it may be gymnastics, aerobics, an exploited version of so-called yoga, or eating and not-eating certain foods. Since this is done without paying any attention to stamina or constitution, it contributes in vitiating a humor. Another factor that plays an important role in vitiating humors is a change of residence without adapting it to our individual lifestyle.

When I explain vitiation of the humors or the humors in the context of the individual constitution, you must keep in mind that they are not only referred to in terms of their quantity, although it sounds like that from the illustrations as well as from terms like "enhancing," "pacifying," etc. You must try to visualize the complexity of humor theory. Humors are the three vital forces of the body and are responsible for all the physical and mental functions. In fact, our physical and mental being (besides the power of discretion or intellect) is constituted by the three humors. These vital forces are not measured by mere quantity but also by their complex performance. For example, a humor may be vitiated if it diverts from its place or it begins to accumulate somewhere else, or it may not coordinate with time, or it is not in harmony with the other two humors in terms of its functions. To feel excessively hungry denotes a *pitta* vitiation, and a

---

[5]*Caraka Saṃhitā, Sūtrasthāna*, XII, 8.

state of indigestion is also due to the vitiation of this humor. If the digestive juices are secreted when there is no food to be digested, they will only cause what we call "heartburn." This is also a state of *pitta* vitiation.

Kapha builds the body, and even in an adult, the body cells are constantly renewed. The inner lining of our intestines is made of epithelial cells which are gradually but constantly renewed. These cells have protective and secretory functions and keep the inner part moist. If they are not renewed, or they cease to secrete, it is *kapha* vitiation, and if their formation is in excess, that is also a state of pathology caused by *kapha* malfunction. Abnormal blood pressure (low or high) is due to *vāta* vitiation. *Vāta* is mobile, and if it stops its smooth flow and accumulates at one place, it creates a pathological effect. Joint pains are an example of this.

Despite the fact that each humor performs its specific function, all three humors are interrelated and interconnected. Blood circulation is the function of *vāta*, but blood, itself, is the product of *kapha*, and it distributes the nutrients supplied by *pitta* to the whole body.

Vāta is all-pervasive. It carries nutrients through specific channels. In case its functions are deranged due to its vitiation, the body will begin to suffer due to the imbalance of the other two humors. If *pitta* is vitiated, there will be an imbalance relating to the intake of food, its digestion and assimilation. Soon this will cause a lack of nourishing materials in the body. If this state prevails for a long time, it will vitiate the other two humors. *Pitta* provides fire or energy for the movement of *vāta* and nutrients for *kapha* which carries out the functions of bodily secretions, and the renewal and replacement of different body cells, such as skin, blood, intestines, uterus, etc. Vitiated *kapha* may block the channels, thus hindering the passage of *vāta* and the distribution of nutrients provided by *pitta*. The blocked channels will also vitiate *vāta* at those places where *kapha* is accumulated. *Vāta's* vitiation will also cause *pitta* vitiation.

In the description of the three humors, tastes are specifically mentioned in all cases. The tastes described that cure the humor-vitiation not only refer to food but also to the humoral qualities of the medicinal products. You do not have to limit yourself to foods, medicinal plants, or other medicinal products described in Ayurveda or in this book. Instead, you must learn to recognize the humoral qualities of the products yourself. Once I attended a conference given by a very learned Ayurvedic physician, Professor Acharya Niranjan Dev, at the Ayurvedic College of Gurukul Kangri, in Haridwar. He is a professor emeritus there. Speaking on Ayurveda, he said that in this holistic system of medicine, it is not the drugs which are important, as they keep changing with time and place. The most valuable contribution of Ayurveda is its concept of humors.

You must remember that Ayurvedic medicines are unlimited, as in this holistic system *everything* around us affects us in one way or another and therefore changes our humoral balance. Since the principle of health and curing ailments is to maintain an equilibrium of the humors within us, anything can act as a medicine, depending upon the need of that particular time. A glass of water, some milk, going out regularly for a walk, taking a bit of garlic every day, ginger, a cup of coffee, a change of climate, controlling the emotions—all these simple aspects of daily living can act wonderfully as medicines. Learning to use this wealth of medicines means that you must learn to know yourselves in the Ayurvedic way, by learning the humoral nature of the things around you. Having learned this, the use of an appropriate medicine at the right time comes automatically.

Human beings have a tremendous intuitive knowledge about the body and the psyche. This intuitive knowledge is often left unused because of the prevalent notion of the body-mind dichotomy. In this modern civilization that originates in the West, we are taught that if something is wrong with the body, it is not our duty to think about our trouble, trace its origin, remove the causes, and cure ourselves. It is the duty of the doctors to "mend" all our ailments. Isn't this a terribly irresponsible attitude?

After having read the details of the three humors, I am sure that your minds are already working to find out your predominant humor. Perhaps some of you are confused and find in yourself the characteristics of two humors. Besides the three humoral types, varying of course in their degree, there are also other combinations. They are *vāta-pitta*, *vāta-kapha*, *pitta-kapha* and *samdosa*, or the equilibrium of the three humors. As you know already, there are variants due to the proportions of humors in relation to each other but also due to the difference in gradation of the humors. In the same relative proportion, you may have them in lower or higher quantity. This obviously will change your physical as well as your psychological reactions.

For knowing yourself with respect to humors, you have to be very sensitive to your actions and reactions. You must follow very carefully the effect of all that you eat or do. You must notice changes within yourself during the seasons, places, the time of day, in social situations and because of the food you eat. When you learn the effect of your surroundings on yourself, and you relate it to time, then you will be able to find your Ayurvedic identity. With keen observation, you should make a list of your physical and mental reactions and problems. Then you must notice the factors that increase these reactions or problems. When you have these facts, take out the humor tables and try to see where the features which enhance your problems fit in.

Let us look at a few examples to illustrate what I am trying to convey. Imagine that you find you are rather sensitive during the summer and autumn months, that you feel a lack of appetite during this time, and you are irritable. You may also have skin eruptions, allergies, etc. You generally do not like these months because of your intolerance to heat and other allied health problems. However, you might realize that many of these problems go away as the winter sets in. This should make it clear to you that you are a *pitta*-dominated person. To get rid of your problems, you cannot remove summer and autumn from the calendar! However, you can do everything that decreases *pitta* during that time of the year. For example, you should not eat oily, salty foods, or nuts, hot drinks, garlic, etc. Take cold baths, drink plenty of cold water and cold drinks so that *pitta* does not accumulate in your system. You should follow all the suggestions to alleviate *pitta*.

Those of you who are quick and swift in your actions, as well as in emotional reactions, are surely *vāta*-dominant. If you tend to shiver rather quickly and are sensitive to cold, are quick to catch cold, and tend to develop respiratory troubles, then you are certainly a *vātika* person. During the rainy and humid season, all your ailments seem to emerge and weakness in body and mind come to the surface. You may wake up tired in the morning, with a feeling of pain in your body. Do not think of taking pain-relieving tablets to suppress this pain. You are a *vātika* person and this humor gets vitiated during certain times of the year. Cure your vitiated humor with proper measures rather than ignoring and suppressing the symptoms. Drink a glass of water with fresh lemon and salt everyday. Do not let yourself be constipated and take an enema from time to time. Take a *vāta*-lowering diet, appropriate rest, avoid situations which make you hyperactive and excited, do yogic exercises to get proper sleep, use massage and anointing, take a hot bath, adopt a slower pace of life; you will see that with all these precautions, your *vātika* disorders will vanish.

If, contrary to *vāta* people, you are inactive, sedentary, sleep too much, dull in your activities and reactions, then you have *kapha* constitution. Unlike *vāta* people, who tend to react quickly, who are impulsive and excessively emotional, those of you with dominating *kapha* have delayed and subdued emotional reactions. If, despite appropriate sleep, you feel drowsy, you yawn and often get a sweet taste in your mouth, you sure have excess of *kapha*. Eat hot and spicy foods, go for a Turkish bath, do yogic exercises regularly, get involved in various activities rather than submitting yourself to your fatigue and sleeping. *Kapha* fatigue is different than the fatigue caused by over-activity. You must have heard some people grumbling and saying, "I don't understand why I feel so tired these days. I sleep eight to nine hours every night and have restful weekends." This statement comes from a person with vitiated *kapha*. He or she needs help! If this is your case, do not delay taking action, for you will go on increasing the *kapha* disorders if you don't make some changes in your life.

The above discussion does not mean that you cannot have another humor vitiated than the one which dominates you. These descriptions apply to your dominating tendencies. Many times, due to sudden climatic, nutritional, or other changes, carelessness, and doing excesses with yourself, you may be prey to the vitiation of other humors as well. For example, when you are traveling in hot countries, stay out in the sun and eat spicy food that you are not used to, you easily are victimized by *pitta* disorders. I have seen this happen to the European travelers in India, who, despite all warnings, venture to travel in the peak summer months of May and June. Suddenly, these people lose their appetites, get nausea, have burning sensations in the stomach, etc. In a reverse situation, that is, traveling in excessively cold and windy climates when you are not used to it, you may get *kapha* and *vāta* disorders. Talking about a sudden change in one's situation, during my stay in Germany, I observed that people who were unemployed began to suffer from *kapha-vāta* disorders due to the sudden change from an active to an inactive life. They were dealing with shock, insecurity, resignation, followed by an excess of sleep.

THE ENVIRONMENT AND THE HUMORS

There are hundreds of factors in our modern, largely westernized lifestyle that increase *vāta*. Many vaidyas (Ayurvedic physicians) are of the opinion that eating foods sprayed with pesticides and grown with chemical fertilizers increase *vāta* tremendously. Eating fried, preserved, or dried foods also increases *vāta*. Taking cold drinks during the winter and the rainy season also enhances *vāta*. A hectic way of life, a lack of real rest, the idea of doing something even during leisure and a constant stress of keeping pace with time are additional *vāta*-promoting factors in our times. In addition, these days, we really do not know what we are eating for many chemicals are added into our foods to increase their shelflife. Few pure products are available. In our consumer society, the influence of the media is such that people are buying and eating what they are "told to," or in other words, manipulated to buy. They are not eating according to time, season, and their own intuitive feelings about the right kind of nutrition. Foods are grown everywhere and in all seasons in artificial climatic conditions. The balance in nature indicates that seasonal fruits and vegetables, and their combination, maintain our natural equilibrium. Consumption of foods out of season challenges this natural balance.

Looking at the changes that have taken place in our way of living due to technological advancements, we can say that our modern civilization is made up of largely *vātika* people. Diseases caused by the vitiation of *vāta* are on the increase. Some examples are hypertension, diabetes, digestive disorders, insomnia, asthma, infections of the respiratory tract, rheumatic pains, gout, fatigue, numerous aches and pains, etc.

What is the solution to all this? For an overall solution, we need a tremendous change in our social, political and economic policies on a global basis. To start making changes, let's consider individual consciousness. When the number of self-aware individuals passes certain limits, systems are forced to change or they will crumble. We, as individuals, form the foundation for the very systems which, in a way, force pesticides on us (slow doses every day and, from time to time, big doses like the one in Bhopal in 1984), an awful lot of industrial drugs, chemicals added in our foods and much more. If we really think that there is something wrong with our present way of living, then we must begin to shake the foundations of the systems that allow this way of life to exist. We change the way we eat by becoming aware of what we eat.

Coming back to the basic human constitution and the role of humor equilibrium in maintaining good health, people wonder where the humor theory stands in the case of epidemics, for example. In this context, it is said in Ayurveda that while people differ in constitution, etc., there are certain common factors that cause derangements and diseases that have a similar period and symptoms can arise and destroy the community. These factors in communities are air, water, place, and time. Air . . . not in accordance with the season, excessively moist, speedy, harsh, cold, hot, rough, blocking, terrible sounding, excessively clashing, whistling, and affected with unsuitable smell, vapor, gravel, dust and smoke. . . . Water [is] devoid of merit when it is excessively deranged in respect [to] smell, color, taste, and touch, is too slimy, deserted by aquatic birds, aquatic animals are reduced. . . . Places [are] unwholesome when normal color, smell, taste, and touch is too much affected. . . . contains excessive moisture, is troubled by reptiles, violent animals, mosquitos, locusts, flies, rats, owls, vultures, jackals etc., birds and dogs cry there, painful conditions of various animals and birds; abandoned virtues like truthfulness, modesty, conduct, behavior and other merits, rivers agitated and overflooded, frequent occurrence of meteorites, thunderbolts and earthquakes . . . the sun, the moon and the stars with rough, coppery, reddish white and cloudy appearance.[6] Time should be known as unwholesome if it is having signs contrary, excessive or deficient to those of the season.[7]

To explain further the causes of the above mentioned derangements, Caraka said that "the root cause of the derangement of all is unrighteousness or *adharma*. That arises from misdeeds from a previous life, but the source of both is intellectual error. [Unrighteousness is] . . . when the heads of the country, city, guild, and community having transgressed the virtuous path, deal unrighteously with people, their officers and subordinates, and people of the city and community and traders carry this unrighteousness further. Thus, this unrighteousness makes the righteousness disappear. . . . Consequently, when righteousness has disappeared, unrighteousness has the upper hand and the gods[8] have deserted the place, the seasons get affected and because of this, it does not rain in time, or at all, or there is abnormal rainfall, winds do not blow properly, the land is affected, water reservoirs are dried up; herbs give up their natural properties and acquire morbidity. Then epidemics break out due to polluted contacts and edibles.[9]

Since all the universe is made of the same five elements, everything around us affects us, but we also affect our surroundings. Caraka has pointed out the impact of moral degradation on environmental factors and subsequently the appearance of epidemics and the destruction of communities. What Caraka stated 2500 years ago still applies in our times, but at a dangerously broader scale. It seems that in former times, these destruc-

---

[6]These days, almost all big cities of the world have the features described by Caraka.

[7]*Caraka Saṃhitā, Vimānasthānam*, III, 6.

[8]In Indian tradition, the word "god" is used to describe various forces of nature. Caraka's description of *vāyu* (or air) will illustrate my point. "*Vāyu* is all-powerful and indestructible; [it] causes negation of the positive factors in creatures and brings about happiness and misery; he is death, *Yama* (the god of death), regulator, *Prajāpati* (master of the creatures), *Aditi, Viśvakarmā* (creator god), taking all sorts of forms, penetrating into all, executing all the systems, subtle among the things, pervasive *Viṣṇu* (protector), *Vāyu* himself is the Lord (all powerful)." *Caraka Saṃhitā, Sūtrasthāna*, XII, 8.

[9]*Caraka Saṃhitā, Vimānasthānam*, III, 20.

tive degradations of morals, environment, flora and fauna were at a limited or smaller scale. With the possibility of rapid transport all over the globe, moral degradation spread rapidly through the traders, as Caraka suggested. Caraka's notion of *adharma* and its spread is applicable in our times, for when a substance is sold to the public despite its harmful effects and when such sales are done only to promote personal financial gains, this is *adharma*. Today's traders are multinationals who manage to sell toothpaste with flourides, formaldehyde, sodium dodecylsulphate, shampoos with dioxin, and food and drink with many other toxic products used to increase shelflife. In addition, large quantities of industrial waste goes to rivers, pollutes the air and pierces through the protective covering of the atmosphere. Various governments participate in spreading this *adharma* by allowing obviously harmful products on their land. It is done because economic gain means political gain. In this cycle of gains, our most important interests are ignored, that is, life itself. Due to intellectual error, we forget that what we do to our surroundings will come back to us sooner or later as all is cyclic in this universe. Caraka has stated very clearly that "there are abnormal conditions of stars, planets, moon, sun, air and fire and also of the environment which derange the seasons. After all these [conditions prevail], the earth also does not provide properly the *rasa*, *virya*, *vipaka*, and *prabhava* (various pharmaceutical properties and their effect) to herbs, consequently, due to the absence of these requisite properties, the spread of disease is certain.[10]

In this holistic system of medicine, our humoral nature is not independent of our surroundings and our surroundings will not remain unaffected by our deeds. The moral degradation has lead to the ruin of our environment. Ayurveda warns us not to take environment and natural resources for granted.

This discussion should make you aware that your efforts should also be directed to your surroundings. If we are to work with Ayurvedic medicines and foods, we need to be aware of the way our plants are grown and how our food is prepared.

---

[10] *Caraka Saṃhitā, Vimānasthānam*, III, 4.

AYURVEDIC TERMS

After having discussed the practical application of the humor theory, let us now briefly look at some other aspects of Ayurveda that also form the basis of this system. I do not want to go into too many technical details because this book is meant to be a practical guide for a general reader, nevertheless, it is necessary to talk about some fundamental concepts so you are aware of various terms used in Ayurveda. *Dhatus, ojas, malas,* and *agni* are the four topics we are going to talk about. Do not be frightened by this formidable terminology; it has no appropriate translation and I will explain each term in an easy-to-understand way.

Dhatus: The word *dhatu* literally means to support or to nourish. It also means "metal," but it is not used in this sense here. *Dhatus* promote the growth of the body and provide structure and nourishment to it. *Dhatus* are actually the resultant materials of the functions of the three humors. There are seven *dhatus*: 1) *rasa,* 2) *rakta,* 3) *māṃsa,* 4) *meda,* 5) *ashti,* 6) *majjā,* and 7) *śukra.* *Dhatus* are either temporary or permanent. Temporary in this sense means that they are constantly renewed; the old is destroyed and the new is formed.

Rasa dhatu is the essence of nutrition. All that we eat, drink, lick and devour, as Caraka puts it (*Sūtrasthāna,* xxviii, 3), turns into two products: 1) the essence of food absorbed in our system and known as *rasa;* and 2) the waste products, known as *mala,* are thrown out in the form of sweat, urine, feces, dirt of ears, eyes, nostrils, mouth, genitals, nails, etc. After absorption, *rasa dhatu* circulates through *sarotas* (channels) with the help of *vayu* or *vāta* in the whole body. The *rasa* also nourishes the other *dhatus.*

Rakta dhatu is blood and its circulation. It also nourishes all the other *dhatus. Rakta* is made from the combination of *rasa dhatu* and *pitta.* It provides color and luster to the body. In Ayurvedic literature, it is said that the blood is circulated by heart (*hṛdaya*) with specific channels for *rakta dhatu.*

Māṃsa dhatu is responsible for the formation of muscles. It is produced by *rakta* and *rasa dhatus*. *Māṃsa dhatu* provides a structure to the body and supports the *meda dhatu*. *Meda dhatu* (adipose tissue or fat) provides a kind of padding to the body and protects the *māṃsa dhatu* as well as *asthi dhatu* (bones). If it is in low quantity, it may produce weakness, and if in excessive quantity, it becomes the cause of obesity.

Asthi dhatu is permanent as compared to the other *dhatus*. It is not renewed. It gives structure to the body and support to *māṃsa* and *medas*. *Majjā dhatu* is the bone marrow produced by *asthi dhatu*. It oils the body and nourishes the *śukra dhatu*.

Śukra dhatu is white, viscous, and liquid. "It is not expressed during childhood and dries up in old age. Like a full bloom, it is blossomed and sensuous during youth. It is produced in monthly cycles. Its chief function is to provide sensuous pleasures, fondness and pregnancy."[11]

Ojas are the essence of the *dhatus*. It seems from Caraka's description that the *ojas* are the living thrusts of a person. "As the bees collect honey from fruits and flowers, organs of a person constitute the *ojas* with their activities. (1) Excessive exercise, fasting, anxiety, rough, little and measured diet, wind and sun, fear, grief, ununctuous drinks, vigil, excessive discharge (of mucus, blood, semen and other excreta), time factors (old age) and injuries are the causes of diminution of *ojas*."[12] *Ojas* prevents decay and degeneration of the body and saves it from disease. Thus, in modern medical terminology *ojas* can be equated to the immune system.

Malas have been already defined under the description for *rasa*. What is absorbed from the nourishment (*rasa*) and what is excreted out (*mala*) should have an equilibrium. This equilibrium maintains balance of the *dhatus* in the body. If there is too much absorption and less excretion, the *dhatus* are over-nourished and

---

[11]P. V. Sharma. 1989. *Ṣoḍaśānghṛdayam*, Padma Prakasana, Varanasi, p. 12–13 (Sanskrit and Hindi).
[12]*Caraka Saṃhitā, Sūtrasthāna*, XVII (1), 76–77.

all the toxins are not excreted from the body properly. This would give rise to obesity and other disorders. When excretion or waste products exceed their normal limit, it is also not healthy, as the *dhatus* are not getting adequate nourishment. This leads to weakness and underweight.

Malas are very important in Ayurvedic diagnosis. They provide us with important information for finding our humoral constitution as well as the information about various functions of the body. We should very minutely observe excretion from the body with respect to color, smell, form, etc. We will discuss this in detail in the next chapter.

Agni is included in *pitta* in the body and is responsible for producing wholesome or unwholesome effects in balanced or vitiated states—such as digestion or indigestion, vision or nonvision, low and high temperature, normal and abnormal complexion, prowess or fear, anger or exhilaration, confusion or clarity or other such duals.[13] See figure 18 on page 64.

> There are four categories of bodily fire (*agni*) according to intensity—such as intense, mild, regular and irregular. Among them, the intense fire can tolerate all sorts of improper regimen while the mild one has the contrary character. The regular fire gets affected by improper regimen but otherwise remains normal; the irregular fire has the character contrary to that. These four types of fire are found in four types of people. People having normal constitutions with *vāta*, *pitta* and *kapha* in equilibrium have regular fire; in those of the *vātika* constitution, because of the seat of fire having been subdued by *vāta*, fire becomes irregular. Likewise, in people having the *paitika* constitution, the seat of fire is affected by *pitta* and thus the fire becomes intense. When people have the *kapha* constitution, the seat of fire is subdued by *kapha* and the fire becomes mild.[14]

In Ayurvedic literature, three major groups of *agnis* or fire are described according to their specific functions:

1) *Jathragni* is located between stomach and duodenum, it is responsible for digestion and assimilation. It separates the part of

---

[13] *Caraka Saṃhitā, Sūtrasthāna,* XII (11).
[14] *Caraka Saṃhitā, Vimānasthānam,* VI, 12.

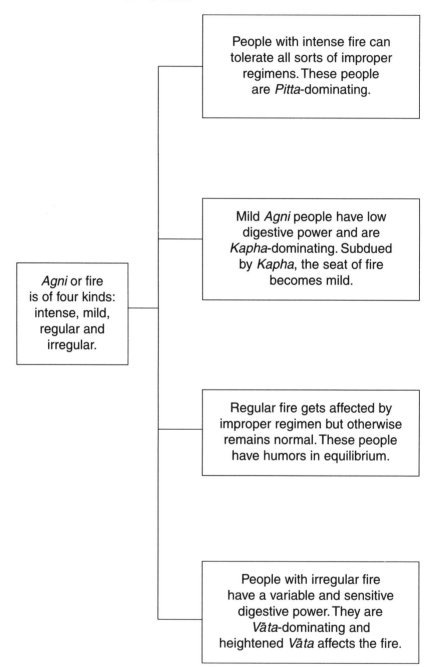

Figure 18. *The various types of bodily fire (or* agni) *and their relationship to the three humors.*

the food to be utilized by the body to nourish itself (*praśāda*) from *mala* (the waste product). This is the principle *agni* and all other *agnis* are dependent on it.

2) *Dhatvagni* is that *agni* which separates the essence of absorbed food for different *dhatus*. This *agni*, of course, depends upon the *jathragni* which is also responsible for the principle assimilation of the food.

3) *Bhutagni* is related to the five basic elements. All material substances are composed of the five basic elements—this means us, as well as the food we eat. Why is there so much variety in this universe? It comes from the varied organization of these five elements and their subgroups. The *bhutagni* actually assimilate five different elements in food in one way and convert them to another form required by the *dhatus*. To facilitate understanding, consider an example from researches in modern biology. Our bodies have proteins and we also eat proteins. Proteins are composed of amino acids. When we eat proteins, they are not assimilated as such in the body. During the process of digestion, they break down into amino acids and these amino acids are assimilated by the cells. The reconstitution of the proteins takes place inside the cells according to the particular needs of the cells. It is this aspect of digestion that *bhutagni* refers to. However, the details and the point of view is different in this holistic system than in the reductionist approach. Fundamentally the idea is the same. There is a supply (of food) in one form, the process of breakdown, absorption, and distribution. After that, a reorganization takes place according to specific needs.

As I said earlier, Ayurveda is a vast subject and in this book I will only be able to explain the fundamental way of life that Ayurveda recommends for good health and preventing illness. Therefore, I will not go into more detail regarding the anatomical and physiological aspects of Ayurveda. Interested readers may consult the original texts mentioned.

3

AN INTEGRATED
WAY OF LIVING

A FTER HAVING DISCUSSED the practical application of the humor theory and some other principal aspects of the Ayurveda, we need to learn some practical techniques for daily living. Every facet of life is important and we should perform our activities very consciously. Ayurveda teaches us to be "with ourselves" all the time, to feel involved with all our physical and mental actions. "Being with ourselves" means to be present mentally with every activity we undertake. For example, if we are eating, we should concentrate on food, on the process of eating, and on the digestion and absorption of the food consumed. "May this food bring me goodness of nature, fill me with energy, and keep me healthy," should be the thoughts before beginning to eat. None of our actions should be mechanically performed—the process of waking up, beginning a new day, the act of excretion, cleaning ourselves, etc. Somatic consciousness is a very important part of Ayurvedic way of life. When we perform various bodily actions with mental involvement the bodily parts involved in our various physical activities are involved from another dimension than just their physiological role. This leads to a communication between soma and the mind, and heightened self-awareness and self-observation develops. Since Ayurveda greatly emphasizes preventive health care methods, it is essential to learn to observe oneself minutely in order to act well-in-advance to ward off ailments. We have to develop a keen observation so that we don't miss the ignorable, subjective, pre-symptoms which usually warn us of an ailment. However, this does not mean that we should become obsessed with ourselves. We have to learn to look at ourselves in a detached way by distancing from our physical being. We have to learn to look at ourselves like a work of art—a painting, a drama, a sculpture, a piece of architecture, or a dance performance; that means going into all the minor details and yet keeping a distance.

HEALTH IN RELATION TO COLOR, FORM, SENSATION, AND SMELL

Nothing happens without reason, and everything has a cause. If you feel a bitter taste in your mouth, or the color of your urine is deeper than usual, or you have difficulty in passing stools, or you have bags under your eyes, or your tongue has a white coating, or if you notice a smell on your breath, or you were sweating despite the cold weather, or your hands or feet stay colder than the rest of your body, or if your eyes get swollen after sleep or have a different color or expression than usual, or you have a blister in your mouth, or a pimple somewhere on your body, or a burning sensation in the vagina, or an irritation on the scalp, and so on and so forth, none of the symptoms should be ignored. They should be keenly observed in detail and should be attended to immediately.

Let us examine some principal aspects you should regularly check and attend to immediately in case there is an indication of an irregular functioning. These minor but important health care instructions form the basis of good health and can save you from many health hazards. As I have already said, ailments and diseases are due to an accumulated effect of minor malfunctioning that was left unattended for a long period of time.

Stool and its Examination

When I was a little girl, it was usual that parents asked us (children) every morning about the details of our stools. If, one day, a child did not succeed in passing stools, he or she was immediately attended to, given some sort of decoxion, a rose petal marmalade, or made to drink hot water, etc. If the problem still persisted, an enema was applied. Also we were questioned about the characteristics of our stool, such as color, smell, and hardness, etc. These good old Ayurvedic traditions are getting lost in a considerable section of Indian society now. Like elsewhere in the world, with rapid industrialization, people have no time either for themselves or for their children. Thus, health is left to professionals.

Stool takes out an important part of *mala*, or the waste product from our body. Passing stool is the end result of our digestive process. It is that state when the body has taken out what it needs and the rest is thrown away. Although what we throw out everyday is a waste product, nevertheless, it carries very important information about the process of digestion. It indicates the state of digestion as well as the humoral composition of an individual. The color and form of the stool can reveal whether our humors are in equilibrium. A proper excretion of this *mala* should be ensured. If the excretion does not take place in time, and the *mala* is accumulated inside, it can cause serious consequences for health. When you do not throw out your kitchen garbage on time, the kitchen begins to smell foul due to fermentation and decay. Similarly, the delayed evacuation causes ill effects on the body.

It is very important that the stool should pass with facility, and evacuation should be done once or twice a day. The stool should be neither too hard nor too liquid. It should not have a foul smell and it should float in water.

Hard, dry, rough, gray, or black-colored stool is indicative of vitiated *vāta*. Greenish, liquid stool is due to vitiation of *pitta*, whereas whitish, sticky, mucus mixed stool is caused by an excess of *kapha* in the body. After getting an indication of the onset of humoral imbalance from the stool examination, you should attend to it immediately and appease the vitiated humor.

It is possible that you may have different types of stools on different days. This indicates that you have more than one humor vitiated. In that case, an enema should be applied and it should be followed by proper nutrition and lifestyle. Fasting, light diet, and medications are required. We will discuss the treatment aspect later in the book.

I have discussed in the previous chapter that our modern civilization is of *vātika* people. A great many people suffer from constipation. They mostly do not realize the seriousness of this malfunction and consider it all right if they evacuate every other day or once in three days. Remember that your intestines are a passage for the purpose of excretion. They are not meant to serve as a reservoir for keeping waste mater. This gives rise to *vāta* and related *vātika* ailments. It also causes hemorrhoids (piles), headaches, and skin problems. When feces remain stored too long in the bowels, they start to smell, ferment, and decay. All this causes problems of gas in the system. In Ayurveda, it is believed that this fermentation, smell, and gas does not remain limited to the place of its origin. The body is a single unity and through the blood the "poisons" are spread all over, causing various ailments. Constipation over a long period of time makes for various minerals and organic deposits in the bowels that are hard to get rid of, and they give rise to various ailments related to impure blood. Thus, you should always clear the bowels every day and should not let the dirt accumulate inside. Do not let your insides smell foul!

Some very simple remedies will be suggested in the later part of the book for curing constipation. From time to time an enema is suggested for a complete evacuation and cleaning and getting rid of any other *vātika* disorders.

Examination of Urine

Urine is another form of throwing out *mala* or waste products from the body. You should always keep watch on the color, quantity, frequency, and other qualities of your urine. This examination will also help detect vitiated humors. The urine of a healthy person should be clear and without much foam. Muddy, thick, dull-colored urine in reduced quantity is indicative of vitiated *vāta*. If the urine becomes reddish or dark yellow, strong smelling, it is vitiated *pitta*. A whitish, foamy urine is due to an excess of *kapha*. When all three *dosas* are involved, the urine is blackish in color.

Sometimes, the above mentioned signs, such as color and smell, are due to some foods we consume. For example, eating beet root gives a red color to the urine. Eating cabbage, cauliflower, or garlic may give a strong smell to the urine. Therefore, you should not be alarmed if you see these temporary signs.

If you get the urge to urinate too frequently, and each time in low quantity, you should take some teas with anti-diuretic properties. On the contrary, if you urinate after a long interval, and also in small quantity, it is due to *pitta*. It should be cured by taking lots of liquids, cold water, and diuretic teas (mentioned later in the book).

For proper functioning of the urinary system, you should always drink lots of liquids, and a pint of water in the morning after getting up. *Never* delay or postpone the urge to urinate. In the case of a vitiated humor, you should begin the treatment by curing the vitiation.

An increase or decrease in the frequency or quantity of urine accompanied by pain when passing urine, or slimy and turbid urine with blood, indicates some serious infection or disorder. A physician should be consulted immediately in such cases.

Sweating

Sweating is another form of excretion of *mala* from the body. There is always a loss of water from our bodies' outer surface. During hot weather, sweating forms a protective mechanism for the skin. It humidifies the skin and evaporation cools it. Sweating also helps excrete toxins from the body, and therefore it is used as a therapy. It is used to alleviate *vāta* disorders, especially stiffness, heaviness, and cold.

Excessive sweating is a sign of vitiated *pitta.* In normal conditions, the sweat should be color and odor free. However, a smelly and untimely sweat is indicative of dominating *pitta.* For example, to sweat in relatively cold weather indicates a *pitta* derangement. If this is the case, it should be attended to and cured by the use of *pitta* diminishing substance. A temporary smell in the sweat may also be due to some nutrients. So you should not be alarmed immediately by a smelly sweat. If the smell is persistant, and there is too much sweat, then measures should be taken to cure *pitta.* Those of you who sweat relatively little should make an effort to sweat, as it is an important cleaning process of the body. Turkish baths, sauna, or simply a hot shower or bath followed by wrapping the wet body with a towel are some of the measures to force sweating.

Breathing

As you know, breathing is the most vital activity of all the living organisms. When breathing stops, other vital functions of the body also stop and life ends. That is why breathing is called *prāṇa* in yoga and Ayurveda. *Prāṇa* means life, and breathing, or the intake of air that is activity which sustains life. Air is one of the five fundamental elements of this universe, and when it enters inside us through the process of respiration, it becomes *prāṇa śakti*, or the life-giving force.

Breathing should be smooth and unrestricted. Both nasal passages should be kept clear by various yogic methods (see the chapter on yoga). Obstructed nasal passages, the frequent occurrence of colds or other factors causing restriction in the breathing lead to many problems, such as headaches, snoring, throat and ear pain, weakening of the eyesight and pain under the eyelids. Many people suffer from chronic headaches in one half of the head due to a restricted nasal passage. If you suffer from too much sneezing due to change of temperature, or due to some allergic reaction (hay fever), it should be cured to ensure smooth breathing.

Breathing should be deep, and the process of breathing should be conscious. Every day, you should have at least a minute or two when you take deep breaths with a conscious feeling that the air which you are inhaling is life-giving and vital. It is indispensable—even for a moment—you need to be thankful to this energy for keeping you alive. Let the air which you take in bring you goodness and equilibrium, and let the air which you exhale take out imbalances of energy from your body. May the air which you inhale be intellect-promoting and give you the power of discretion (*buddhi*). Let coherence, equilibrium, and *shanti*[1] prevail.

Short and rapid breathing makes you pale and dull looking. You are advised to do various *prāṇāyāma* practices. The control of the breathing process helps control activities of the mind and increases the power of concentration. Concentration is also required in healing. *Prāṇāyāma* and the process of healing are directly related to each other and have been described elsewhere in detail.[2]

---

[1]I have not translated the word *shanti* as "peace," as *shanti* signifies more than peace; it denotes a feeling of equilibrium and stillness.
[2]See my book, *Ayurvedic Instructions on Nutrition, Healing and Sexual Behaviour* (Freiburg: Aurum Verlag, 1991). This book is only available in German.

It is also important to notice the smell of your breath. A foul smelling breath is indicative of problems with teeth, gums, or stomach disorders that are related to digestive juices (*agni*). The reason should be searched with careful observation in case of a foul smell and a proper cure should be done without delay.

Sensitive and conscious breathing will make you observe very minor symptoms if there is any infection setting in the nasal passage, throat, larynx, etc. It is easy to cure an infection at a budding stage with some yogic exercises, *prāṇāyāma* practices, or mild herbal teas. However, if these symptoms are ignored and the infection has a chance to develop, then it takes much longer to cure and it involves suffering. Different types of breathing practices also serve a purpose of cleaning the respiratory channels.

Body Temperature

The external body temperature and a skin examination should be done by feeling the body, as it is indicative of humoral disorders. The skin temperature is low and the skin feels rough in the case of vitiated *vāta*. *Pitta* raises the body temperature and makes the skin moist with perspiration. Excessive *kapha* makes the skin oily and cold.

When you touch your arm or leg with your hand, the hand should not feel too cold or too hot. Many people have this complaint—their hands and feet are either too cold or too hot. Both are indicative of an imbalance of the distribution of the body's energy. It is *pitta* which regulates body heat. To resolve this problem of variations in body heat, proper functioning of *pitta* should be ensured. Special yogic exercises for hands, feet and fingers should be performed.[3]

In a healthy person, the forehead should be slightly colder than the hands and feet. A hot forehead indicates either a fever or an excess of *pitta*. Fever can also be due to some external attack (exogenous disorder).

Pulse Examination

Examination of the pulse is very important in modern-day Ayurvedic practice. However, it seems that pulse examination

---

[3]See my book, *Yoga for Integral Health* (New Delhi: Hind Pocket Books, 1991).

was incorporated in Ayurveda very late–perhaps during the Middle Ages, as in the classical texts there is no description of pulse examination. Pulse examination can reveal the humor character of a person. In fact, some Ayurvedic physicians work with their patients without asking them about their complaints. They examine the pulse and tell people about their health problems along with providing the diagnosis.

A good vaidya's (physician) diagnosis is always correct and the patient almost feels as if the physician is also a magician or a clairvoyant. However, to acquire such expertise needs years of experience and intuitive power. Intuitive power depends upon the stillness of the mind and the power to concentrate.

For the examination of the pulse, you should be reclining. The pulse should not be examined after eating, or directly after any other physical activity such as walking, taking a bath, staying in the sun, while hungry, thirsty, sleepy, or under emotional stress. The pulse should be felt at least three times in order to get accurate findings. It is customary to feel the pulse at the root of the thumb of the right hand.

In a normal, healthy person, the pulse should be strong, regular, neither very slow nor very rapid. You might say that it is a very obscure description. Actually, the examination of the pulse can be learned only through experience. When you, yourself, feel well and healthy, try to feel your own pulse. Similarly, you can learn by feeling the pulse of healthy and emotionally balanced persons. This way, you will get an experience of feeling the pulse.

The pulse of a *vātika* person moves in a zigzag fashion; that means in the highs and lows at intervals. The pulse shows sudden, unpredictable jumping in the case of a *pitta* person. *Kapha* people will have a slow motioned and low sounding pulse. It is possible that you get a zigzag pulse which also suddenly shows jumps, or the pulse shifts from slow to fast motion. This indicates that the person is suffering from the vitiation of two humors. With someone suffering from the vitiation of all the three humors, the pulse is irregular and arhythmical.

A weak and slow pulse also indicates low blood pressure and/or low body temperature. A very slow, nearly imperceptible and interrupted pulse indicates fatal signs. In fever, the pulse is rapid. Sexual activity and hunger also make the pulse rapid. Emotions like anxiety and fear also make the pulse weak.

Examination of the Tongue

A healthy tongue should be pink, clear, and with a luster. It should have no white coating on it. A dry and rough tongue indicates *vāta* vitiation. A feeling of burning, reddish in color, bitter taste, and frequently growing painful bristles on the tongue are due to excessive *pitta*. When *kapha* is vitiated, the tongue has a white coating, and it remains wet and slimy. A white or black lusterless tongue is indicative of vitiation of more than one humor. You should always examine your tongue in the morning while cleaning your teeth, and you should attend to any negative signs and make an effort to remove the causes.

General Appearance and Examination of the Eyes

The appearance of a person gives very important diagnostic clues. Every morning, you must examine yourself very carefully. You will notice that there are slight variations in your looks from one day to another. There are days with a healthy, cheerful, and radiant look, and on other days you may notice that your face and eyes are slightly swollen or there are bags under your eyes, or you have a fatigued expression, or a pale and tired look, or a lusterless complexion, or a lack of brightness in your eyes, etc. You must learn to correlate your looks to the factors responsible for them and try to eliminate the causes of a tired and unhealthy expression. A late dinner and going to bed immediately after may give rise to a swollen look and a tired expression the next day. Too much salty and spicy food, or large quantities of food may do the same. Lack of sleep and too many worries, indigestion, changing weather, intake of alcohol and tobacco, will also have negative effects. However, all these effects vary with different people. What I am trying to convey is that you should see for yourself in accordance with your constitution and always make an effort to avoid those activities that give you a lusterless and fatigued expression upon waking up. After a night's rest, you should look fresh like a flower.

A close examination of your eyes also reveals the humoral constitution. Rust colored and smoky eyes with dull movements of eyeballs indicate *vāta* vitiation. Excessive *pitta* is indicated by pink, red, or yellowish eyes with a burning sensation and photophobia (fear of light). The *kapha* vitiation makes the eyes white and wet. You must observe your eyes very minutely every day.

Some people get bags under their eyes when they are tired or suffering from some disorder or ailment. If they take timely care, the bags disappear, whereas neglect slowly makes them into a permanent feature. Such people acquire a persisting tired look and begin to appear old at a young age. An irregular lifestyle, the intake of tobacco and alcohol, not attending to a vitiated humor, indigestion, and lack of sleep are some of the factors which are responsible for bags under the eyes.

There are two reasons for teaching you to examine yourself minutely and closely in the above-described manner. First, it should teach you self-awareness, and make you live in a way which will lead to consciousness and wholesomeness of your being. We are often aware of what is going on outside in the world, how people are behaving around us, and the ways in which their behavior affects us. We are also aware of political changes taking place in the world, of earthquakes, floods, or other such events. However, we remain indifferent to the changes, transformations, and deformations happening within ourselves. In other words, this discussion attempts to bring somatic consciousness to you and to stop automatism. The second purpose of the self-examination is to acquire a sensitivity toward yourself in order to detect very minor, still subjective symptoms of an ailment. This forms the basis of preventive medicine and Ayurveda strongly propounds to stop an ailment before it expresses itself fully. At very early stages, you can easily cure yourself and avoid a sickness "not yet come."

This latter can be achieved by making every effort to maintain a humoral equilibrium in the body. This equilibrium not only cures and keeps us free from the inborn ailments, but also gives us the capacity and strength to fight against external attacks. You will see during the course of this book that it is not a difficult task to maintain humoral equilibrium. There are simple ways to do it. A sensitive diagnosis, hygiene, revitalization of external and internal parts, living in harmony with time (age, weather, day, night, etc.), nutrition, self-control and mild medicines are some aspects which have to be learned in reference to Ayurveda. The initial process of learning demands a considerable effort, but later, all this will become a part of your daily routine. Once you learn to swim, bicycle, or drive, you do not forget these all your life, and you do these activities spontaneously. Similarly, you will see that the simple ways of Ayurveda will get assimilated in your life with time.

While using Ayurvedic methods, you must keep in mind that in this cosmos everything is interlinked and interconnected, and all these move with a rhythm. You should make every effort to move with this rhythm and not to create disharmony. To follow this cosmic music, first, establish a good relationship with your own physical and mental self. Then create a harmony with your immediate surroundings and the larger environment.

4

CLEANSING
THE BODY

C ARE AND HYGIENE of the individual organs of the body
is an essential feature of Ayurvedic education. Ayurvedic
methods of hygiene and care play an important role in the prevention of disease by keeping the humors in balance. They also
save us from external attacks by increasing our vitality. Cleanliness is not limited to external body parts, such as nails, hands,
feet, head, etc. It is equally important to clean the inner parts
through various cleansing practices, such as enemas, emesis,
sweating, and some other practices. We have already learned in
chapter 2 that these practices are essential to cure vitiated humors.

Cleaning the internal parts of the body revitalizes them
and insures their proper functioning until old age. Ayurvedic
sages calculated for a lifespan of 100 years. According to them,
youth ends at 60. For them, the aim of health practices was to
insure an active and healthy last part of life. Therefore, all
measures were taken to lessen and prevent the decay which is
a part of aging. Longevity in Ayurveda does not mean just
long life; it means a good quality, disease-free old age. For this
latter, it is essential that we do something to keep up the
youthful vigor and vitality of every part of the body and its
functions. It is important to remind ourselves that the time to
act is now. The time to invest in our old age in terms of good
health is now.

EXTERNAL CLEANING

Cleaning the Mouth, and Teeth and Tongue

There is more to cleaning your mouth than brushing your teeth with toothpaste twice a day. Many people suffer from weak teeth, ailments of the gums, and a foul smell in their mouths. Bristles in the mouth cavity is another frequently heard complaint. With appropriate care, all this can be avoided.

First of all, the mouth should be always kept clean and small food particles should not be left to rot there. For that, you should get into a habit of rinsing your mouth after every meal. This should be done by filling the mouth with water and then pushing the water around with the help of the air inside the mouth. You will also use your face muscles in this process. This practice will make a little noise. Do it with pressure so that the water makes a jet inside your mouth and pierces the spaces between your teeth and between the teeth and gums to take out any remains of food. Rinse your mouth after every meal, or each time you eat something. This is a protective method for the long life of your teeth and gums. Whenever it is not possible to rinse your mouth after you have eaten something, then eat a cardamom or a clove immediately after, to get rid of the ill effect of sugar or other food particles. Both cardamom and clove help prevent tooth decay. They also refresh the mouth and remove the bad smell.

In the West, many people are addicted to eating chocolates, candies, or a variety of other sweet things. In India and in some other parts of Asia, they are addicted to Areca nuts (betel nuts), betels, tobacco, or other products like that. Both addictions are terribly bad for the inner lining of the cells of the mouth (epithelial cells) which constantly function to produce a secretion for keeping the mouth moist. Sugar is an irritant, and so-called sugar-free candy perhaps contains more harmful products than the sugar. Too much of areca nut dries up and erodes the mouth skin. A constant irritation to the inner cells of the mouth generally gives rise to bristles. Chronic bristles over a long period of time may cause some irreversible morphological alterations. Mouth cancer is frequent in betel addicts and tobacco chewers. Therefore, take care of yourself before it is too late. Also avoid chewing gums and other such products, and use your mouth and the chewing process only when you need to nourish yourself with good and tasty food of your liking. Eating something all the time, however little it may be, has an ill effect on the mouth as well as on the digestive juices.

You should clean your teeth with care and indulgence. Remember that your teeth are like a very fine, intricate, and exclusive piece of porcelain. Imagine how carefully you would clean such a piece of porcelain after having used it to serve some food. You will try to take out leftovers of food from all its corners with probably a very soft sponge or brush with an effort not to ruin the polish of this exclusive piece. Extend the same love and care to your teeth, and stop brushing them rapidly and mechanically without even thinking about them. The tiny deposits left on them and in between them cause them to lose their luster, color and strength in time.

Do not use a hard toothbrush as it will ruin the tooth polish as well as harm your gums. Be very careful about the choice of toothpaste. There are two major problems with commercial toothpastes: 1) Some of them contain nasty chemicals like formalin or sodium dodecylsulphate, etc., which do more harm than good to the teeth. Formalin-containing toothpastes are suggested by some dentists to cure bleeding gums. In fact, formalin is a very dangerous chemical for the living tissue as it slowly causes cell death even in low quantities. This chemical is used in biological laboratories to fix and preserve the tissues of laboratory animals. 2) The commercial toothpastes contain many harmful preservatives or else bacteria tend to grow in them.

Ayurveda recommends various herbal and salt powders for cleaning teeth, or else the use of tender twigs from several trees like *neem* (margosa tree or *Azadirachta indica*), *kikar* (*Babul* or *Acacia arabica*), *tejphal* (Toothache tree or *Zanthoxylum armatum*), is recommended. This twig is chewed from one corner to make a kind of brush and then rubbed on the teeth and gums. In fact, leaves and twigs from the above plants are also used in Ayurvedic tooth powders. These tooth powders are available everywhere in India and NOW makes one tooth powder based upon Ayurvedic principles. However, if you do not have access to these readymade tooth powders, you may make your own. Choose the herbs, twigs, fruits, etc., which are edible (not toxic) and which should have astringent, pungent, bitter qualities and add these to some available varieties of rock salts. Some common examples of these ingredients which are also available in the West are clove, pepper, cinnamon, camomile, thyme, bay leaves, etc. These herbs and salts should be ground very fine and then this powder should be passed through a thin cotton cloth to obtain an extremely fine powder (see chapter 9 for details). If the tooth powder is not very fine, it will get stuck between the teeth. To clean your teeth you need only a pinch of this powder which you may stick to your wet brush. The tooth powder not only cleans the teeth but also removes bad smell, tastelessness, and cleans the tongue.

Some tribal people in Rajasthan have extremely white, lustrous and beautiful teeth. On inquiring about their cleaning process, I found that they polish their teeth with charcoal.

In Ayurveda, it is suggested to chew some plant products for strengthening teeth. Chewing cardamom or clove purifies and disinfects the mouth. From time to time, chew sesame seeds for strengthening the teeth. Chewing a raisin from a tree called Mastic also strengthens the teeth. This raisin is used in many Ayurvedic tooth powders and medicines for gums. The Mastic tree originally comes from the Aegean Sea area.

Tongue-cleaning is very important in Ayurveda. "The dirt which is collected at the root of the tongue creates obstructions in respiration and produces a foul smell; hence one should scrape one's tongue."[1] It is recommended to make tongue scrapers of gold, silver, copper, tin, or brass. However, these days the tongue scrapers are available in plastic. You may also use your tooth brush for cleaning your tongue.

After brushing your teeth and rinsing your mouth well, stick out your tongue and clean it softly with your brush. During this process of tongue-cleaning, stick out your tongue far enough so that there is a sound from your throat. Spit out all the saliva and rinse your mouth again.

This process not only cleans the tongue, but also activates the salivary glands and cleans and revitalizes the throat. It saves you from throat and mouth infections. This practice is highly recommended to those who complain of a frequent bad throat.

---

[1] *Caraka Saṃhitā, Sūtrasthāna*, V, 75.

They have a little irritation and pain in their throat especially in the mornings upon getting up. This is due to an accumulation of *kapha* during the night. When *kapha* is accumulated, it blocks the passage of *vāta* and renders the organism weak, due to the hindered circulation of energy. This situation increases your vulnerability to an external attack of bacteria and virus. However, when the above-described practice is done regularly, the excessive *kapha* and any minor infection is thrown out. It is also a very beneficial practice to combat atmospheric pollution as well as the ill-effects of smoking on the throat. To cure a chronic bad throat, also do gargles with hot water and salt, or camomile tea, or a tea made from pomegranate and *kachnar* (*Bauhminia variegata*) rind, or with a decoction made from *makoe* (*Solanum nigrum*). I give many different possibilities so that you can use whatever is available in your surroundings.

During the tongue cleaning practice, the stomach is temporarily retracted and relaxed. Thus, this practice revitalizes stomach muscles.

Cleaning and Care of Nasal Passages

The two nostrils, with a fine hair-growth within them, form the passage for inspiration and expiration. The fine hair growth provides a filter for the in-going air. To insure a proper passage of air, which is absolutely indispensable for your subsistence, the nasal passage should be cleaned every day. While bathing or taking your shower, try to blow your nose with force two or three times, so all accumulated dirt is thrown out and the nostrils are rinsed. However, if you suffer from a blocked nose, or your nose tends to get blocked during sleep, then you must rinse your nose thoroughly using *jal neti*, a yogic practice described in the next chapter.

Do not ignore the problem of a blocked nose, as it can lead to serious consequences. You may get headaches, migraines on the blocked side of your nose, or pain in the jaw, ear, shoulder, etc. Therefore, always check that both your nostrils are fully open and there is free passage of air through them. A daily practice of *jalneti* removes the accumulated phlegm and clears the nasal passages.

In Ayurveda, it is also recommended to sniff or smell something which causes sneezing. Sneezing removes nasal obstructions and opens the related channels. Something easily available all over the world to cause sneezing is pepper. A common daily preventive practice done during the bath is to put some oil inside the nasal passage with the fingers and then inhale it slightly. It might make you sneeze. This practice is good as prevention against nasal infections, or dry nose, which often occurs in North India in winter due to the very dry and cold Himalayan air. In the West it is due to central heating which lowers the humidity of the air.

Cleaning the Ears

Cleaning and care of the ears is necessary to sharpen and maintain the sense of hearing. The ear cavity is constantly moistened by a sticky secretion which helps prevent the entrance of dust or small insects, etc. inside the ear. Since this secretion is constantly renewed, the waste product (*mala*) needs to be removed from time to time with soft cotton. The outer ear also needs to be well cleaned with the fingers because of its intricate pattern. While taking a shower, rub your ears properly to give them a light massage and to clean them well. Oil massage on the ears is very soothing and saves you from ear diseases due to *vāta*.

Care of the Eyes

Eyes bring us the universe of color and form. They should be properly taken care of to get a bright and shiny look. Eyes should be washed every morning after getting up by splashing clean water on them. The water should not be hot, neither should it be very cold. Excretion from the corners of the eyes (*mala*) should be regularly removed. In Ayurveda, it is recommended to use eye drops. You should use mild eye drops at night before going to bed or whenever you feel dryness in the eyes. In India, there are many Ayurvedic eye drops available. Elsewhere, one may use some mild herbal eye drops. I do not recommend that you should make your own eye drops as there is a risk of infection.

The importance of eye drops and collyrium is described as follows in Ayurveda: "As various types of metals, like gold, etc., become stainlessly clear after washing with oil, cloth, brush, etc., the vision in the eyes of mortal ones brightens like the undisturbed moon in the clear sky with collyrium, eye drops etc."[2]

There are many types of collyrium described in Ayurveda, like antimony oxide, soot by burning some specific herbs and woods in ghee, etc., but the use of these collyriums is disputed by modern researchers and they are declared harmful. However, I do not agree with this opinion as there is no direct relationship established between the use of these collyrium and eye troubles. Besides, the use of these products stands thousands of years of testimony. Some experimental results on laboratory animals can give us very distorted data because of a very high dose of the products used in these experiments. According to Ayurveda, anything will be poisonous if used in abundance.

If you have a persisting redness in your eyes, besides using eye drops, you also need to check on excess of *pitta* in your body.

Vision is specially susceptible to *kapha*. Vitiation of *kapha* effects the vision immediately. It is necessary to keep a check on your *kapha* and all measures should be taken to throw out an excess of *kapha* from the body. A constant accumulation of *kapha* blocks the channels and passage of energy. This will lead to vitiation of *vāta* and *pitta* both. If there is an accumulation of *kapha* in the head region, it may lead to the weakening of the vision. The problem of sinusitis in relation to *kapha* and vision is discussed later in this book.

To keep your eyes healthy and your sense of sight strong, you should regularly do yogic exercises for the eyes by moving the eyeballs.[3]

Care of the Skin

Until now, I have been discussing the cleaning and care of the four senses. Last is the sense of touch and this involves your outer skin. This will include your whole body and individual parts, their cleaning and care by massage.

Oiling the body is highly recommended in Ayurveda. It is said that the skin is highly prone to *vāta* and for its health and beauty, an oil massage is essential.

---

[2]*Caraka Saṃhitā, Sūtrasthāna*, V, 18–19.
[3]Vinod Verma, *Yoga for Integral Health* (New Delhi: Hind Pocket Books, 1991).

When a pitcher is moistened with oil or the axis of a wheel is rubbed with lubricant, they become strong and jerk resistant. Similarly, with an oil massage, the body becomes firm, smooth-skinned, free from disturbances of *vāta* and tolerant of exertion and exercise. . . . The body of the one who uses oil massage regularly becomes more resistant to injuries or strenuous work. By using oil massage daily, a person is endowed with a pleasant touch, trim body parts, becomes strong, charming, and less affected by old age.[4]

We will soon discuss the details of healing and curative massage. In this section of cleaning and care, we will learn the practice of a daily routine which can be done in a relatively short time. Two principal things that account for beauty are the brightness of the eyes and the glow of the skin and complexion. We clean our houses and decorate them so that they look beautiful and attractive. This is an innate human desire and is irrespective of whether one owns a hut or a palace. A beautifully kept hut decorated with plants can look more beautiful and attractive than a neglected palace. Similarly, the beauty of a person does not depend upon standard concepts of beauty. A so-called ordinary looking person can acquire an attractive appearance by taking proper care, while people with standard norms of beauty may look rough and unattractive due to neglect. Let us see what we can do to look attractive and beautiful.

Cleaning the Skin

These days, nearly everywhere in the world, soap is considered as the supreme means of cleanliness. No doubt it is. However, it dries the skin. The traditional people of India are well aware of this fact and that is why you will notice that in public bathing ponds and on riverbanks people use oil along with soap. This is one way to counteract the dryness of the soap. The soaps which claim to contain oil do not suffice as the quantity of the oil in them is too little. Therefore, it is best to oil your whole body before washing it with soap. Alternatively, you may rub soap first between your palms and then mix some oil with it. Mix the soap and the oil by rubbing them well between your palms and then apply this mixture on your body.

---

[4]*Caraka Saṃhitā, Sūtrasthāna*, V, 85–86, 88–89.

Clean all the parts of your body well by rubbing between joints, between fingers, under the knees, armpits, ear lobes and behind them, genitals, etc. The body should be rubbed well and firmly either with hands or with a light massage brush. This revitalizes the outer skin, insures proper blood circulation, and gives luster to the complexion.

Your choice of soap should be made carefully. It is best to get a soap that does not contain artificial perfumes and colors. It needs some oil in it. In France, a large variety of such soaps are available under the name of Savon de Marseille. These soaps are being marketed elsewhere in Europe. In India some sandalwood soaps (Mysoor Sandalwood soap) are available. I do not recommend the use of liquid soaps or bathing shampoos, as they leave the skin very dry, which gives rise to excess of *vāta* in the outer skin. Besides, these liquids stick to the body and it's difficult to wash them off completely.

The use of milk for cleaning the body is highly recommended. Put about 150 ml full cream milk in an open container. Fill your hands with it and rub it on various parts of your wet body. Milk cleans very well and does not leave the skin dry. It lends a glow and softness to the skin.

For special care and beauty for the face, it is recommended to clean it with milkskin mixed with almond powder. It is best to take the milkskin from nontreated fresh milk that comes direct from the cow. When this milk is boiled and then cooled down, a thick creamy layer forms on its surface, and this should be used as a paste. The paste is made from almond powder. Make a mask of this paste and put it on your face. Leave it for some time and rub it off when it is dry. Then wash your face with warm water. If you can not obtain milk in its natural form and have only homogenized milk, then cook it for about ten minutes, uncovered, on a low fire. You will obtain a thick creamy milk which can be used to mix with the almond powder. This treatment is good for both dry and oily skin and leaves the face smooth and glowing.

If your face has a dry and drab look, it is due to excess of *vāta*. Pay attention to this humor and at the same time give your face a massage with ghee or milk skin. On the contrary, if your skin is too oily, then clean it with whole wheat flour or preferably with chick pea flour if available. Mix three teaspoons of one of these flours with 1/4 spoon of ghee, 1/8 spoon of curcuma powder, and make all this into a paste by adding some water. Mix all ingredients well and then apply this paste on your face. Rub your face with your fingers a few times. Be careful not to put this mixture on your clothes as curcuma has a very strong color which leaves a stain.

In Ayurveda, it is strongly recommended to oil your whole body. You should rub oil on your body at least once a week. Do this a few hours before your bath. Rub all your body well by applying pressure so that the oil pierces in the skin. Rub each place a few times and do not ignore any part of your body. Concentrate especially on joints (ankles, knees, wrists, elbows, shoulders, and hips). Keep warm after oiling yourself and take a warm bath after some time has passed. The bath water should not be too hot. Take pure coconut, sesame, mustard, or olive oil, or ghee for the purpose of oiling. If you are using ghee, warm it a little before massaging.

Care of the Hands and Feet

Hands and feet are very active parts of the body and we should take good care of them. Nails should be kept clean and should be cut every week. The spaces between nails and skin should be well cleaned with the help of a soft brush. After having walked a lot, you should take special care of your feet. Massaging your feet well with oil, and then dipping them in warm, salted water alleviates fatigue and pacifies *vāta*, promotes vision, keeps the soles from cracking, avoids fungus infections on the feet, and avoids the constriction of veins and ligaments.

It is essential to wash our hands well and often. It saves us from infections. Since the hands are washed so frequently and they are also used to wash other things, take care of them properly. It is recommended to apply some oil, ghee, or cream on the hands from time to time. Our hands should not feel rough and hard. Press the hands by crossing the fingers of both hands to revitalize them.

The yogic exercises for the hands, feet, and fingers[5] revitalize them and they are also beneficial to make the joints flexible. These are preventive measures against arthritic pains.

---

[5]See *Yoga for Integral Health.*

Care of Head and Hair

The scalp should be regularly oiled and washed. You must oil your scalp at least once a week and leave the oil on it for a few hours, preferably overnight. Use pure coconut, sesame, or olive oil for this purpose. Do not use oils with perfumes and other chemicals in them, take pure oils just as they are used for cooking. In Ayurveda, these oils are cooked with many hair growth-promoting and hair-beautifying herbs. At NOW, we make one such product with fourteen different herbs for preventing graying and falling of the hair. The products available in the market are not that effective, as the concentration of the herbs in them is not high enough. In any case, even if the oils with herbs are not available to you, use one of the above-described pure oils.

Usually you use shampoo to wash your hair. By the way, the word shampoo originally comes from India, from the Hindi word *champi*, which means "head massage." Shampoos are petroleum products which usually make the scalp too dry. Besides, some of them are known to contain chemicals like dioxin. Therefore, you should be very careful about your choice of a shampoo. Take a light shampoo or a hair washing soap. Hair can also be washed with Savon de Marseille. Do not think that the herbal shampoos available in the market are made of herbs alone. Some herbs are added to a shampoo base. In any case, take a very small quantity (as little as possible) of the shampoo and do the cleaning of the scalp by rubbing and massaging well. Take time to massage your head well while washing your hair. This will help relax your whole body. Make sure that you rinse long enough to take out all the traces of the shampoo.

Do not hesitate to use alternative methods for washing your hair. In Europe, there is a recipe for washing hair using a mixture of beer and egg whites. The plants containing saponine can be used to wash hair. In Ayurveda, the famous mixture of *ritha*, (soap nuts or *Sapindus trifoliatus*), *amla* (*Emblica officianalis*) and *shikakai (Acacia concinna)* in a ratio of 1:2:2 is used to wash hair. *Ritha* and *shikakai* contain saponine, whereas *amla* is used to give an attractive and shiny look to the hair. At NOW's Center we have tried to make a hair-washing powder with the above ingredients along with five more hair growth promoting and beautifying plants, but we did not get satisfactory results with it for people with blond hair. Besides, the users wanted something with foam, like a shampoo. We gave up this project and instead made the above described oil which is very beneficial, especially to prevent hair loss and baldness.

It is very easy to make your own hair conditioner. Add two teaspoons of sugar or honey, one spoon of lemon juice or vinegar, and five spoons of water. With this ratio of 2:1:5, make the quantity according to the length of your hair. After washing and rinsing your hair well, put this mixture into your hair and rub it thoroughly. Rinse it after about a minute.

If you have dry scalp or if the skin keeps peeling off, use a decoction of liquorice for rinsing your hair after you wash it. This plant is called *Glycyrrhiza glabra* and you use its roots. It is available anywhere in India and at herbal shops in Europe and America. The mode of preparation of a decoction is described later in the book. After washing your hair, put this decoction on your scalp by rubbing and massaging with your fingers. Leave this for 2-3 minutes and then rinse once again with water. Liquorice root is extremely sweet. It has fifty times more sweetness than sugar. This decoction leaves the hair soft and fine.

Do not use very hot or cold water for washing your hair; the water should be mildly warm. It should be less hot than the water you use for washing your body. Hot water on the head can cause giddiness or headaches.

It is essential to comb your hair well. Many people use hair brushes but the use of a comb in untangled hair is recommended at least once a day. Take a soft comb which should not be too fine and pass it through your hair several times. This revitalizes the scalp by providing a kind of massage.

Care of the Vagina

The vagina is a cavity, like the mouth, and women need to take care of it regularly. From time to time, the vagina should be washed with a warm water jet or with some herbal decoctions. You may use an enema apparatus for this purpose. Use a bitter herbal tea or decoction to wash the vagina in order to get rid of any possible attack of infection. A decoction of *neem* leaves (*Azadirachta indica*) or camomile is very beneficial. In Europe, some herbal mixtures are sold as "liver teas" which are usually bitter. You may use these for washing the vagina and its external parts.

One should always make sure that there is no swelling in the vagina. Such a swelling is usually due to *vāta* vitiation in this region, or is due to an infection. Excessive vaginal excretion or dryness speaks for an unhealthy state. Proper measures should be taken in this direction. Some measures regarding these problems are discussed later in this book.

The undergarments should be changed daily. During menstruation, the sanitary towels should be changed frequently so that excessive humidity may not cause sore skin. Use of some kind of internal soaking materials during menstruation is not recommended as they cause undue stress on the vaginal epithelial cells that provide vaginal secretions. Remember that the vaginal cavity is like your mouth. Putting an absorbant material in the vagina will damage the cells in the long run, just as something kept in your mouth for several days will cause bristles, inflammation, and sore skin.

For revitalization of the vaginal muscles, exercise them regularly as described in the next chapter.

INTERNAL PURIFICATION

In Ayurveda the internal purification of the body is as essential, as is external cleaning. For curing various disorders originating from the vitiation of humors and for maintaining good health, vigor and for a long life, five principal types of purification therapies are described. These are unction, fomentation, emesis, enema, and purgation. If all the humors of the body are vitiated, one suffers from many ailments, and Ayurveda recommends a thorough inner purification treatment using all these purification methods. This is the only way to uproot the vitiated humors, especially when the vitiation is old and the patient suffers from many different ailments. A complete purification therapy is also beneficial for those who suffer from side-effects from chemical drugs taken over a long period of time, or for those who are addicts of narcotic drugs.

After applying all the purification methods in a specific sequence, the patient is put on a light, nourishing and balanced diet. This complete set of purification methods is supposed to uproot disorders of the body. However, in this book, we will not be dealing with the complete purification methods we did for the treatment of extreme cases because these patients require the help of a physician. This is primarily a self-help book and I will describe simple methods of purification that you are able to use yourself. It is recommended to do the internal purification practices twice a year, preferably at the beginning of autumn and in spring, leaving a gap of six months.

In classical Ayurveda, five purification practices are described. They are known as *panchakarma* (*pancha* means five, and *karma* means action). They are very elaborate and there are a number of practices which should be done as preparatory to panchakarma (*purvakarma*), and another set of methods should be followed as after care (*pascatakarma*). Panchakarma is used in Ayurvedic therapeutics but for the appropriate management of a disease, the help of a physician is required. However, I have described below the simplified version of inner cleaning of the body which are inspired from ways and methods of Ayurveda as they are practiced in many traditional Indian homes. A detailed book about panchakarma as they should be used by physicians in therapeutics will be written separately. Keeping in view our modern lifestyle, which is considerably anti-health, and because our air and water are also polluted, I have added two more purification practices to the classical five. These are blood purification and cleaning of the urinary tract. I discussed this with the Ayurvedic sage of our times, Professor Priya Vrat Sharma, in Varanasi (on February 28, 1994). He declared that *panchakarma* should be *saptakarma* (seven actions) from that day. Thus, hereafter, the classical *panchakarma* will be referred to as *saptakarma* and you are recommended to do seven purification practices.

Enema Treatments
_____

"Enema, though done in a localized part of the body—the colon—draws up impurities from the soles of the feet to the head by its power, as the sun situated in the sky evaporates the humidity from the earth."[6]

_____
[6] *Caraka Saṃhitā, Siddhisthānam*, VII, 64.

Internal purification by enema is a tremendous therapeutic value in Ayurveda. Enema cures *vāta*. Since *vāta* is the most vitiated humor of our times enema therapy is important in preventing and curing many of the prevalent ailments of our era. You should also remember that *vāta* is a very powerful force in the body and is responsible for the movement and distribution of the other two humors. *Vāta*-related disorders are numerous, and this humor enhances during old age. Therefore, enemas are important for preventing ailments related to aging. Timely and appropriate enema treatment saves us from many aches and pains, restlessness, sleep disorders, and gives us a healthy and long life. Besides alleviating *vāta*, enemas are used to pacify *pitta* (cold enemas), and to remove accumulated *kapha* that has localized in the colon. It is a preventive for colitis and hemorrhoids. I recommend highly that you should regularly practice taking enemas, according to your constitution, age, season, etc. Following are some citations from Caraka that highlight the importance of enemas and some instructions for its use.

> Enemas are commended particularly for those who are stiffened, contracted, lame, afflicted with dislocation, and in whose extremities aggravated *vāta* is moving. Enema is prescribed in tympanitis (distention of the abdomen due to the presence of gas), knotted feces, colic pain, aversion to food, and other such disorders of the gastrointestinal tract. Enema is beneficial for those women who do not conceive . . . due to complications caused by *vāta* and for those men who have deteriorated senses and are debilitated.
>
> Those who are oppressed with heat should be given cold enemas and those who are oppressed with cold should be given warm enemas.
>
> Enemas should not be administered to those suffering from chest wounds, excessive weakness, fainting and already evacuated.
>
> As *vāta* is responsible for the release and conjunction of feces, urine, bile, etc., there is no remedy other than the enema for pacification when there is malformation and disorders relating to these. Thus, enemas are called half-medicine and even whole-medicine by some.[7]

Enema Apparatus: Enema apparatus is simple and is normally available in medical supply stores, but if you cannot find one,

---

[7]Ibid, I, 32–35, 37, 39.

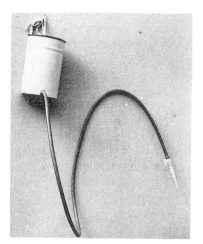

Figure 19. A homemade enema apparatus.

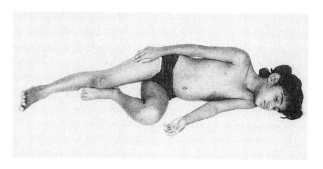

Figure 20. Enema position.

you may make your own. It consists of an enema pot with a capacity of nearly two quarts. It needs an outlet. To this outlet, a 5 or 6 foot rubber tube is attached, and the end of this tube has a catheter with a small outlet tap to control the flow of water (figure 19). The enema pot should be hung at a higher level than the person undergoing this treatment. After cleaning it properly, it is filled with the appropriate enema liquid.

First of all, open the outlet tap to check the free flow of the liquid from the apparatus and to get rid of any air bubbles in the tube. Then put some oil on the catheter to facilitate its introduction in the anal opening. Introduce the catheter very slowly and gently, and open the tap for introducing the enema fluid.

You should be in a relaxed state before introducing the enema. Lie down and take some deep breaths. Make sure that all your body parts are free from tension. It is better to massage your body a little before taking an enema. Get into an "enema posture" by turning on your left side with your left leg folded and your right leg straight (figure 20, page 94). Then insert the oiled catheter slowly and gently, and open the tap to introduce the enema liquid. Sometimes the anal passage is obstructed due to feces or hemorrhoids. Introduce the nozzle slowly and with care.

Non-unctuous and Unctuous Enemas

I will describe two principal types of enemas which can be easily managed on your own without the help of a physician. A non-unctuous enema consists of introducing liquid without any fat. It is generally warm or cold water, or salted warm water, or some herbal decoction. An unctuous enema consists of fatty substances. Both types of enemas should be taken one after the other to maintain the equilibrium of humors.

The dose for non-unctuous enema is 40 ml (about 1 fluid ounce) for a 1-year-old child and this dose should be increased 40 ml per year up to age 12. After 12, the dose should be increased 80 ml ($\frac{1}{4}$ cup) per year up to age 18. That makes a dose of 960 ml (nearly 4 cups) for adults. After 70, the dose for the next sixteen years should be reduced (800 ml or $3\frac{1}{2}$ cups).

A non-unctuous enema may consist of simply warm water with a little salt in it ($\frac{1}{4}$ teaspoon in one quart) or a decoction you wish to introduce as a curative measure. For example, for the purification of blood, as well as an anti-infection agent, you may make an enema decoction of *neem* or camomile, or some other such herbal teas, according to the requirement. The temperature of the enema liquid should not be too hot. It should be pleasantly tolerated by your system. Similarly, in case of a cold enema, the liquid should not be too cold. It should not give a shock to your system and make you shiver.

Some of you may have a strange urge to evacuate after introducing only a small quantity of the liquid. This happens particularly when you are not relaxed. If this is the case, begin again after evacuation. The correct procedure is that after introducing the enema, the water should be held inside for at least 10 or 15 minutes. You should walk around after introducing the enema so that the liquid inside can "rinse" the intestines well and remove the *mala* which is sticking inside. This will help open channels, purify the blood, and activate the cells of the inner lining of the intestine for they have both protective and secretory functions.

After enema therapy, you may have to evacuate several times. The accumulated wind will also be released. You will have a tremendous feeling of well-being and you will feel relaxed after this treatment.

A non-unctuous enema should be followed by an unctuous enema. People who are delicate and who are agitated by evacuation treatments need to try the unctuous or oily enema. Here are some recipes.

1) Take 160 ml ($\frac{5}{8}$ cup) of milk and add equal quantities of honey, oil, and ghee so that the total mixture is 240 ml (1 cup). Mix all these ingredients well. This enema mixture alleviates *vāta* and promotes strength and complexion.

2) Mix 80 ml ($\frac{3}{8}$ cup) each of oil, white wine, honey, and ghee well. This mixture also alleviates *vāta*.

3) Take honey, oil, milk, and ghee (80 ml each, $\frac{3}{8}$ cup) and mix all these with 5 grams ($\frac{1}{2}$ tsp.) of rock salt and 10 grams (1 tsp.) of mustard paste. This mixture is very good to alleviate skin disorders and bladder infections. This will also help alleviate *vāta-kapha* disorders.

An unctuous enema should be kept inside for a long period—from one to several hours. The duration of retention increases with practice. In the beginning, most people are not relaxed, and their rectal muscles are tense. This leads to a quick desire to evacuate. Unctuous enemas will not be effective if not retained inside the intestines for a long time. After an enema treatment, rest for a while and eat light and warm food.

If you are overweight, suffer often from constipation, or are a *vāta*-dominating person, you may take an enema once a week. It is advised to take an enema after every season. If you are a restless person, have trouble sleeping, or suffer from intestinal problems, you should also take an enema once a week.

Very weak and sick people should not take enemas. You should also not take enemas if you are feeling very fatigued.

Emetics
_____

Emesis is a process of purification that involves voluntary vomiting. This vomiting is incited by first consuming some especially prescribed drinks and then throwing them up voluntarily by tickling the deeper part of the throat. This practice serves to wash and rinse the upper part of the digestive tract. This purification is essential to keep the upper part of the digestive tract clean, to activate the cells of the inner lining (epithelial cells) in order to insure proper secretory and immunological functions.

The capacity to vomit is related to the degree of *kapha* in the body. People with dominating *kapha* vomit easily, whereas when *kapha* is deficient, the emetic drugs come out with difficulty.

As a daily or frequent cleansing practice, it is suggested that you follow a yogic practice called *jaldhauti*. This practice involves drinking about a pint of slightly salted warm water after getting up in the morning. After drinking this water, move around a little bit for about five minutes. Then try to throw out this water by tickling your throat with your finger. The first time you do this, the water may come out in a small quantity. Repeat this two or three times until you feel that the water you drank is emptied out. This practice will take out excess *kapha* from your stomach, throat, and tracheal region, and will revitalize these organs. This is a very beneficial preventive practice against stomach and respiratory ailments.

In case you feel that you are unable to digest your food and undigested food is causing trouble in your stomach, then do the above-described practice. It will provide you relief immediately from the headaches and discomfort caused by stomach problems. Similarly, if you have taken a toxic substance by mistake, practice emesis without losing any time. In this case, you will have to do it repeatedly by drinking water and throwing it out.

As has been said earlier, emesis is very important to cure vitiated *kapha*. The above-described practice is beneficial to cure chronic coughs, to relieve asthma, or to relieve other problems related to the respiratory tract. These curative measures are discussed later.

In the Ayurvedic practice of emesis, the patient is made to drink a meat soup made from domestic, aquatic or marshy animals, or a soup of black gram (an Indian grain) or milk. Vomiting impulses should not be more than eight. Excessive vomiting gives rise to thirst, mental confusion, fainting, vitiation of *vāta*, loss of sleep and weakness.

After emesis (excluding yogic practice of *jaldhauti*), you should rest for a while and then take very light food, like vegetable juice, soup, or well-cooked rice. You should not eat too much after emesis. You should take one or two light meals daily.

Caution: Do not practice emesis, when you are sick or very tired.

Purging

Purging treatments are beneficial to cure vitiated *pitta*. It is done by administering medicines that stimulate the liver function, and the mucous membrane and musculature of the large intestine. This therapy helps revitalize the liver functions and throws out accumulated *pitta* in the form of liquid yellow stools.

Purgation treatments should not be confused with a simple purgative which one takes to cure constipation. Purgatives taken for this cure are very strong and the idea is to clean the system thoroughly and throw out the accumulated *mala*. People who look pale, who are weak, or who have blood-related disorders, loss of appetite, frequent fevers, or skin problems are especially recommended to take this therapy.

In every country there are herbal mixtures available for the purpose of purging. In Austria, an herbal mixture called "Mai cur" is available. It is a very effective cleansing preparation for this purpose. In France, a milder purgative called "Herbasen" is available, but a double or triple dose of what is prescribed should be used for proficient purgation. Some purgative plants described in Ayurveda are the following: 1) Mexican poppy (*Argemone mexicana*) (the dose of its powdered root is 1–3 grams); 2) *jamalgota* or purging croton (*Croton tiglium*) (the dose for its powdered seeds is 25 to 50 mg or oil half to one drop); and 3) *seeg* or common milk hedge (*Euphorbia neriifolia*) (dose for its powdered root is half to 1 gram); or 4) *kaudtumba* or bitter apple (*Cirullus colocynthis*) (dose for its powdered root is 1 gram. (1 gram would be a pinch.)

Purgative substances should be taken before going to bed so they can react on the body during the resting period and the system is cleaned in the morning.

It is advised not to give this treatment to children or old persons. The dose of the purgation should be well-controlled, as an excess will cause weakness, loss of weight, insomnia, and depression. Even a healthy person without any problems should take a purgation treatment twice a year as a purification therapy. It is suggested to take this treatment if you have been overeating due to festival periods or some other reason. It will keep you from putting on weight.

Unction or Fat Cures

This treatment consists of administering fat in the body for a temporary period. It destroys the vitiated *vata* and makes the body soft. It does the purification by accumulating the internal waste and opening blocked channels. The fat used for this cure may be of animal or vegetable origin according to the need. "Ghee alleviates *vata* and *pitta*, is beneficial for *rasa*, semen and *ojas*; it is cooling, softening, and improves voice and complexion. Oil alleviates *vata*, but at the same time, it does not aggravate *kapha*. It promotes strength, is beneficial for skin; it is hot and provides firmness and cleans the female genital passage. Muscle-fat is used in fracture, injury, prolapse of the uterus, earache and headache. It is also useful for enhancing virility. Marrow promotes strength, semen, *rasa*, *kapha* and fat. It gives strength to the bones. Ghee should be taken in autumn, fat and marrow in spring and oil in the early rains. One should not take unction substances in too hot or too cold weather. With aggravated *vata* and *pitta*, and in summer, one should take unction at night. With aggravation of *kapha*, and in winter, one should take unction during the day."[8] An average dose is around 25 grams (2 tablespoons) for an adult weighing between 120–140 pounds. The dose should be calculated according to body weight and one's power of digestion. As a cloth absorbs water according to its capacity and releases the rest, similarly, unction substances are assimilated according to digestive power and the excess is thrown out.

The simplest and most commonly used treatment is to put a teaspoon or two of ghee in hot sweetened milk and drink it before going to bed. Some people eat the ghee by itself, but perhaps this is difficult for Westerners to do.

---

[8] *Caraka Saṃhitā, Sūtrasthāna,* XIII, 14–19.

Another way to do fat or unction treatments is to administer ghee or other fats through the anus. This can be easily done either with a plastic syringe with a nozzle, or with enema apparatus (fig. 19, page 94). Take care that the fat administered should be held inside for several hours and not thrown out immediately. Some people are very sensitive to anal administration, and they have an immediate urge to evacuate. However, with practice, the time can be increased. One has to concentrate and relax the anal musculature completely.

I have already discussed the importance of oiling one's body. However, for the penetration of oil inside the body, one requires an Ayurvedic oil massage which is described in the next chapter.

If your skin feels rough, if you are experiencing extreme dryness in some parts of your body, or if you have some other symptoms of vitiated *vāta*, do not hesitate to use some simple methods of fat treatment.

Before doing unction, take a light, liquid, warm meal without much fat. Do not take anything cold or drink cold water before or after taking the fat treatment.

Caution: Pregnant women, people with an excess of *kapha*, with slow and weak digestive power, with an excess of secretion in the mouth, with an aversion to food, with any weakness of the body or mind, or with depression, should not take this cure. Unction will further increase these disorders. Drug addicts should be given this treatment only after they are off the drugs.

Fomentation or Sweating Treatment

This treatment purifies the body by eliminating toxins from the skin, and opening the finer channels of the skin by stimulation and instigation. It is very beneficial to remove *vāta-kapha* or *vāta* or *kapha* disorders.

This treatment should be done when the food consumed is already digested. There are various modes of sweating. You may use various methods, but take care that you do not expose yourself to drafts after fomentation.

If you live in a hot climate, it is easy to sweat, and this purification process is naturally performed. However, even in these countries, if you stay mostly indoors in cooled rooms, or in countries with a cold climate, this purification treatment should be done from time to time. It is very beneficial to cure minor fevers, common cold, cough, an exposure to cold, body pains and other *vāta* and *kapha* disorders.

A simple way to sweat is to wrap yourself in a towel after a hot bath or a shower. Lie down covered until after you stop sweating. Then slowly get up and dress warmly and take every precaution not to expose yourself to cold or drafts. Another mode of sweating is to apply external heat, like a hot water bottle, or other heating mechanisms, like hot sand bags or heated stones. A steam bath is another mode of sweating described in Ayurveda. It is advised to put *vāta*-alleviating drugs in water, and you should be fomented with the vapors.

Another mode of sweating frequently used in Ayurveda is to take a hot decoction which is not only hot in temperature but also hot in its Ayurvedic nature. This means a decoction made of substances which are *pitta*-inducing, like ginger, pepper, big cardamom, etc. After taking a hot decoction, lie down and cover yourself well with a warm blanket. Do not take off the blanket when you start sweating. Otherwise you will get an exposure to cold. Let yourself sweat as much as you can and get up only when your body is no longer wet.

Caution: Fomentation should be stopped when the cold and pain subsides, when stiffness and heaviness is controlled and sweating is produced. It means that the heat should be regulated in such a way that you should not get excessive heat. Overfomentation causes vitiation of *pitta*, fainting, malaise, thirst, burning sensation, weakness of voice, and general fatigue. Do not do fomentation during pregnancy, vitiation of *pitta*, if you have diabetes, diarrhea, poisoning or jaundice, when angry, thirsty, or hungry. It is said that fomentation treatment should be done when any food consumed has been digested. Thus, this treatment should be done at least two hours after eating and not later than four hours after your last meal. However, you should calculate this time according to your digestive system.

Urinary Tract Purification

Purification of urinary tract is done by taking something strongly diuretic for a day—accompanied by consuming plenty of liquid to clean the urinary system. In Ayurveda, barley salts are recommended for this purpose. In nearly every country, diuretic herbal teas are available, but mostly people use them to cure bladder or kidney infections or other problems in this system. For the purpose of purification, you use these teas for a day and drink plenty of liquids. Excessive urination will activate and revitalize the urinary system and will flush out dirt from it. Continue to take a light and warm liquid diet, like vegetable or chicken soups, etc., on the following two days of this purification practice so that the loss of fluid is compensated from the body. Take appropriate rest during the day you do this purification practice; keep warm and avoid air exposure.

Caution: Do not take diuretics in excessive quantity as they will vitiate *vāta*. They may lead to stiffness in the body.

Blood Purification

We eat a variety of food products and inhale air which is at times polluted with different chemicals. Some of these substances, which we take inside our body willingly or unwillingly, may not agree with the nature of the body. This gradually makes our blood impure and leads to various skin ailments, allergies, a bad smell in the body, diminished vitality and immunity, thus, making us more vulnerable to external attacks. A periodic purification of the blood, with the intake of some natural substances, will save us from various ailments and will have a rejuvenating effect on body and mind.

There are many products in nature which act as blood purifiers. Normally the substances with bitter taste (*rasa*) perform this function. The blood-purifying substances also work on the liver and regulate *pitta* functions. Thus, the blood purifiers also cause mild diarrhea. However, their function is more than just eliminating waste products from the digestive tract.

Blood purifiers should be taken in very small doses over a period of one week. People with a strong body smell, or blood-related ailments like allergies or skin problems, may need them for a longer time. In Ayurveda, there is a description of several plants which purify blood, and usually a combination of some of these is used for the routine twice-yearly blood purification. The two famous plants exported from India in large quantities

are Neem(*Azadirachta indica*) and atees (*Aconitum hetrophylum*).
One cannot buy ready made blood purifiers in the West, but
various combinations of bitter herbal teas are available, and
they also perform this function. It is recommended to use
these teas regularly for a fortnight twice a year. There are several other substances which purify blood and are easily available in the West either in health food stores or Indian food
shops. Fenugreek, kalongi, garden cress, coriander, dill, ajwain,
basilica, turmeric and garlic are some examples. Turmeric is an
excellent blood purifier and may be taken alone in case nothing else is available. A simple recipe for its consumption is
given later in the book.

Surgery

In addition to internal and external cleaning to alleviate the vitiation of humors, surgery is the third measure suggested. "A
surgical operation consists of excision, incision, puncturing,
rupturing, scraping, extraction, probing and the application of
alkali and leeches."[9] Surgery is beyond the scope of this book
and therefore I will not go into detail. Surgery in modern medicine is very advanced but one needs a wise physician before
making a decision to undergo an operation. Surgery should be
used only when all other alternatives are closed. One should
seek the opinion of several physicians and make an effort to
use all available methods to cure before making the decision to
undergo an operation. However, in allopathy, the alternative
options are limited and a surgical intervention is prescribed
very quickly.

---

[9]*Caraka Saṃhitā, Sūtrasthāna*, XI, 55.

REVITALIZATION
THROUGH MASSAGE AND YOGA

MASSAGE AND CERTAIN yogic practices play a very important role in Ayurvedic therapeutics. They revitalize the body organs and slow down the decay due to aging. There are many preventive and curative therapies both in Ayurvedic massage and yogic practices and it is important to learn them for health care. The concentration and breathing practices of yoga are also used in curing psychic disorders and healing.

MASSAGE

You have already learned that massage appeases vitiated *vāta* and *pitta*. There are different types of massage in Ayurveda to cure various disorders. Besides therapeutic massage, there are methods of massage for maintaining the equilibrium of the humors and for revitalizing the whole body. Massage helps open all channels in the body, insures good circulation of energy in all parts, and brings vitality and vigor.

Massage in India, where the Ayurvedic tradition began, is not only done by professionals but also forms a part of the family tradition. I would suggest that you should get a massage once a week by exchanging massages with friends or family. If such a possibility is not there, you should massage yourself by using the simple methods described in this chapter. However, this latter is less effective, but better than no massage at all. Therapeutic Ayurvedic massage is very extensive and can be the subject of another book. Here I have chosen simple preventive and curative methods of massage taken from the family tradition. You can easily learn these techniques and add them to your routine. You will learn five different kinds of massage: 1) pressure and pressing massage; 2) foot-pressing massage; 3) oil massage; 4) head massage; and 5) healing massage.

Before beginning any massage, make sure your subject is completely relaxed. Let the subject take an appropriate position according to the type of massage you are going to give. Check that all parts of the body are loosened and relaxed. Usually, people are tense in the joints of the hands, feet, and shoulders. Some people have a frown and a tense musculature in the forehead. Look at all these parts carefully and help the subject relax.

Pressure Massage

There are several methods of doing this massage.

Hand Pressure: In this massage, you should press with both hands by applying proper pressure (figure 21). Move your hands around so that you reach all parts of the body. Apply equal and smooth pressure. You should be firm and gentle. If the pressure from your palms is not well distributed, you may hurt the person you are massaging.

Begin massaging from the feet by pressing each individual toe. Press well on the joints of the toes, and apply pressure on the spaces between the toes by applying pressure from the upper part of the foot. Hold each toe individually and pull it out. Proceed further on the ankle and then the leg. Pay special attention to all the joints and press them between your fingers (figure 22). Press the pelvic joints of both legs. Now you reach the abdominal and thoracic region. Press this part very gently and make small, circular movements with your hands. Press well on both sides of the body by putting your hands in an elongated position. This way, you will press the sides of the ribs and the waist. After this region, begin to press the hands and arms. Press the joints of each finger and pull each finger slightly. Press the half-closed fist by applying pressure from both sides on the folded fingers (figure 23). Press the palm and center of the hand between your fingers and thumb. Proceed further by pressing the wrist from all the sides and then press

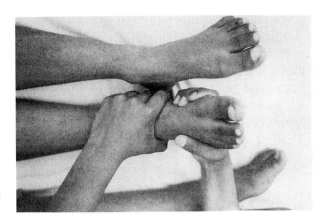

Figure 21. Apply pressure with both hands.

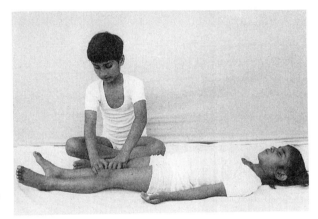

Figure 22. Apply pressure to all the joints.

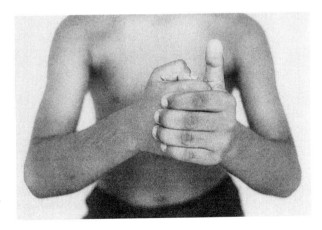

Figure 23. Massage the hands.

the arm by putting your hands around the arm. The elbows should be pressed well with fingers. While doing this massage, you may discover some sensitive and painful spots around the joints. Take care of them and apply some pain-relieving oil after the massage. These painful knots indicate an accumulation of *kapha*. Press the shoulders and the sides of the neck and head. Press the ear lobes gently between your fingers. Press the head

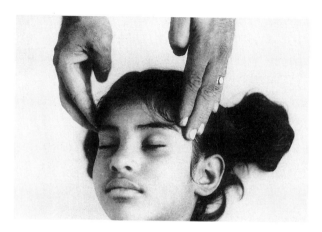

Figure 24. Massage the temples gently.

Figure 25. The walking massage.

Figure 26. Pressure is applied by standing on the body.

from all sides and then press the forehead gently. Apply pressure with the fingers of both your hands on both the temples simultaneously and make small circular movements with your fingers (figure 24).

Now the subject should be made to lie down on his or her stomach so you can press the back. Press the neck region close to the head by pressing with both your hands simultaneously. Press the back muscles and the back of the shoulder region. Do not put too much pressure on the vertebral column. Instead, feel each vertebra between your fingers and make small round movements on them to revitalize them. After the pressing massage, let the subject rest for a while. Do not expose the subject to cold or let him or her take a cold bath after a massage.

Pressing by Applying Body Weight

This is a type of massage which may not be suitable for Westerners. It is done by making a person with less body weight than you stand and walk on you. This is a familial mode of massage and generally children are requested to do it for adults. It is done on the legs and back either by standing and walking on these parts (figure 25) or by simply sitting on them (figure 26). This massage involves applying more pressure than the previously described pressing massage. This is particularly good for corpulent and overweight persons.

Calf-Pressing Massage

This is a peculiar mode of pressing the lower parts of the legs and is useful when the legs are aching due to fatigue and heat, or feel lifeless. Pressing strongly increases blood circulation in the legs and revitalizes the leg muscles. It gives an immediate feeling of well-being to a fatigued person who has aching legs and feet.

Make the subject lie down on his or her back in a relaxed posture. Press the lower part of the leg by taking it between your calf and thighs and by applying pressure (figure 27). This pressure is applied by bringing your calf and thighs closer together. Be careful not to apply too much pressure. Ask the subject each time if the pressure you are applying is tolerable. Repeat this process on different parts of both the lower legs.

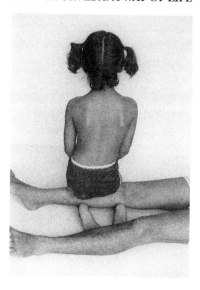

Figure 27. Applying pressure using your legs.

Foot-Pressing Massage

This is not massage of the feet but massage done with the feet instead of the hands. It is a very pleasant mode of massage and is easy to do. The procedure is the same as for hand-pressing massage but the pressure is applied with the foot and you are usually standing while doing this massage. You require training to learn to apply varying degrees of pressure with various parts of the sole of your foot. It is also important to learn to make circular movements with the front part of the sole. Most of the work is done by the front part of the sole and you should take care that the pressure you apply should be well-distributed over a large surface of your sole. If you apply pointed pressure, it will hurt the subject and also it is not good for your legs. You will feel tired after doing massage. While doing this massage, your knee is usually bent and you apply force from the knee downward. Try to revitalize various parts of the body of your subject with sensitivity just as you would do with your hands. Many people have difficulty in relating their minds to doing work with the sole of the foot, for we are used to working exclusively with our hands. Feet are used only for walking, standing, or driving, and these activities are done with the shoes on. To develop the same sensitivity in your feet as you have in your hands, you may use your sole on a pillow and practice applying smooth pressure.

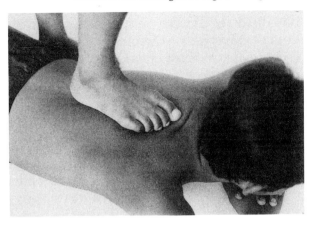

Figure 28. Using the feet to massage the spine.

Massage done with the hands requires much more energy, is tiring, and the pressure applied may be insufficient. Therefore, foot pressure massage can be very beneficial.

Have your subject lie down on his or her stomach. Begin the massage from the feet and proceed upward (figure 28). Follow the same pattern described earlier for the hand-pressing massage, except you cannot massage the sides, the front region, and the head.

Oil Massage

This massage is done by applying some oil or fat to the body and then applying smooth pressure by sliding your fingers on it. Take sesame or coconut oil or ghee. To get rid of some skin infections, you may use mustard oil, but otherwise it is too strong and thick in consistency. According to Ayurveda, the ghee is considered to be the best for massage because of its fineness and better penetration capacity in the skin.

The oil massage should be started from the central region of the body, between the abdomen and thorax. This is called the *hrdya* or solar plexus (figure 29, page 112). This part is the seat of the body's fire or the central distribution system for energy. When this part is properly massaged and made to relax, the rest of the body relaxes automatically.

Make the subject lie down on his or her back in a relaxed position. Take the oil or ghee in an open container and dip your fingers in it. Apply it gently with your fingers on the above-described region. Go on massaging gently with the fingers of both your hands in a rhythmical manner. Make sure your subject is completely relaxed and does not get tense with the procedure of this massage. Gradually, come to the lower abdominal part and massage it well and softly. Go on applying oil or ghee again and again because it not only helps your fingers to slide on the subject's body, but it also penetrates into the skin and cures vitiated *vāta* from the surface of the skin. The skin is liable to *vāta* vitiation and the penetration of the oil makes it stronger and more beautiful. While massaging the abdominal part, softly press with your hands to check if there is any stiffness or pain in the internal parts. If pain is caused with pressing, it speaks for some internal injury, inflammation, constipation, or infection, etc. It should be immediately attended to by appropriate diagnosis and cure. Massage well the parts below the navel. This is the urinogenital area. Do not massage the abdominal part if the subject needs evacuation.

Massage the chest and shoulders, and then slowly work down the arms, one by one. Massage the wrists, the thumbs, and the finger joints. Then begin massaging from the feet and particularly pay attention to the toes. Massage on the toes promotes vision. Massage each toe well. Massage the spaces between the toes by making inward movements (figure 30). The ankle should be massaged from all directions and the region above the heel should be especially attended to. While massaging the legs, work on the region along the side of the central projecting bone of

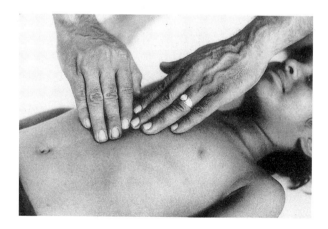

Figure 29. Start the oil massage in the solar plexus area.

Figure 30. Massaging the toes.

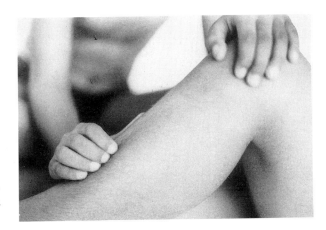

Figure 31. Massage the bones in the legs.

the calf. Make linear movements from down to upward in this region by sliding your fingers along the bone (figure 31). This massage should be done along the outer side of this bone. This massage is good for tired feet and soles and removes pain from the soles.

At the knee, make the massage movements in two opposite directions—clockwise and counterclockwise. Massage well all parts of the thighs and use your palms to apply force on this highly muscular region. After massaging the loins, let the subject turn on his or her stomach and massage the back. Massage the hips and lower part of the back above the hips, paying attention to the musculature and applying pressure accordingly. Continue like this going upward on both sides of the vertebral column to

Figure 32. Massaging the neck. -

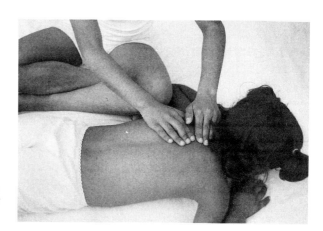

Figure 33. Work from the bottom of the spine upward.

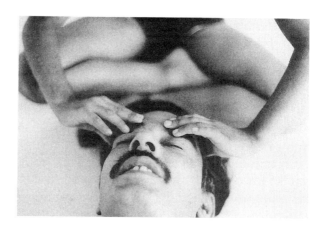

Figure 34. Gently work on the forehead.

the shoulders. Massage the neck with one hand by taking it between your fingers and thumb (figure 32).

Begin massaging the vertebral column from below. There are three principal energy channels in this region. One is along the spinal cord and represents *sattva*. On the left and right of the spinal cord two channels represent *tamas* and *rajas*, respectively.[1] The Ayurvedic massage of this region has a special importance because of the three energy channels here. Massage the base of the vertebral column (near the last vertebra) first by making circular movements in both the directions. Afterward, put the fingers of both your hands on the left and right sides of the vertebral column respectively, press them and make circular movements in both the directions. Slowly proceed upward to the neck region. Then begin again from below starting from the center. Make the movements in the same way by putting your hand on each vertebra (figure 33).

After completing the back, let the subject lie down once again on his or her back and now give a gentle oil massage on the forehead. Apply some oil and put the fingers of both your hands in the middle of the forehead with the thumbs on the sides. Slide them in the opposite direction to the temples (figure 34). Repeat this many times. End the massage by gently stroking your subject's head. After the massage, the subject should rest for some time and then take a hot bath.

Suggestion: It is suggested that massage be done once a week by alternating an oil massage and a pressure massage. It helps maintain the body's vigor and vitality. Massage energizes the whole body by opening fine energy channels and cures vitiated *vāta*. It helps cure minor pains and digestive disorders. Massage also helps discover any inflammation or malformation taking place in the body. Abdominal oil massages are good for women to cure painful menstruation and other minor disorders related to uterus and vagina. It also cures constipation. The massage on the solar plexus insures good appetite and a bright complexion.

---

[1]For details, see my book, *Yoga for Internal Health* (New Delhi: Hind Pocket Books, 1991).

Head Massage

Head massage or *champi* is considered extremely important in Ayurveda. It is memory-promoting and gives longevity. It cures headaches. It keeps *kapha* from accumulating in the head region and is beneficial for disorders like chronic colds, migraine, and sinusitis.

For the head massage, let your subject sit on a lower seat than you in front of you. You sit or stand behind, whatever is convenient so your hands can move freely without causing you discomfort.

The first part of the head massage includes a gentle oiling of the scalp. Use coconut, sesame or olive oil. Put the oil on your fingertips and apply it to the scalp by running your fingers through the hair and by rubbing gently. Do the oiling systematically. Begin at the front and move downward each time. When you have finished oiling the whole scalp, begin massaging by moving the fingers of both hands on each side of the head (figure 35). Massage all parts of the head and then gently massage the ear lobes.

The next step of the oil massage is doing a stronger and more forceful massage. This should not be done to all subjects, as some weak and delicate people cannot tolerate this massage. It consists of moving both your hands on the subject's head as if you are doing a drum beat (figure 36). The movements of the palms and fingers should follow each other. Both the sides of the head are massaged simultaneously. After this strong massage,

Figure 35. Massaging the head.

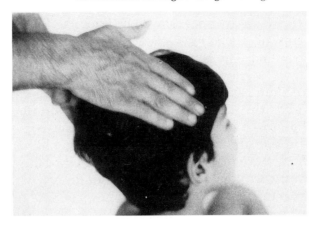

Figure 36.
A strong head-massage.

stroke the head gently a few times and then do the last step by pulling the hair. Hold some hair and pull gently. Do this with all the hair. This practice revitalizes the roots of the hair and makes them firmer. Never do this on dry hair. This is to be done only after an appropriate oiling massage.

Healing Massage

This is a very soft massage and is done generally without any oil. It consists of putting your hands softly on the subject's forehead or any ailing part of the body and gently stroking it. This has to be done with the determination of curing the person and helping him or her to enhance the process of healing. An ailing person requires consolation and reassurance which should be provided with this gentle massage by family members or friends. This massage is very helpful for curing disorders from *pitta* vitiation and psychic disorders. While doing this massage, you are barely touching the subject. This massage needs a special feeling of love and care, and people who are gentle and tender in nature can do it effectively. This may be done on any part of the body.

YOGA

Let us first talk about what yoga is and how it relates to the science of Ayurveda. Before attempting to understand yoga, it is essential to comprehend *Sāṃkhya* thought and review the concepts of *saṃskāra, karma,* and *saṃsāra* already described in chapter 1. The aim of yoga is to achieve immortality; that is, to attain freedom from *saṃsāra,* the cycle of life and death. This freedom can be attained by an ultimate union, or yoga[2] of the "Self" (the individual soul or *ātman*) with the Universal Soul– the *Puruṣa* or the Absolute. As is clear from the *Sāṃkhya* description, the *Puruṣa* is bound to karma only as far as it is united to *Prakṛti* or the Cosmic Substance. Once the Self or the part of *Puruṣa* within us is separated from the *Prakṛti* through individual effort, it reunites with the Universal soul or the *Puruṣa.* This union makes an individual immortal; that means the individual attains freedom from the cycle of life and death and becomes a part of the immutable, indestructible, eternal *Brahman, Puruṣa,* or the Absolute.

The path to achieve the ultimate aim of yoga is long and difficult. It involves tremendous individual effort to gain control over one's senses and mind. This spiritual development is not possible without a healthy body and strong mind. If one is unhealthy, one's mind remains involved with one's physical self and one is unable to reach the higher realms of consciousness. The body is considered holy because it houses the soul which is indestructible, unchangeable and is a part of the *Puruṣa.* Yoga teaches a harmonious development of the body and mind and their relationship to the cosmos. The body, along with senses and mind, is the cause of involvement with this world, but freedom can be obtained only through the effort of the mind by gaining control over the senses. In the classical literature, this idea is illustrated as follows:

> The body is like a chariot
> of which soul is the owner
> the intellect is its driver
> the mind plays the part of reins,
> as for the horses–those are the senses,
> the world is their arena.[3]

---

[2]See *Yoga Sutras of Patañjali* and the *Bhagavad Gītā* for details.
[3]*Katha Upaniṣad,* III, 3.

It is the intellect (the driver) which should lead the horses (senses) by using the reins (the mind) to take the chariot (the body) along with its owner (the soul) toward its goal (the Absolute). This illustration makes clear that physicality is very important to achieve any spiritual goal, as no chariot can go without the horses. The sick or uncontrolled horses will bring a bad end to the chariot. The maintenance of chariot, and the control over the horses through reins (mind) is a very important message as, without these, the chariot will not be able to bring its owner to the desired destination.

It is essential to harmonize our microcosm with the macrocosm in order to realize our inner light and the power of the soul which is above this ever-changing, temporary material world. In Ayurveda, various yogic practices are used for keeping an equilibrium between the body, mind, and the self, in order to establish harmony with the cosmos. Both yoga and Ayurveda have a holistic view of life and the cosmos, and neither of them is exclusively for the well being of the body in the disintegrated sense. They comprise our entire existence—personality and outlook. This idea is illustrated in figure 37, page 120. In the present context, we will deal with some yogic practices, *pranāyāma*, and concentration practices. All these are specifically oriented for physical and mental well-being, as well as for healing.

Yogic exercises (*yogābhyāsa*), yogic postures (*yogāsanas*) and breathing practices (*pranāyāma*) energize and revitalize the internal as well as external organs of the whole body and bring peace to the mind. They help in an unrestricted flow of the body's energy and bring harmony with cosmic energy.

For an Ayurvedic way of life, it is essential to comprehend yogic principles and learn some fundamental practices. If you are not prepared to do the yogic practices described here, and your body is stiff, you will naturally force yourself to achieve success. This will do you more harm than good. In yogic practices, it is forbidden to use any force. All the movements are linked to breathing and concentration of the mind on the particular practice. The yogic exercises and asanas coordinate your mind and body and help you to become self-aware. Therefore, I request that you attain proper knowledge and a gradual practice in this direction. Following are some comprehensive yogic practices and their benefits.

1. Forbearance or *yama*	A. *Ahiṃsā*: not killing or causing others pain. B. *Satya*: veracity or truthfulness. C. *Asteya*: not stealing. D. *Brahmacarya*: continence, i.e., self-restraint from yielding to impulse or desire. E. *Aparigraha*: not coveting, i.e., not desiring for oneself the means of enjoyment.
2. Self discipline or *niyama*	A. *Śauca*: purification — Physical. Mental. B. *Santoṣa*: contentment. C. *Tapa*: austerity. D. *Japa*: silent repetition of a mantra. E. *Īśvarapranidhānād*: a profound devotion to the *Īśvara*.
3. Yogic postures or *āsana*	The special postures devised for the purpose of yoga. They should become steady and pleasant with continuous practice.
4. *Prāṇāyāma*	*Prāṇāyāma* is the expansion of vital energy. Its practice involves a progressive deceleration of respiratory rhythm, increasing the intervals between inhaling and exhaling, and vice versa.
5. Restraint or *pratyāhāra*	*Pratyāhāra* is the indifference of the senses to their objects and their uniformity with the nature of the mind. Objects of senses are color for sight and sound for hearing, etc.
6. *Dhāranā* (attention)	*Dhāranā* is concentrating the thinking principle on internal space (*deśa*).
7. *Dhyāna* (contemplation)	*Dhyāna* is a continuous state of *dhāranā*.
8. *Samādhi* (meditation)	*Samādhi* is when *dhyāna* reaches a state where only the awareness of its meaning remains and even personal identity is lost.

Figure 37. A summary of the eight yogic practices of Aṣṭāṅga Yoga. It is not possible to find the exact equivalent in English for the last three yogic practices. However, the tentative translation has been given in parentheses. It is better to learn these words as such.

Sūrya Namaskāra (Prostration to the Sun)

The sun provides us the energy for life and health. It is symbolic of time, as the rising and setting of the sun represents one day. In the *Ṛg Veda*, which is the oldest of the four Vedas, it is said in relationship to longevity and the sun: "Witnessing always the rising sun, may we at all times remain pure in our mind."[4] In the *Atharva Veda*, which is largely a Veda on medicine, while praying to the element water, it is said: "Give me medicament so that I remain healthy and may continue to see the sun for a very long time."[5]

Plants and animals grow with the sun's energy. We reuse this energy in the form of food. The light from the sun is the medium for our power to see. With the practice of *Sūrya namaskāra*, we unite ourselves to cosmic energy.

The *sūrya namaskāra* is always done facing toward the direction of the sun. If you do this after sunset, then face toward the West. It involves a set of twelve comprehensive postures which are rejuvenating and provide long life. If *sūrya namaskāra* is done properly for fifteen minutes daily, it revitalizes the whole body and brings vigor. It helps you detect if there is any stiffness or hidden pain in any part of your body, including the internal organs.

The yogic postures are done on an empty stomach, and the body should be free from unsuppressible urges. For example, the bladder should be empty and the bowels should be cleared. There are twelve different positions in the *sūrya namaskāra*. For your convenience, you may learn these positions individually at first and combine them later on. Once you get rid of the initial hazards in the process of learning, you will be able to do the twelve postures smoothly, shifting from one to another spontaneously. After arriving at this stage, you must learn to concentrate on the sun's form and energy while doing these asanas.

Position 1:

Stand straight with folded hands. Your legs should be slightly apart. (See figure 38, (left), page 124). The folded hands should touch the middle of your chest. Try to relax completely and check that your shoulders and arms are not stiff or tense. Once

---

[4]See the *Ṛg Veda*.
[5]*Atharva Veda*, I, 6.

you feel completely relaxed, concentrate on the image of the sun and imagine its form in the middle of two eyes at the *Ajñā cakra*.[6] When you are fully concentrated, you will feel a slight swing in your body. Your breathing will automatically slow down.

Position 2:

Slowly start raising your folded hands upward until your head is between your two arms. Maintain this posture and bend backward (figure 38, page 124). Take care that only your upper part should bend, your legs should be straight and your head should not bend more backward than your arms. In fact, the arms should nearly cover your ears and this position should be maintained while bending backward. Go as far back as you comfortably can. The air will be pushed out from your lungs in this position. A slow and superficial (not very deep) breathing continues if you remain slightly longer in this position.

Position 3:

Slowly come out of this position by straightening your body. When you are in a straight position, unfold your hands and make your arms straight, with palms facing forward. Allow yourself time for two or three deep breaths in this position. Now slowly bend forward and then downward until you touch the ground on both sides of your feet (figure 38, p.124). Your legs should stay straight and your knees should not bend in this position. While doing this posture, you will exhale. If you stay in this posture a little longer, continue breathing slowly. Never try to hold your breath forcibly. Do not force yourself to touch the ground if you cannot reach so far down. This will give you bad cramps in the legs and shoulders. Try to achieve this posture slowly by regular practice.

Position 4:

From Position 3, while inhaling slowly, make Position 4 by putting your weight slightly on your hands and one leg, and simultaneously putting the other leg behind you. Straighten this leg at the back, resting the knee and the front part of your foot

---

[6]See *Yoga for Internal Health.*

on the ground and bend your head backward (figure 39, page 124). It is mostly the right leg that one tends to pull out in this position. It does not really matter which leg you pull out. What is important is that in Position 9, you should stretch out the other leg. Air will be partly pushed out from your lungs when you are in this position.

Position 5:

In this position, your body should be in a straight line, and your body weight should be put on your hands and the front part of your feet (figure 40, page 124). From Position 4, come to Position 5 by starting to put your body weight on your hands and by pulling back the second leg also. Let your body weight be distributed between your hands and toes and between these two, your body should be in a vertical line. Do not lift your head upward, align it with the rest of your body. Breathe softly in this position.

Position 6:

This position is also called *sāṣṭānga praṇam*. It means a salutation with eight limbs. In all, eight parts of the body touch the ground in this position. Exhale slowly, lower your body toward the ground from the previous position and let all eight parts touch the ground. Four parts of the body were already touching the ground in the previous position (two feet and two hands). Touch the ground additionally with two knees, your chest and forehead (figure 41, page 125). Your stomach and thighs should not touch the ground and that is why these two parts remain slightly uplifted from the ground. You may either hold the breath if you stay in this asana very briefly, or breathe very slowly if you stay in this position slightly longer.

Position 7:

Slowly raise your head from the previous position by putting your weight on your hands and straightening your arms. Bend your head backward as much as you can without straining yourself (figure 42, page 125). Your lungs retain very little air in this position. You should continue breathing softly if you stay longer in this position.

Figure 38.   Left: Legs apart, hands folded (Position 1); Middle: Arms raised (Position 2); Right: Palms to the ground (Position 3).

Figure 39.
Position 4.

Figure 40.
Position 5.

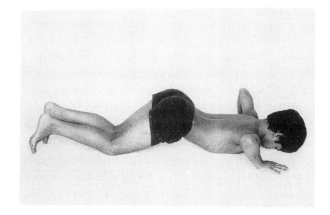

Figure 41.
Position 6.

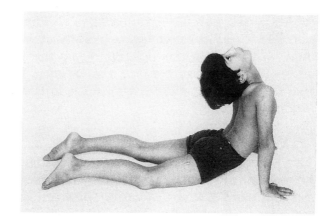

Figure 42.
Position 7.

Figure 43.
Position 8.

Position 8:

This position comprises making a hillock of your body. Slowly lower your head from the previous position, raise your body from the middle while putting your weight on your hands and feet. Your head should remain between your two arms, whereas your feet should be in a flat position (figure 43, page 125). From feet to hips, one straight line should be made which should be the highest point of the hillock. From hips to head, and then to your arms, there should be another straight line which descends on the other side. The body makes two sides of a triangle on the ground. The body weight rests on the hands and feet. Continue slow breathing.

Position 9:

This position is the same as Position 4. Do not forget to alternate the leg in this position as compared to Position 4 (figure 39). For example, if you had stretched behind the right leg in Position 4, then do the left in this position. From the previous position, bring one leg forward, bending it at the knee. The other leg stays resting on the knee and the toe just like in Position 4. Bend your head backward.

Position 10:

This position is the same as Position 3 (figure 38). From the previous posture, bring your stretched out leg forward and put this foot parallel to the other foot between your two hands. In this process, your body will be slightly lifted and you will bend forward. Keep your head close to your knees and lift your back.

Position 11:

This position is the same as Position 2 (figure 38). Straighten your body from the previous position and raise your arms upward, fold your hands and bend backward as you did in Position 2.

Position 12:

This is the last position of *sūrya namaskāra* and comprises coming back to Position 1, that is, to stand straight with hands folded (figure 38).

These twelve positions together make one *namaskāra* or prostration. You are recommended to repeat these 12 times as a daily practice. After one prostration, give yourself a small rest in Position 1. It will take rather a long time to achieve perfection in doing all the twelve positions with spontaneity. Do not force yourself and do not tire yourself too much; try to learn gradually. Learn the individual positions. Then learn to change from one position to another smoothly and by the prescribed methods. Remember that your feet should not change their place from Position 1 to Position 12 whenever they are required to be in their original position. For *sūrya namaskāra*, you need space behind you and not in front of you. When you displace one of your feet and stretch it backward, for example in Position 4, the forward foot should not change its place from Position 1. Remember exactly where you put your feet when you began. If they do not remain at the same place at the last position, then you are making some mistakes.

After doing *sūrya namaskāra*, lie down in *śava asana* for a while in order to relax and feel the goodness and energy this yogic practice brings you.

Note: There are many versions of *sūrya namaskāra*. These slight variations are from different schools of yoga. My version does not lay emphasis on one breath for one position. The breathing is generally automatically regulated for the various positions. I find that prolonged positions are more beneficial than quick ones coordinated to one breath each. In the latter, either you end up feeling breathless or do the various postures too fast.

Benefits: As has been already stated, the *sūrya namaskāra* energizes the body's internal as well as external organs, and helps detect hidden pains and ailments. It brings the mind in harmony with cosmic energy. A regular practice cures constipation, menstrual problems, and minor digestive disorders. It improves the general body condition and is highly recommended to healthy individuals for maintaining good health and for long life. According to my personal experience and from the experience of several others, I would like to add that the practice of *sūrya namaskāra* is very powerful and energy-providing if done right, regularly and twelve times at a stretch daily. I recommend it highly!

Now I will describe some specific yogic practices which can be useful for curing some frequently occurring health problems and can also help women in menstruation, pregnancy, and menopause. These practices are therapeutic and curative.

Jal Neti

Jal neti is a yogic practice for cleaning the nasal passages with water. The reason I have chosen to describe it here is that many people complain of sinus problems and some allergies related to nasal passages (like hay fever or sensitivity to sneezing for other reasons). The practice of *jal neti*, coupled with other measures, can provide a remedy for these problems.

For doing this practice, you need a small pot with a nozzle. Fill it with clean drinking water. The water should not be too cold; lukewarm water is preferable. Hold the pot in your right hand. Tilt your head slightly backward, then on the left side, and then slightly forward. Relax in this position, open your mouth and breathe freely from it. Insert the nozzle of the pot in your right nostril and tilt it softly. Let the water enter through right nostril and come out through the left (figure 44). Let the water flow smoothly by continuous tilting until the pot is empty. Blow your nose after this practice in order to clear the passages. Now repeat the same from left to right nostril.

Note: Jal neti activates the mucous-secreting cells of the nasal passage and some mucus is secreted after this practice. Spit it out and blow your nose a few times. You might have a momentary feeling of having a slight cold. The epithelial cells of the mucous membrane of the nasal passage are activated by *jal neti* and this practice keeps them active to fight any attack of virus, bacteria, or polluted air. After *jal neti*, some of you may experience that your sense of smell has been very much enhanced. You may feel a sensation of smell which you may not have experienced before. Some call this as a "celestial sense of smell." From my personal experience, I feel that the process of cleaning the nasal passages with water activates also the sensory cells, and one becomes capable of smelling nearly undetectable odors as well as odors from the internal parts of one's body. Perhaps the experi-

Figure 44. Practicing Jal Neti.

ences of persons who do not otherwise have a sharp sense of smell can provide some more information in this.

Caution: It is advised that this practice should be learned with a teacher. If the position of the head is not accurate in order to allow the gravitational flow of water from one passage to another, there is a danger of water entering in the wind pipe. This may cause an obstruction in breathing and coughing.

Benefits: As said above, *jal neti* cures sinus problems. It also makes the nasal passages resistant to infections and irritations. Therefore, it is particularly beneficial for people prone to allergies related to breathing (dust, hay fever, etc.). Since this practice clears the nasal passages and allows a free flow of air, it gives a feeling of well-being in the head. People prone to catching cold are highly recommended to do *jal neti* regularly.

Śirsāsana (head posture)

Most people find it hard to do the classical *śirsāsana* or standing on the head. This is a relatively easier version of the head posture. Do this asana either on a carpet or use a blanket or a thin cushion and rest your head on it.

Sit on your heels and bend forward a little to rest your hands in front of your knees with palms touching the ground. Bend forward a little and let your chest rest on the upper part of your arms. Shift your body weight gradually on this part of your arms while bringing the head forward on the ground in

Figure 45.   Head position.

front of your hands. Put the top of your head on the floor while slowly raising your body and shifting your weight on your hands. This way, your chest will raise and your hind-arms and legs will straighten. Bring your knees upward and rest them on your elbows. This way, your feet will be up in the air and your body will rest on the upper part of your head (figure 45). Stay in this asana a few seconds initially and gradually increase the time.

Caution: People with cervical problems should never attempt to do this asana. Do not do this asana if you are suffering from cough or cold. Do not stay in this position more than your capacity, and stop immediately if you feel giddy. It is advised to learn this asana under the guidance of a teacher.

Benefits: This asana improves blood circulation in the brain and therefore it is invigorating for the nervous system. It also enhances retention power, it is beneficial for blood circulation in general, and it brings a youthful look to the face.

Makarasana (crocodile pose)

This is rather a relaxing asana and can be done after the above-described asana, or to relax when you are tense or hyperactive.

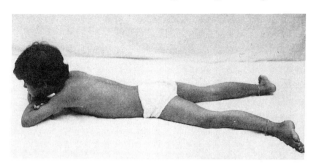

Figure 46. The crocodile pose.

Lie down on your stomach, widen the gap between your legs and let the heels of your feet face each other. The toes should face outward. Now cross both your arms in such a way that your right hand is on your left shoulder, and your left hand is on the right shoulder. Rest your chin where your arms cross, close your eyes and relax yourself completely (figure 46). Feel that your body is getting heavier and heavier on the ground. Follow the rhythm of your breathing with your thoughts. Do not let your mind wander. Stay in this asana for a few minutes and then get up gradually.

Benefits: This relaxing posture is beneficial when you are tired or tense. It is recommended to people with hypertension. People suffering from sleep disorders or insomnia should do this asana before going to bed.

Pavanamukta Asana (the wind-releasing pose)

This asana is for releasing accumulated wind from the intestines. Lie down on your back, relax completely and release yourself. Now slowly bend one of your legs and bring it to your chest. Keep your lungs filled with air while in this position. Bring both your arms around your bent leg and clasp your hands together. Stay in this position for a few seconds and then exhale. Raise your neck and touch your knee with your nose (figure 47, page 132). Slowly return back to normal and then do the same with your other leg. The next step is to repeat the same with both your

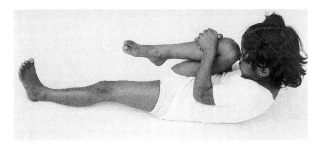

Figure 47. The wind-releasing pose.

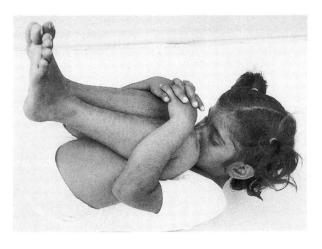

Figure 48. The second part of the wind-releasing pose.

legs together and bring your nose between the two legs (figure 48).

Benefits: This asana helps release the accumulated wind from the intestines and relaxes the intestines. It helps cure the problems of gas and clears the digestive tract.

Konāsana in Sarvāngasana (angular pose)

The word *kona* means corner (e.g., of a triangle). There are several types of *kona* asanas which involve making different angular shapes while being in other asanas. This particular asana is made after making *sarvangāsana*. The principal purpose of this asana is to release wind from the uterus as well as to provide exercise to the urinary system and genital organs. Lie down on your back with both hands on your sides and legs together. Relax yourself. Slowly raise your legs and when your legs are at a right angle to your body, stay for a few seconds in this position. Then bring the legs toward your head. Your waist will be slightly raised in this process. Put both your hands at your back to provide a support in order to straighten your whole body. Once your body is in a straight line and your whole weight is supported by your shoulders, neck, and the back of your head, put your legs as much apart as you can (figure 49, page 134). Your breathing will be slow and superficial in this position. Now slowly start bringing your feet together in such a way so that the soles are facing each other (figure 50, page 134). Your knees will bend in this process. Slowly bring the joined feet as much downward as you can (fig. 51). Stay a few seconds like this. Take your joined feet up and down slowly a few times (see arrows). These movements will provide exercise to the internal organs of the lower abdomen and will push out air from the uterus. While in this position with feet downward (figure 51, page 134) women should try to contract and relax their vaginal musculature.[7] Normally, while making these positions, your breathing will follow the rhythm of your movements, but never force yourself to hold your breath too long during a particular movement. You should not feel breathless. Your breathing should not be too fast, or as though you are making a tremendous effort. Therefore try to learn all the positions described here very slowly.

Caution: People with cervical problems or with any injury in their shoulder region should not do this āsana.

Benefits: This practice is particularly beneficial for urinogenital organs. Women are advised to do this practice regularly, especially as a preparatory exercise before conception for a healthy pregnancy. It makes the pelvic joints flexible and therefore paves way for an easy delivery.

---

[7]Women should do the contraction and relaxing exercises for vaginal muscles in a sitting posture. These exercises should be done every day to revitalize the vaginal muscles and inner lining of the cells. This practice insures proper vaginal secretions and saves one from minor vaginal infections. When doing this practice, sit cross-legged in a relaxed posture. Begin to contract the vaginal muscles while you inhale slowly and smoothly. After you have finished inhaling and have contracted the vaginal muscles as much as you can, stay a few seconds like this, holding your breath and contracted vaginal muscles. Then slowly relax the muscles while exhaling. Do not let the muscles loose abruptly. You should exercise your control on the phenomenon of muscle relaxation so that you let the muscles loose very slowly with the rhythm of exhaling.

Figure 49.
Angular pose.

Figure 50.   Bring your feet together.

Figure 51.   Bring your feet down
slowly.

Upavistha Konāsana (angular pose in erect position)

In the previous āsana, you were making an angular posture of your legs while in *sarvāngāsana*, whereas here the same will be done while sitting in an erect position.

Sit straight on the floor with your legs stretched out and your hands on your thighs. Take some deep breaths and relax. Make sure that you have an erect posture and you have no curve in your back and shoulders. Slowly put your legs apart as much as you can. Stretch out your arms to touch your feet with your hands (figure 52, page 136). Do not bend your spine in this process, just bring your whole back forward. Breathe slowly and stay in this āsana as long as you can. If your body is flexible enough, try to bend forward to touch the floor with your forehead (figure 53, page 136).

Benefits: This *āsana* is beneficial for both the thoracic and abdominal regions. It makes the pelvic joints flexible and therefore is helpful for an easy delivery. It exercises lower abdominal organs, particularly the urinogenital organs. It makes the uterus flexible and hence makes more room for the movements of a fetus. This āsana, like the previous one, is suggested as a preparatory āsana for pregnancy.

Baddha Konāsana (sitting with folded legs)

This āsana should be followed by *upavistha konāsana*. Put your legs apart while sitting erect as described above. Slowly bring your legs closer to each other in such a way that the soles of your feet are facing and touching each other. Your knees will bend in this process. Bring your clasped feet toward yourself. Hold them with both your hands and pull them toward yourself as close as possible by applying force from your hands (figure 54, page 136). After acquiring this posture, release tension from your body. Keep your back straight. Your knees should be as close to the ground as possible. Breathe slowly and smoothly. Remain in this posture for about a minute or as long as you can do so comfortably.

Figure 52. Stretch your arms and touch your feet.

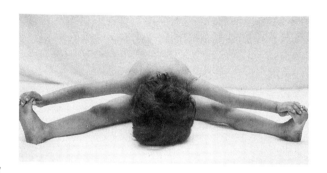

Figure 53. Bend forward if you can.

Figure 54. Sitting with hands and feet together.

Benefits: This āsana is beneficial for making ankle, knee and hip joints flexible. It works on these joints from a different angle than the two above-described āsanas. This āsana is particularly beneficial for the urinogenital system and is especially recommended to those suffering from these disorders. Like the above two āsanas, this āsana is also recommended before conception for a healthy pregnancy and delivery.

Prāṇāyāma

Prāṇāyāma is the fourth of the eightfold yogic practices described by Patanjali (see figure 37, page 120). In the yogic and Ayurvedic traditions, the process of breathing is not only a mechanical phenomenon of taking the air in and out. It is our link to the cosmos. The vital cosmic energy pervades everything and also the air we breathe in. Thus, by inhaling, we are taking this vital energy or *prāṇa* within us. To become conscious of this vital energy and to develop an ability to control the respiratory rhythm is called *prāṇāyāma*. In the present context, it is important to learn the fundamental techniques of this practice in order to use them for various curative methods and to develop one's mental power for healing.

For learning *prāṇāyāma* practices, first of all you must learn to coordinate your breathing with your thought process. The mind and the breathing process are linked together and control of one requires the other. Sit down in a relaxed posture, preferably with folded legs, and breathe normally. Concentrate your thought process on your breathing. Follow the movements of the air you inhale inside your body. Feel this *prāṇa* (or vitality) inside you by following its inward journey, its stay inside you, its outward journey and the emptiness inside when you have thrown out all the air. In fact, these are the four steps of the *prāṇāyāma* practice which you should prolong with a conscious effort. Try to make the process of inhalation slow and steady. Do the second step by holding the vital air inside you. The third step is to let the air out in a similar slow and steady manner as for inhalation. The fourth step is prolonging that moment of time when you have exhaled all the air. In other words, the fourth step involves increasing the interval between two breaths.

These were some preliminary preparations for the practice of *prāṇāyāma*. I will describe four simple practices of *prāṇāyāma* which you can do easily in the morning and at night before going to bed for attaining a tranquil mind and good sleep. In the end, we will discuss the application of these practices to enhance the process of healing.

1) Sit down in a relaxed posture, preferably cross-legged or in *padmāsana* (figure 55, page 139). Put your hands on your knees, or stretch out your arms so that the front part of the arms can rest on your knees. Keep your back and shoulders straight. Loosen yourself and begin to inhale the vital air very slowly and smoothly. Inhale as much as possible without feeling uncomfortable. Once your lungs are full, pause a little, let loose the back and the shoulder which were stretched during the process of inhalation. Now hold the air inside you and when you can not hold it any more, release it slowly and smoothly. Let all the air out and pause for a very brief interval before inhaling a second time and beginning the whole process again. You should concentrate on the vital air during this process and should keep your eyes closed. You should shut yourself from the external world and concentrate entirely on the cosmic vitality inside you. Repeat this five or six times or more.

2) The second practice of *prāṇāyāma* is the same as above except that this time, when you are holding the vital air inside, or you are holding your lungs without air, you should shut your nostrils with the help of your thumb and ring finger. This ensures that no air leaks in or out when you are doing this practice. When you have filled your lungs completely with air, slowly raise your right hand and close your nostrils (figure 56). When you want to exhale, put your hand in its original position on the knee. Do not keep the hand near your nostrils in a tense position. After

Figure 55. Inhale vital air slowly and smoothly.

Figure 56. Use your thumb and ring finger to shut your nostrils.

exhaling the air, close your nostrils again, but this time with the thumb and ring finger of your left hand.

With practice and effort, you should try to increase the timings of all four steps of the *prāṇāyāma* This should not be done with force, but with a gradual effort. Always let yourself completely relax. If your muscles and other parts of your body are tense during this practice, you require more energy, and your capacity to hold the vital air will decrease.

3) This practice involves doing the above-described four steps with one nostril while the other is kept closed with the thumb.

Acquire the *prāṇāyāma* position and slowly raise your left hand to close the left nostril with its thumb. Now do all the four steps of *prāṇāyāma* with only the right nostril. During the second and fourth step, when you need to shut both your nostrils, shut them with the ring finger of the left hand. Do this practice five or six times or more, and then slowly put back your left hand on your knee again. After an interval of a few breaths, do the same practice with your left nostril. This time the right hand is used to close the right nostril. This practice purifies two of the three principal energy channels of the body described earlier in the section on massage.

4) The third energy channel is straight. It lies in the middle of the left and right energy channels which cross each other at six different points of the central channel. After having purified the left and right energy channels, this practice is done to balance the three qualities of nature in the body. Here, you will inhale from the right nostril, exhale from the left, followed by inhaling from the left, and so on. In other words, you will let the vital energy flow in your body in a circular manner, involving the three principal energy channels and activating the *cakras* (or the confluent points of energy) which are located at the crossing points of the three energy channels.

Benefits: The *prāṇāyāma* practices help harmonize the body and mind. They strengthen the nervous system, increase memory, bring calmness and longevity. They are helpful in curing headaches. Minor nasal infections are cured by these practices and it makes one resistant against the common cold and other respiratory infections.

Prāṇāyāma practice is also used for various curative methods described later in this book. For enhancing the healing process with *prāṇāyāma*, you need to learn to guide the vital energy in various parts of your body. For example, guide the vital energy to your head and let it make circular movements there. If you get a minor injury somewhere, guide vital energy immediately to the part which is hurt and hold this energy there. However, for healing practices, you need to acquire mastery over *prāṇāyāma* by doing this practice every day. It involves developing a mental capability present in all of us. This capability remains in a dormant state due to lack of effort. By concentrating on the vital energy, we bring our minds to stillness. A still mind has the same nature as soul–pure energy which is our power or *śakti*. To evoke this power, we need mastery over our minds through *prāṇāyāma* practices. We will talk about this subject again during the course of this book.

6

HABITS AND MODERATION

THE AYURVEDIC WAY of life is a holistic system that involves the body, mind, and spirit. Your basic constitution involves psyche and soma, and coordinating them with the cosmic rhythm is the key to good health. Balancing the humors is maintained by coordinating your basic nature (in Ayurvedic terms) to external factors, such as place, time, nutrition, behavior, etc. You have learned to observe yourself in order to recognize factors that cause disorders. You have learned the importance of hygiene and inner purification to establish humoral equilibrium. You have learned to revitalize external and internal body parts and the mind. Now, you will learn about moderation, which also plays a crucial role in maintaining good health, or getting rid of minor health problems.

The subject of food in relation to health is very expansive and it is not possible to discuss this in detail here. I will only discuss some principal concepts. When we look at the kinds of disease suffered fifty years ago and those of our times, we see a clear shift. People used to deal with more exogenous disorders caused by the lack of hygiene; now we suffer more from innate and psychic disorders. The previous pattern of disease is only seen now among poor communities of the world. This became evident to me when I was working with a slum-dwellers around Delhi. These people frequently suffered from diarrhea, malaria, cholera, typhoid, etc. None of them ever complained of backache, neck pain, stomach ulcers, colitis, diabetes, sleeplessness, or depression. However, some of these people suffered from the malnutrition that is caused by poverty. Poor people could not afford a comprehensive diet and children suffered from the diseases caused by a lack of vitamins, minerals, and proteins. The diseases of the rich in India are not different from the diseases of the affluent West. A poor worker's malnutrition is different than a rich person's malnutrition all over the world. Diseases of the rich are generally caused by excessive, untimely eating and consuming too much alcohol, tobacco, or other drugs. The eating habits in the West after World War II have changed. This change may be due to the development of food technology and industrialization. I have already discussed this in the context of Ayurveda in chapter 2 to show you that our modern civilization is *vāta* oriented. The Ayurvedic way of life requires an alteration to these recently established norms of quick eating, and fast foods prepared with preservatives and other technical alterations.

QUANTITY AND QUALITY OF FOOD

Ayurvedic nutrition does not mean that you eat insipid food or that you become a vegetarian, or eat like an ascetic. It only implies that you strike an equilibrium between the quantity and quality of your food, and that you eat according to the place, time and your constitution. Always remember that if the food is delicious and you are enjoying it, it does not mean that you should prolong this joy by eating too much. Prolonging this joy will only give rise to ultimate pain. Tell yourself the following when you are tempted to eat too much: "I want to keep this joy as joy; I do not want this prolongation of joy to give me the ultimate pain in terms of obesity, stomachache, liver problems, etc. Therefore, I will eat what I require and what my body needs."

Another extreme for people who overeat is the new habit of weighing, measuring, and counting calories. You are not a machine that needs a definite quantity of oil, water, fuel, etc. Your consumption of food may vary according to your inner and outer environment. You all have desires, emotions, feelings, tastes, smells, and the process of eating is related to social activity and joy. When you spend all you energy measuring and counting, there is hardly any joy left. Instead, you could develop a sensitivity to yourself so that you eat an appropriate quantity of food according to your needs. Stop eating at the stage when you feel comfortably satisfied. Hunger is a phenomenon which gradually increases by eating too much and decreases by eating too little.

Some children suffer from the problem of eating too little and then they loose their appetite. In the beginning, they eat less due to some minor health problem or for emotional reasons, or they find the food monotonous. Slowly, their bodily fire diminishes. Since childhood is *kapha*-dominating, the bodily fire is easily suppressed. After that, they begin to suffer from a lack of appetite. Therefore, eating less is as dangerous as overeating.

Some people suddenly reduce the quantity of food consumed in order to lose weight. This also vitiates *agni*. Always reduce or increase your diet gradually if needed. Check overeating and overweight immediately otherwise you will be trapped in a vicious cycle. Sometimes this process begins during festival periods when people eat too much for about ten days. This increases the appetite and they put on weight during this period.

You should not eat again unless you have digested the previous meal because ". . . if one eats during the process of digestion, the products of the earlier meal mix together with the later and vitiate all the humors."[1] It is also important to consider that the intervals between the consumption of food should be appropriate with its quantity. It is said in Ayurvedic literature that you should consume food presuming that the stomach has three parts. The first part is for the solids, the second part for the liquids, and the third part is for the three humors located there. It is advised that you fill two-thirds of the stomach and leave space for the humors. "Food in inappropriate quantity is of two types—deficient and excessive. Food in deficient quantity causes loss of strength, complexion, and development. It causes upward movements of *vāta*, is harmful to the lifespan, virility and immunity, is damaging to body, mind, intellect, and the sense organs. Food taken in excessive quantity is said to be vitiating all dosas. After taking solid food up to the saturating point, if liquids are taken up to the same point, *vāta*, *pitta* and *kapha* situated in the stomach presses too much and gets vitiated simultaneously. . . . *Vāta* produces colic pain, hardness in the stomach, body-ache, dryness of the mouth, fainting, giddiness, irregularity of digestion,

---

[1] *Caraka Saṃhitā, Vimānasthānam*, I, 24.

stiffness, constriction, and spasms in the blood vessels. *Pitta* produces fever, diarrhea, internal heat, thirst, narcosis, giddiness and delirium. *Kapha* produces vomiting, indigestion, fevers with cold, lassitude, and heaviness in the body."[2]

When people consume low-quality food, it is said that, "The use of foods and drinks which are heavy, rough, cold, dry, disliked, distending, burning, unclean, antagonistic, or taken untimely, are while afflicted with psychic emotions—like passion, anger, greed, confusion, envy, bashfulness, grief, conceit, excitement and fear—also cause the above-said disorders."[3]

The right quality in Ayurvedic nutrition lies, first, in preparing various combinations which have humoral balance. This balance may be created by adding herbs and spices. One has to know about adding appropriate spices in food which is excessive in a particular humor or which might threaten to cause imbalance. The humoral qualities of various foods depend upon *rasa* or taste.

Ayurvedic nutrition means that you should eat according to your basic Ayurvedic constitution. For example, if you are predominant in *pitta*, you should avoid *pitta*-promoting food, and if you eat this food, you must balance it with other nutrients which decrease *pitta* so that the humoral balance of the body is maintained.

If you want to work with Ayurvedic nutrition, you should try to cure minor ailments at the preliminary stage by bringing in harmony the vitiated humors. Here the food acts as a medicine. For example: suddenly you feel excessive heat, and your blood pressure may go down, What you need to do is drink plenty of cold water mixed with some sweet syrup. Similarly, a spell of sudden heat may cause pain in the calf muscles and feet due to an excessive loss of salt from the body. All you need to do to cure this problem is to drink cold water with some salt and lemon. Similarly, you may cure stomach acidity by taking a glass of cold milk every night before going to bed. A hot cup of tea or coffee may cure a headache, or a glass of hot milk may alleviate fatigue.

Now we come to the subject of eating according to place and time. Place denotes climatic conditions and your geograph-

---

[2] *Caraka Saṃhitā, Vimānasthānam,* II, 7.
[3] *Caroka Saṃhitā, Vimānasthānam,* II, 8.

ical location. You require different food in the mountains than while living near the sea or in a desert. The humoral quality of these places differs. By not taking this aspect into consideration, many people get ill when they change locations. Forest areas are *vāta*-dominating, whereas climate near the sea is *kapha-pitta*-dominating. The desert is predominant in *vāta-pitta*, mountains, in *vāta-kapha*, and marshy places in *kapha*. You should carefully study your problems and find their relationship with your location, and cure them by altering your diet.

When people move from one country to another, there is a change in both climate and food habits. They need to pay special attention to changes in the body. For example, if you move from a cold country to a warm one, you need to decrease your quantity of food and change the quality of your food. *Pitta*-promoting diets should not be eaten in a warm climate. You need a more liquid diet and you need to take cold baths. You need lighter food, less cheese, more fruits and salads, cold mild, yogurt, and plenty of cold water.

Coordination between time and Ayurvedic nutrition is also something to think about. The first thing to consider is your age. As you have learned, each age (childhood, youth, and old age) has a particular dominating humor; therefore, you should consume food according to the particular cycle of your life. The time of the day, weather, the seasons also should be taken into consideration.

OBESITY, ALCOHOL, AND TOBACCO

I want to discuss three important subjects which are the major causes of ailments among the economically secure. These are excessive eating and the excessive intake of alcohol and tobacco. An excessive intake of food and drinks causes obesity. Obesity can cause many health problems over a period of time. In Ayurveda, eight defects of an obese person have been described: "shortening of the lifespan, hampered movement, difficulty in sexual intercourse, debility, a foul smell, profuse sweating, too much hunger, and excessive thirst."[4] It is further said that obesity

---

[4] *Caraka Saṃhitā, Sūtrasthana,* XXI, 4.

is caused by over-saturation (with food), intake of a heavy, sweet, and cold diet, day sleep, exhilaration, lack of mental and physical work and hereditary defects. In an obese person, there is an excess of fat due to imbalance of *dhatus*.

Remember when you are overweight, you have to carry this weight with you always. You have the same heart, lungs, kidneys, liver and other organs as when you had less weight. These organs have to work harder to take care of the extra weight you are carrying.

If your weight is healthy, you should have well-covered bones, no hanging and loose flesh, and well-developed muscles. Thighs, abdomen, and hips should not be over-covered with flesh. Some people are fat at a particular body part. They should do specific yogic exercises to get rid of this fat. For curing overall obesity, you should do yogic exercises, physical and mental work, control your diet, don't sleep during the day and you should take a not-unctuous enema. To get rid of obesity, you need to control your senses and develop a disciplined routine. You need tremendous courage not to yield to temptation. You must be persistent in your effort to lose weight and if you give up in between, you will regain the lost weight.

Obesity is caused because of excessive *kapha* and *vāta*. To get rid of obesity, Caraka suggests food and drink that alleviate *vāta* and *kapha*, rough, hot and sharp enemas and anointing. One should give up the sweet, cold, and oily diet, and gradually increase vigils, sexual intercourse, physical exercise, and mental work.[5]

Contrary to the problem of obesity, sometimes, I come across people who are too thin and despite consuming sufficient food, they do not gain weight. In order to gain weight, you should not worry about business or other responsibilities. You should take a sweet, cold diet, use ghee, massage, and get plenty of sleep. "Sleep, exhilaration, a comfortable bed, a relaxed mind, calmness, keeping away from mental work, sexual intercourse, physical exercise, cheerfulness, new cereals, fresh wine, curd, ghee, milk, sugarcane, rice, various grains, wheat, fragrances, garlands, white clothes, the timely treatment of vitiated humors and a regular use of bulk-promoting and aphrodisiac formula-

---

[5] *Caraka Saṃhitā, Sūtrasthana*, XXI, 21, 28.

tions remove the over-leanness and provide good development to a person."[6]

Ayurveda does not forbid us the pleasures of life, rather it tells us the means to promote them. It advises us to heighten our sensuality and intensify the pleasures of living. However, the joy of living should not be accompanied by self-destruction. True joy in any form is not destructive. If you are convinced that what you call joy is also destructive, then you should rethink the concept of joy. If you are smoking cigarette after cigarette the whole day, or you empty bottles of alcohol day after day, and find these pleasure-giving, it is very doubtful. Looking at the sunset and sunrise is a great pleasure for some. But imagine if our planet moved very fast and there was a sunset every ten minutes: would we really pay attention to it? Or imagine someone who likes looking at the sunset and goes to a specific point to watch the sunset every day. This person is very particular and fussy about this evening action. Don't you think it becomes more a mechanical activity than a joy? It is rather an addiction than pleasure. Don't get enslaved by certain habits.

Neither smoking nor drinking is forbidden in Ayurveda. You will find detailed descriptions of various herbs which can be smoked and a large variety of wines and beers. It is recommended to enjoy both smoking and drinking in a ceremonial way. Preparation of smoking material, the equipment used, and the fire to light the smoking material are prepared carefully by the smoker. The act of inhaling and exhaling should also be a conscious process, watching the exhaled smoke carefully.

Various medicinal qualities of different wines and beers are described in Ayurveda, and among their pleasure-promoting qualities are their aphrodisiac effects. Wine is suggested with food, but some kinds of wines are forbidden because of their drastic humoral nature. It is advised to use moderate quantities of wine.

Be very particular about the quality of alcohol you drink. Low quality alcohol causes stomach ulcers, colitis, destroys the liver and may give rise to even more serious health problems. It slowly destroys the memory, the power of discretion, and the in-

---

[6]*Caraka Saṃhitā, Sūtrasthāna*, XXI, 29-33.

tellect. You all know that excessive smoking gives rise to a wide range of ailments ranging from minor respiratory trouble, asthma, to lung cancer. Smoking in closed places and polluted areas is more harmful than in fresh air, open spaces, or a clean environment. In big cities, we are already inhaling lots of harmful particles which cause various ailments. They say that living in Mexico City is like smoking a pack of cigarettes every day. New Delhi is not better. Imagine that if you live in such a city and are a smoker, it is like adding another pack of cigarettes to the quantity you actually consume.

Don't let your habits enslave you. You are the master and you should have the capability to direct yourself. A mentally healthy person should be able to control his or her senses and should have self-control and self-restraint. Remember that mind controls mind and to develop that control of mind, the previously described *prāṇāyama* practices are very helpful. If you learn to control your mind to get rid of certain habits that damage your health, this will also make you stronger to face other life situations.

I suggest the following ceremonies for getting rid of the smoking and drinking habit. These are based on old Ayurvedic principles of *Atharva Veda*.

At least once a day, make a smoking ceremony. Wash your hands and feet before beginning the ceremony. Sit down in a relaxed posture and keep with you your smoking equipment. Take some deep breaths and concentrate on smoking. Repeat the following mantra: "I am going to smoke." First repeat loudly and then slowly repeat it silently in your thoughts. Concentrate completely on this mantra. When you have reached the state that all other thoughts are gone out of your mind and you are concentrating completely on this mantra, then slowly and gently begin to prepare your smoking material, repeating this mantra all the while. Now slowly light the fire. Look at the flame carefully by repeating the mantra once again. Light your cigarette or pipe. Inhale gently while repeating in your mind: "I am smoking now." Let the smoke slowly out and look at it carefully. Go on repeating: "I am really smoking, I am smoking now." Smoke the whole cigarette like this while repeating the mantra. Try to do this ceremony at least once a day—if possible, twice. It will make you pause and think each time you begin to smoke. When the process of mechanization breaks, and you are prepared to think, the wisdom follows.

Do the same ceremony for drinking. The process of pouring, looking at the color and form, and the slow and gentle sipping should be accompanied by this mantra: "I am drinking—I am really drinking now."

Tobacco and alcohol both increase *vāta-pitta* in the body and vitiate *agni*. They may cause hypertension. Tobacco gives rise to nervousness; it effects the peripheral nervous system and gives rise to a foul smell in the urine, especially in *pitta* persons.

In brief, we should adopt moderation in life. Extremes of anything, or being a fanatic about certain things, disturbs our humors and becomes the cause of Ayurvedic imbalance.

7

ADJUSTMENT TO
NATURAL FORCES

AFTER HAVING DISCUSSED about the humors in relation to nutrition, we proceed a step further to see how other
life activities, physiological as well as emotional, affect our humoral equilibrium and how we can learn to live in harmony with
our surroundings to keep good health. It is important to
Ayurveda to establish harmony with the natural forces. What are
natural forces? In nature, there is nothing static. Everything is
constantly changing and this change, itself, denotes "time." Life
is a series of changes from one state to another. Within us, it is
the same person (or *jīva*) which was there when we were in our
mother's womb, little babies, young men or women, old persons
and finally reaching toward the end of our journey. This self is
the living essence in all of us. It is what we call soul or *jīva* in
Ayurveda, and it does not alter, grow old, or die. It is an essential
part of life to learn to establish harmony with the "outer" material and the "inner" essence. Natural urges are divided into two
categories in Ayurveda—the suppressible and the non-suppressible.[1] I have detailed these in Figure 57 on page 154.

NON-SUPPRESSIBLE URGES

If we suppress the non-suppressible urges described in Figure
57, it leads to many health problems. There are people who ignore their natural urges due to their professional obligations or
just due to carelessness and laziness. For example, some people

---

[1] *Caraka Saṃhitā, Sūtrasthāna*, VII, 3–35.

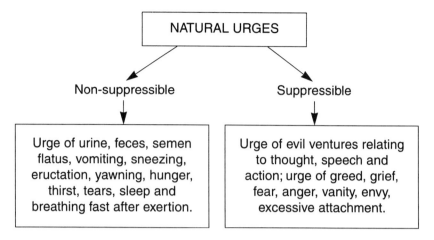

Figure 57.   The suppressible and non-suppressible natural urges.

sit for long hours in meetings and think that it is not polite if they leave. If this is done over a long period of time, it leads to serious consequences. "Pandits, government servants, courtesans and businessmen are ever ill persons. . . . They always suppress the impelled natural urges, do not take meals on time and excrete and move untimely. Others who also behave this way are also always ill."[2]

Pain in the urinary bladder and passage, dysuria, headache, stiffness in the loins are conditions caused by a repeated suppression of the urge to urinate. To cure these problems, sit in a warm water bath and do fomentation (sweating therapy) and massage.

Suppression of the urge to evacuate (defecation) causes colic pain, headache, retention of flatus and feces, cramps in the calf muscles and flatulence. To cure these problems, an enema is prescribed. Oil suppositories, massage, fomentation and an evacuative diet are some other helpful measures.

By retention of the semen, the symptoms caused are pain in the penis, scrotum, pain in the cardiac region, and obstruction of the urine. To cure this, massage, baths, wine, chicken soup, rice, milk, non-unctuous enemas and sexual intercourse are prescribed.

Suppression of flatus causes retention of feces, urine, flatulence, pain, exhaustion and other abdominal disorders due to

---

[2]*Caraka Saṃhitā, Sidhisthānam*, XI, 27, 30.

vāta. To cure these problems, an enema and oiling the whole body is recommended.

When we suppress the urge to vomit, itching, black spots on the face, anemia, fever and nausea are caused. Induction of vomiting after eating, smoking, fasting, or light diet, physical exercise, and purgation are prescribed to cure disorders.

Suppression of sneezing gives rise to stiffness in the muscles of the neck, headache, migraine and weakness of sense organs. Neck massage, nasal drops, smoking, and taking ghee after meals are prescribed.

The suppression of eructation causes hiccups, tremors, and obstruction in the cardiac region and chest. Chest and back massage and eating some crystal sugar is helpful to remove these disorders.

Suppression of yawning causes convulsions, contraction, numbness and tremors. Treatment to alleviate *vāta* should be given in this case.

Suppression of thirst gives rise to dryness of the throat and mouth, hearing problems, fatigue, depression, cardiac pain, headache, and deranged blood pressure. Sweet cold drinks are recommended.

If one suppresses tears, inflammation of the eyes, eye diseases, heart disease and giddiness are caused. To cure these, wine, sleep, and consolation are required.

Suppression of sleep causes yawning, bodyache, drowsiness, heaviness in the eyes, nervousness, and forgetfulness. Sleep provides vitality to body and mind, and suppressing sleep causes fatigue and exhaustion. To cure this, sleep and massage are required.

Suppression of fast breathing due to exercise or over-exertion causes tumors, heart disease, and fainting. Rest and *vāta*-alleviating treatments are prescribed to cure this.

SUPPRESSIBLE URGES

The *Caraka Saṃhitā* says that "one desirous of well-being here and hereafter, should hold up the urges of evil ventures relating to thoughts, speech and action. The urges of greed, grief, fear, anger, vanity, shamelessness, excessive attachment and desire to take someone's property should be held up by the wise. One should check the impending urge of speech which is harsh, betraying, untrue and untimely. Whatever bodily actions cause pain to others, like adultery, theft and violence should be checked in their impending urges. . . . The wise should not indulge excessively in physical exercise, laughter, speech, traveling on foot, sexual intercourse, and night vigil even when he or she is accustomed to them. One who indulges excessively in these or similar other activities perishes suddenly (by overstrain) just as a lion dragging an elephant would. The persons who are emaciated due to excessive sexual indulgence, weight carrying, traveling on foot, evacuative measures (like enema, purgation, emesis, etc.) are victims of anger, fear, grief and exertion. The children, the old and those having aggravated *vāta*, those who speak too much and loudly, are hungry, thirsty, should abstain from physical exercise. . . . The one who wants to be disease free should follow the course for the healthy."[3]

From these quotations we see one of the major differences between the health care and treatment methods of modern medicine and Ayurveda. In modern medicine, the body/mind division is very strong. For example, if a person goes to his or her general physician complaining of a headache, the physician will try to cure it, but if it still persists, the patient will be referred to neurology. There, the person will be examined thoroughly for any infection, deformities, or past accidental injuries that could possibly cause this headache. If the neurologists do not find anything, the patient is referred to psychiatry, concluding that the cause of the persistent headache is not physiological, and therefore the patient should be examined by a psychiatrist. However, the situation in Ayurveda is different. The patient with the headache is questioned in detail about his or her nutrition, digestion, excretion, breathing, profession, professional situation, familial situation, other relationships, social situation, emotional behavior, sexual behavior and other specific worries or tensions. The psyche is not separated from the soma and they are considered comprehensive. For example, excessive anger can cause stomach problems and allied headaches. Similarly, excessive

---

[3] *Caraka Saṃhitā, Sūtrasthāna*, VII, 26–29, 34–35, 45.

pitta may be caused by too much heat or eating a *pitta*-enhancing diet in excess, or any other reason that gives rise to anger. A hectic life and over-exertion increases *vāta* and gives rise to *vāta*-related disorders. Similarly, the excess of *vāta* caused by an inappropriate diet or exposure to cold can make one fearful and nervous.

One may say that the basis of Ayurvedic medicine is psychosomatic. However, this is not psychosomatic in the sense this word is used in Western medicine. In the latter, psychosomatic is generally used for bodily symptoms of psychic, emotional, or mental origin. It is considered that there is no problem at the physiological, structural, or chemical level. In Ayurveda, it is not possible to separate body and mind, and conclude that the trouble comes only from the body or from the mind. In addition, this body/mind relationship is further linked to the cosmic reality.

Let us now go into details of suppressible urges, the ill effects caused by non-suppression, and their cure.

We have already discussed that individual variations, like strong or weak constitutions, varied intelligence, gifts, etc., are due to our *daiva*. Our basic nature depends on *daiva*. The basic nature denotes our emotional reactions as well as our humoral nature. By our *purusakara* we can improve upon our *daiva* as well as work for a better *purusakara* for the future. By our sense of discretion or *buddhi*, we should learn to exercise an appropriate control over our senses in order to follow the course for the healthy.

Lobha, which is translated as greed, has actually a broader meaning than greed. It is not only to harbor a desire to have things that belong to others, but also to have an intense desire to accumulate more and more. It is to harbor an insatiable desire to have more and more fame, comfort, money, or anything.

In our times, an increasing number of people harbor the urge of *lobha*. Our modern civilization is very competitive. To nourish this urge is considered a sign of progress. There is a perpetual lack of satisfaction. To progress more, people lead hectic lives, they are over-worked and they have restless minds. All this ultimately gives rise to *vāta*-related disorders, such as nervousness, sleeplessness, tension, stomach problems, blood related disorders, etc.

When people are running around attending one meeting after another, or making deals, they are usually suppressing the non-suppressible urges, inviting ailments, and shortening their lifespan. In the middle of their hectic routine, they should try to pause for a moment and ask themselves, "Why am I doing all this? Why am I doing all these anti-health and anti-life actions?" Running after achievements is of no use when they are life-threatening (with disease) and life-shortening. Remember that the first priority of life is life itself. If that is lost, all else is useless. A mind darkened with the clouds of *lobha* forgets that our stay on this earth is temporary. We are not going to stay here forever. Therefore, it is better to enjoy the small pleasures of life rather than striving for the big, as the journey of life may not take us that far. It is like trekking to a certain point in the mountains. The bliss lies in enjoying the beauty and mysteries of nature. The purpose is not only to reach the destination. If you try to trek too fast to reach the destination quickly, with the thin mountain air, perhaps you are tired by the time you reach up there or you are mountain sick. By trekking in a hectic manner, you gain nothing, you are a loser in every respect. I suggest that you take time for what you would like to do rather than always doing what you are supposed to do.

Indulging too much in grief is unwise and harmful for health. The anguish of grief bursts out in the form of one ailment or another. Dwelling in a state of grief may give rise to stomach ulcers, colitis, cancer, all kinds of body aches, and other *vāta* disorders. People dwell in grief because they exaggerate their pains and perils and think that they are the only ones suffering. They indulge in self-pity and give themselves and their problems too much importance. Grief is also caused by too much attachment to money, property, children, husband, wife, and loss of any of these causes grief.

First of all, always remember that happiness is a state of mind. Happiness is within you. Happiness comes with a state of satisfaction. Do not make yourself a tragic hero or heroine. There is no real tragedy in life. Life is made of pairs of opposites. There is always a good side to everything, and your pain is not bringing an end to this world. Do not drown yourself in the sea of your pain. Even if you see a straw (of hope), try to hold it and swim again. Ayurvedic wisdom teaches us that our sufferings and joys are due to our *daiva* and *purusakara*. *Daiva* is due to previous *karma*. If you are suffering, by grumbling too much, you make the situation worse. *Purusakara* can be made better with *daiva*; that is, your present *karma* and what you should do now. In the face of a bad situation, you should accumulate courage and try to make the best out of the worst. Always remember that pain is a part of life and all of us have it. We must learn to handle it wisely with our *purusakara* so that we do not suffer further. We must learn to break the chain of suffering.

Each individual has his or her *karma* to deal with. Whether they are our sons or daughters or other loved ones, we can only help others to a certain extent. Realize your limitations and do not grieve over what is not under your control.

Too much attachment leads to grief. You must always remind yourself about the short-lived nature of everything, including the physical body and our belongings. Everything is undergoing constant change. You must try to detach yourself.

You must try to inculcate courage, fearlessness, and truthfulness. The emotions of fear are very destructive. Therefore, try your best to get rid of your fears by facing them. If you are fearless, do not generate fear in others. In a situation when you are a parent, or a boss, or in a similar position, try your best not to cause fear in others. Be strong and keep faith in your inner power or light. It is our inner power or *jīva* which is the cause of life, and it is indestructible. Try to concentrate on your inner power in any fearful situation.

Usually, when people tell lies it's because of greed or fear. For speaking the truth, one needs courage and fearlessness. When a child looses or breaks something important to the parents, he or she is afraid. Always give children assurance that if they speak truth, they get a reward for it. Do not create fearful situations for children.

Have courage to speak the truth even if you have to face the consequences. Telling lies also means being in a fearful state and worrying about being caught. A state of fear is bad for the respiratory tract, digestion, nerves, and the heart. When you are in a fearful state, think of those great mountains that stand boldly and strongly in the face of the forceful winds. Think of the limitless sky. Think of the powerful sun and evoke your inner power to get over the fear and have courage to speak the truth.

Jealousy and envy originate from a lack of satisfaction. We want to have what others have, feel frustrated and want to be in other people's places. Try to be satisfied with what you have. Speaking loudly and too much is also injurious to the health. Do not speak louder than what is required for communication. Do not shout. Some people get over-excited and speak very loudly. It is a sign of an excess of *vāta*. Speak softly and gently and use words that do not harm or hurt others. Remember that when we hurt others, we also harm ourselves.

"Anger destroys memory," says the *Bhagavad Gita*.[4] If you wish to live healthy and long, and you want to retain your memory till your last days, then try to get rid of anger. Try to save yourself from this destructive emotion by making an effort to find an amicable solution to problems rather than angry outbursts.

Some people get angry at very minor things in silly situations. In Germany, for instance, many people get angry at parking places or while driving if some other person made a mistake. In India, it is normal that a cow, or a dog, or a donkey, or bicyclists suddenly come on the road in front of your vehicle. Some city people and foreigners get extremely angry at this. Try to take it easy. Anger raises blood pressure and causes nervous and muscular tension. Save yourself from this slow harm you are doing to yourself if you wish to live a long life.

THE BIOLOGICAL CHANGES OF AGING

Many years ago, when I was living in Paris, I once got a letter from my mother complaining that all her sisters, younger as well as older than her, were already grandmothers whereas none of her three children are even willing to marry as yet. After several years, my mother also acquired the status of a grandmother and was extremely happy to take care of the little one, giving him ghee massage, bathing him with milk and all the rest. In Germany, I lived a contrary situation to this. A colleague had a 2-year-old granddaughter who was just beginning to speak. My

---

[4]*Bhagavad Gītā*, II, 63.

colleague's wife, who was around 55, once complained: "It is horrible to be called grandmother (Oma). One suddenly feels so old!" Not that this woman did not enjoy her granddaughter; she was delighted with the little girl as my mother was with her grandson. The difference was that this lady could not face the passing time. The changes which age brought in her made her frustrated and this frustration was also evident through the thick layers of makeup.

According to Ayurveda, the total life span of an individual is divided into three parts—childhood, middle and old age. Childhood is up to 16 years, middle age is up to 60, and above 60 is old age. "Childhood is determined up to 16 years when the *dhatus* are immature, the sexual character is not manifested, the body is delicate with less endurance, with incomplete strength and predominant in *kapha. Dhatus* remain in the developing stage and the mind remains unstable up to 30 years. Middle age is characterized by strength, energy, virility, prowess, acquisition, retention, recollection, speech and understanding. During this time, the qualities of all *dhatus* have reached their normal limit, with physical and mental strength, without degeneration, with a predominance of *pitta*, and this age lasts up to 60 years. Thereafter is the old age up to 100 years. During this period, *dhatus*, sense organs, strength, energy, virility, prowess, acquisition, retention, recollection, speech and understanding gradually degenerate and there is predominance of *vāta*.[5]

At every age, there are changes and alterations. At every moment, we are getting older than the moment before. It is extremely beautiful to see a small baby growing into a child and a child attaining youth. This beauty of change is always there, but after 40 people begin to condemn it. They do not want to grow old and begin to think that the better parts of their lives are over. They are looking at all that was positive and good in the past and at the negative aspects of aging. As it is, many people tend to glorify their past, grumble about the present, comparing it to the past, and worrying about what is not yet there. All steps of life are beautiful in their own way. Do not think that the happiest time of your life was spent when you were taken care of by your mother. A child or a baby is vulnerable, helpless, and dependent.

---

[5] *Caraka Saṃhitā, Vimānasthānam*, VIII, 122.

No doubt the years when one is a student are wonderful but it also involves another kind of responsibility, anxiety, and uncertainty about the future. Besides, many of us do not have much money or comfort during those days.

Another frightful feature of aging for most people is that they associate aging with ill health, deformities, ugliness and dependence upon others. Old age does not have to be like that. It is our own fault to be negligent about our health in our youth and then we reap the harvest of our own *karma* in our old age. Some people think of all kinds of insurances and investments for their old age, but if you tell them to do yogic exercises for fifteen minutes daily, they do not have time for them. For a healthy old age, we have to lay the groundwork in our youth. The body and mind do not forget past experiences. Old wounds give trouble and old accidents cause problems. Smoking twenty cigarettes a day, drinking recklessly, keeping awake late at night, loud speaking, outbursts of anger, and other such factors may not show their effect immediately, but everything is registered. It is very essential to have a multidimensional approach to keep good health and become a healthy, radiating and beautiful old person and not an "old wreck."

Do not try to stay young—try to age beautifully. You have to learn to live according to time, adjusting to time and accepting the passing time. Do not be afraid of the passing time. Accept each day as nature's gift to you. *Carpe diem*—pluck each day. Handle every life situation like a work of art.

Old age does not mean disease and deformity. We can avoid all this by living according to our nature and according to the rhythm of time. Nutrition, lifestyle, and exercise should all change according to age. When we do not follow the rhythm of time and lifestyle, we become victims of humor vitiation. With a constant vitiation of humors, we become vulnerable to other ailments also. We get trapped in a cycle of ill health and *dhatus* are destroyed quickly. Our present *karma* and our mental attitude both play a very important part in maintaining youthful vigor.

Both men and women are concerned about getting old around their late 30s and early 40s. Some gray hairs, a slight decline in vision, or an appearance of a little wrinkle somewhere becomes alarming and they begin to see the body in the process of degeneration. Growing into old age is as much a reality as blossoming into youth from childhood. In fact, the moment we are conceived, we begin to grow old. That means the alteration in the body is taking us toward a definite goal, which is the degeneration and the end of this physical being. The aim of Ayurveda is to reveal various methods to make the journey of life pleasant and comfortable.

Menopause, graying hair, a slow decline in strength, the decrease of sexual power, wrinkling, and ultimately moving toward death are physical alterations which also need the participation of our thought process. You should not consider all these changes as a loss and should not be frightened of them. Rather, you should be prepared for this basic fact of life—nothing stays forever—neither the happiness nor the grief, neither the youthful years nor old age. All of us are moving toward a definite end which is not actually an end but the mere illusion of an end. Our grandparents, their parents and all the other people who lived before us do not live any more but life goes on, seasons change, the Earth goes on revolving around its axis, we see sunset and sunrise and there is a full moon and a new moon. Similarly, when we would not be here, life will go on. There are always new people to replace us. Our bodies are made from the five basic elements and go back to them upon death, and the essence of life within us (*jīva*), acquires a new body in due course and is said to be "reborn."

In this cyclic universe, there is no cause to grieve over physical changes, degeneration, and death. Wisdom lies in accepting these changes gracefully. In fact, most of us take time for granted. We reach a peak and the descent begins. It shocks us. We begin to fight with it in artificial ways, like dying hair, getting wrinkles straightened, or become prey to all those alluring promises from the commercial world to remain young. Actually, to do something more substantial to keep youthful vigor and energy, one needs to do something before the onset of the decline of the *dhatus*. One does not dig a well upon being thirsty.

Many women suffer from menopausal problems. A part of this is caused by the above-described shock regarding the bodily changes. This is coupled with the physiological effect of hormones that cause suffering. The state of mind makes the latter still worse and in some cases the suffering lasts for several years. First, you must understand that the cessation of menstruation is as natural as its beginning which happened to you around age 13. The end of menstruation denotes the end of your reproductive period, and not the end of your sexuality, or the beginning of old age. It only signifies that you will not have your monthly blood release and you will not be able to have children any more.

To facilitate the transitional period of your menopause, you must prepare yourself mentally and physically well in advance. A slight alteration in menstruation marks the premenopausal period. Doing *yogāsanas* regularly, eating a *vāta* decreasing diet, and other measures like massage, enema, etc., will be helpful preparatory steps for menopause. In addition, some concentration practices, *prāṇāyama*, and the use of health-promoting tonics are helpful.

Eyes, hair and skin are other sensitive areas that mark aging. If their proper care is ignored, there is an early onset of graying and falling hair, weakness of vision, and skin problems. The care for these body parts described earlier should be strictly followed.

Wrinkles may appear due to *pitta* vitiation, due to loud and too much speaking, over-exertion, a stressful lifestyle, worrying too much, or making tense and inappropriate postures. A regular practice of *yogasanas*, as well as some specific yogic exercises for avoiding wrinkles should be done.[6] Get enough sleep and watch your diet and take care of your skin. Let the *vāta* not vitiate on the surface of the skin. This makes the skin dry and makes a ground for the early appearance of wrinkles. Make every effort to keep the skin smooth and shiny to delay the onset of wrinkles. Oil your body regularly and take all the other precautions described for the care of skin.

Let us come to the concluding part of this chapter which is also the concluding part of life—death. It is an innate force in all living beings to be alive. Even the smallest unicellular animals have mechanisms of defense to save themselves from death. When life is threatened, we are afraid and use extraordinary means to save ourselves. But at the same time, death denotes a natural process of decay linked to time. It is a basic fact of life that new ones are born and old ones die in due course of time.

---

[6]Refer to my book, *Yoga for Internal Health* (New Delhi: Hind Pocket Books, 1991).

Unlike in modern medicine, death in Ayurveda is not considered as a professional failure, but a natural process. These days, in affluent countries, patients with incurable diseases are kept hanging between life and death with all kinds of advanced techniques. Such patients lie in hospitals for years, either in coma or dispensed with their major vital functions. Contrary to this, Ayurveda does not advise an undue treatment of an incurable disease. Rather, it is advised to keep such a patient in peaceful surroundings in the care of dear ones so that he or she has a good death. In fact, there is no concept of a good and a bad death in modern medicine.

I do not want to give you an extensive discourse on "how to prepare yourself for death," as I think it is suffices to say: do not ever forget death. Always remember that none of us are going to live here for ever. All of us are heading each moment toward a goal, which in this transitory existence, is termed death. Ayurveda does not consider death as a finality. Death is only a transformation which is not different from other forms of transformation of energy. Boiling water transforms into vapors, vapors when cooled down become liquid, and this liquid can be transformed into ice or vapors again. Nothing is really lost. Similarly, with death, nothing is lost. Death is a process of separation of soul (or *Puruṣa*) from the material body (*prakṛti*). The material body goes back to the five elements it comes from. That is why the Hindus ceremoniously burn their dead. This signifies that the material body, without the soul, should be generously given back to the five elements to maintain a balance in nature. With this basic thought, the dead body is not considered important. The real self of an individual is the soul, which is indestructible, a mere essence or energy, without any substance. In the Hindu civilization "death culture" never acquired importance as it did in other ancient civilizations.

It is believed that the soul is reborn in another form. This cyclic, unending process goes on forever. *Kala* is one of the several Sanskrit words for death, and it also means time. Time is defined as transformation.[7] Death is a mere transformation. In Ayurveda, death is not considered as an abrupt end of life. Rather, it is a slow process which sets in with many different pre-

---

[7] *Caraka Saṃhitā, Vimānasthānam*, VIII, 76.

death symptoms. Caraka has devoted one full section (*Indriyasthanam*) to this subject. It is said that there is no death not preceded by pre-death symptoms.

Do not be obsessed by the feeling of death or keep a fear in your mind. Rather, gracefully and courageously accept the fact that death is certain for all those who are born. In fact, there is a story in Hindu mythology describing how the gods cursed human beings once by eliminating death and all suffering and catastrophe this curse brought on earth. At least once a day you should think about the inevitable end but it should not evoke self-pity in you. People generally feel very involved with their possessions and feel sad about leaving them. If you have got rid of *lobha* and excessive attachment, facing death becomes easier. Some others are worried thinking about their dependents. Remember that everybody has his or her own *karma* and you can not be the maker of other people's destiny. We all make our destinies ourselves, and if we are helping others, it is either a past "give-and-take," or nourishment to our tree of *karma* for the future fruits.

8

THE SENSES, MIND, AND THE SELF

H UMAN EXISTENCE IS a combination of body, mind, and soul. The external world is perceived by the senses. This perception is cognized by the mind. The word "mind" is used in a broad sense and includes the power of discretion or intellect. The soul does not get involved in the activities of mind. It is only a *dṛṣṭā*, or passive onlooker. However, without this passive onlooker, no consciousness of knowledge is possible. In other words, without soul, the cause of consciousness, nothing exists for an individual. In fact, the concept of an individual is not there without the presence of soul.

> "Body, mind and self—these three make a tripod on which the word 'living' stands and which is the central theme of this Veda (Ayurveda). Perverted, negative, and excessive use of sense objects, time, and the power of discretion is the threefold cause of both psychic and somatic disorders. Both body and mind are the locations of disorders as well as of pleasure. The self (*jīva* or soul) is devoid of disorders; it is the cause of consciousness in conjunction with mind, and the five elements (the senses—sound, touch, appearance, flavor, odor) and the sense organs (hearing, feeling, seeing, tasting, smelling); it is eternal—the seer who sees all the actions."[1]

Both body and mind are the location of pleasure, whereas the soul is beyond all these. It is said that the balance of body and mind forms the basis for pleasure. You have already learned about the equilibrium of the body in relation to the three humors and the cosmic link through them. The three humors govern the physical and mental functions of the body. For an

---

[1]*Caraka Saṃhitā, Sūtrasthāna*, 46–47, 54–56.

equilibrium of mind and body, a balance of these humors is essential. At the level of thought and psyche, an equilibrium between the three qualities of *Prakṛti*, namely *sattva, rajas,* and *tamas* is essential for maintaining harmony with the cosmic rhythm. These three qualities are responsible for three different psychic states in much the same way as they denote the three characteristics of the Cosmic Substance. These qualities are present in every aspect of life. I will come to this subject later, but first let us see what is meant in Ayurveda by excessive, negative, and perverted use of the sense objects, the power of discretion (*buddhi*) and time, the threefold cause of both psychic and somatic disorders.

THE SENSES, THE POWER OF DISCRETION AND TIME

All the five senses, the power of discretion (the capacity to think, discriminate, decide), and time should be used in an appropriate way. Excessive, negative and perverted use leads to health problems related to innate and psychic disorders.

For example, consider one of the senses—appearance, related to the sense of sight. Gazing at an over-brilliant object indicates an excessive use of the sense of sight. Using the same example, to avoid looking at things will be a negative use, and seeing too much, or seeing fierce, frightful, disgusting, deformed, and terrifying things is a perverted use of sighting visual objects. Watching films full of violence and horror, or watching bullfights, cockfights, or other such activities come in the category of the perverted use of visual objects. Similarly, living in a noisy environment, having a radio or television on all the time, hearing loud sounds like drums or machines, is an excessive use of sound and overloads your sense of hearing. Keeping absolutely away from noise and not hearing at all is a negative use, while hearing hard and frightful words, or those that announce the death of the dear ones, loss, or humiliation, is a perverted use of auditory objects. Smelling too much or smelling sharp, intense, or detestable odors is an excessive use of olfactory objects. Keeping away from all odor is a negative use, and smelling disliked, decomposed and poisoned air, the smell of dead bodies, or the strong smell of some chemicals, is a perverted use of the sense of smell.

Eating sharp, strong, sour, or bitter foods is an excessive use of the sense of taste. Taking tasteless food is a negative use, whereas using substances with *rasas* opposite to one's constitution and strength (see chapter 9 for the description of *rasas*) is a perverted use of taste. Taking too hot or too cold baths, too much massage or anointing is also an excessive use of tactile senses. Abstaining from baths, or massages is a negative use, and touching uneven surfaces, dirty objects, or to injure yourself is a perverted use of touch.

After the explanation of the excessive, negative, or perverted use of the senses, we come to power of discretion (or *buddhi*) and see how the excessive, negative, or perverted use causes ill effect on our health. It is with our *buddhi* (intellect, or power of discretion) that we decide our actions—*karma*. Excessive physical action, movement and overwork are excessive uses of the body, whereas a lack of movement, passivity, the absence of physical exercise are negative uses. The perverted uses of the body are holding up or forcing urges, abnormal posturing, obstructing breath and self-mortification. Speaking too much and loud is an excessive use of speech. Refraining from speech and self-expression is the negative use of speech. Words indicating betrayal, lying, untimely and indiscreet speech, quarrels, harshness, indicate perverted uses of speech.

An excessive use of the faculty of mind is indicated by overly-mental activity or a hectic way of thinking. To have a passive withdrawn mind denotes its negative use, whereas to harbor ill feelings about others, or harming, killing, and paining others are some perverted uses of mind. Perverted use of mind is the perverted use of memory. That is when memory is not used for beneficial and positive purpose, instead, it is used for recalling past (pleasant or unpleasant) situations and ignoring the present. We will soon take up this subject in detail with respect to three *gunas* or qualities.

The excessive, negative, and perverted use of time relates to the changing seasons and their character. For example, too much or too little cold during winter denotes an excessive and negative effect of time. Not coordinating your actions with the changing seasons and their character is a perverted use of time. For example, not wearing suitable clothing in winter or summer are perverted uses of time. Staying too much in sun or exposing yourself to cold air in winter are some other perverted uses of time.

A balanced and wholesome combination of the above factors leads to good health, cheerfulness and strength. On the contrary, their excessive, negative, or perverted use and intellectual errors and an unwholesome way of living give rise to various innate disorders, short life span, dissatisfaction, frustration leading to psychic ailments.

THE THREE QUALITIES OF MIND

The three qualities of *Prakṛti* or Cosmic Substance are *sattva*, *rajas* and *tamas*. *Sattva* is the quality of truth, virtue, and equilibrium; *rajas* denotes the notion of force and impetus; *tamas* restrains, obstructs and resists motion. The application of these three qualities of Cosmic Substance vary from subtle to practical levels. Before discussing their importance in medicine, let us see how they apply to our existence and to cosmic law.

Sattva is an individual's cause of existence—it denotes *jīva* or the soul. It can be compared to the state of wakefulness. The terms sleep, dream, and wakefulness are used in an abstract manner here. The cause of life of an embryo is *jīva*, and it is *jīva* that puts life into the cosmic substance. "The embryo can not be produced without *jīva*. A sprout can not grow from a nonseed."[2] The *jīva* or the self is a "wakeful state"; it means the realization that an individual's real self is not the physical body, but the energy (or soul) which is without substance. The soul is the pure element, it is a state of "wakefulness," enlightenment, or *sattva*.

An embryo is in a state of *tamas* before being born. It is compared to a state of deep slumber, which corresponds to inactivity and the closure to the external world.

---

[2] *Caraka Saṃhitā, Śarīrasthanam*, III, 9.

Rajas is compared to the dream state. It denotes the activities of life that take place with inner subtle energy. This energy has subtle channels or *nadis*.[3]

Thus, in relation to the body, *tamas, rajas* and *sattva* represent the physical, the subtle, and the spiritual aspects of human existence. In the cosmic view, *rajas* denotes the creative principle of the universe, *tamas* is the devouring principle, and *sattva* is the principle of energy and life. Referring to *Sāṃkhya* again for a better comprehension of these principles, these three qualities are unexpressed before the combination of the universal soul and the cosmic substance. The combination of these two denotes creation, and that is *rajas*. When these two are separated again, the phenomenal universe is once again dissolved, and that denotes *tamas*, the devouring principle. *Sattva* is the living principle of life.

Just as *vāta, pitta* and *kapha* are bodily *dosas* (humors), *sattva, rajas* and *tamas* denote the qualities and activities of the mind.[4] Thinking, planning, making decisions, etc., are the *rajas* activities of the mind. During sleep, mental activity is called *tamas*, as the mind is closed to new knowledge during sleep. It is only previously acquired knowledge that preoccupies mind during sleep. This mental activity is in the form of dreams, and even if dreams are absent, the realization of sleep being good or bad, etc., denotes the *tamas* activity of the mind. *Sattva* activities of the mind are those which lead us toward equilibrium, truth, and the realization of self. These are the qualities of self-discipline, self-restraint, control over the senses, *prāṇāyāma*, concentration practices, and stillness of the mind.

In normal worldly living, for sanity and good health, one has to have balance between *sattva, rajas* and *tamas*. I have used the expression "worldly living" because when one is an ascetic, one seeks the path of *sattva* and one withdraws from *rajas* and *tamas*. Let me explain to you in detail about these qualities.

We have already talked about the three priorities of life (see chapter 2). The first priority is to safeguard life itself. The second priority is to earn an appropriate living. The third priority is the

---

[3]See my book *Yoga for Internal Health* for a brief description of *tantric* literature (New Delhi: Hind Pocket Books, 1991).

[4]*Caraka Saṃhitā, Sūtrasthāna,* I, 57.

realization of the self and work for immortality; that is, to end the cycle of birth and death and become one with the Universal Soul. When dealing with the first two priorities, we work and live in a more or less established system in a particular society. Our lives are predominatingly *rajas* as we occupy ourselves with ideas of earning money, having a place to live, getting food, education, and other means of survival. All this gives rise to desires—to earn more money, to build a house, to buy a car or other comforts. All these activities are *rajas* activities.

Emotions like greed, jealousy, laziness, paining, killing, telling lies, stealing, etc., are *tamas* qualities of the mind. To overcome worldly desires, to gain control over the senses, to make an effort to get rid of anger, to get rid of attachments to people and objects, to be free from greed or other activities is called *sattva*.

In our daily routine, we are preoccupied by *rajas*, but *tamas* is also a part of living. *Tamas* balances *rajas* in certain situations, such as over-activity and laziness. Our daily activities cannot be dissociated from *tamas* even as very "good" and "moral" human beings. Eating meat is killing and paining. There are times when we tell lies to handle a situation or save face. *Sattva* is also a part of living, as nearly all people in the world try to find the stillness within them through various means—like religion, nature worship, or some other devotional way.

Our routine activities are a combination of three types of the above-described qualities. Just as an equilibrium of the three humors is essential for good health and longevity, similarly, a balance in *sattva, rajas,* and *tamas* is essential for a peaceful, undisturbed, and strong mind and for keeping sanity. As you know, a disturbed or restless mind will also derange the humoral equilibrium which leads to various innate disorders, which leads further to a disturbed mental state, thus making a vicious cycle (see figure 58).

Let's see how figure 58 works in real life. Imagine someone who earns a lot of money, who is an executive or a top politician, and this person has to make many decisions, attend various meetings, make diverse speeches and think of millions of other matters. He or she has no real leisure. Even when this person comes home from work, he or she still thinks of professional activities. This person has little time for rest and none for making

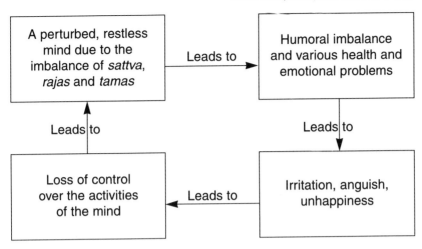

Figure 58. A vicious cycle made by the imbalance of the three qualities of the mind.

an effort to attain peace of mind. Thus, we see this person's mental activity is domineeringly *rajas*; there is a lack of *tamas* and an absence of *sattva*. This imbalance will give rise to excess of *vāta* due to the over-activity of the mind. As you know, too much mental activity, a lack of time, hurried meals, or heavy meals accompanied by business meetings, all lead to a further vitiation of *vāta*. When this situation lasts for a long time, various *vāta* ailments, such as insomnia, hypertension, various aches and pains, and some digestive disorders begin to show their initial symptoms. These busy people do not have time to cure themselves with rest and other time-consuming and health-promoting measures. Because of these nagging ailments, they begin to get irritated, anguished, and unhappy. The capacity to concentrate diminishes. This leads to even more restlessness and nervousness, and the cycle continues. Tremendous will, effort, and external help is needed to get out of this trap and regain balance.

This example is also applicable to people with excessive *sattva* and *tamas*. A person with a *tamsic* mind lacks activity, is dull and slow to reaction. Other *tamsic* feelings are greed, jealousy, too much attachment, and lead to frustration and depression. This leads to *kapha* vitiation and hence to *kapha* disorders. As you know, with the vitiation of *kapha*, a person tends to be inactive, sleeps too much and becomes slow to reaction. This leads further to depression and other *kapha* disorders. This cycle continues unless initiative is taken to balance *tamas* with *rajas* and *sattva.*

The modern materialistically oriented way of living is aimed at fulfilling basic physiological needs of the body-machine and provides maximum comfort and luxury. Training the mind, controlling the senses, developing an inner stillness, and the search for inner power are completely lacking. There is an extreme of *rajas,* and *sattva* is completely lacking. This creates a tremendous imbalance in many societies and leads to our modern social problems. In recent history, it is extreme *rajas* which has led to many reactionary movements from the youth of many Western countries. After so many years of *tamas* during World War II, the West woke up to *rajas* and *sattva* was diminished. People left religion and other spiritual activities. When *rajas* reaches its limit in the absence of *sattva,* it leads to a feeling of emptiness and worthlessness. We are relatively free from material worries but the subtle questions which are basic to human existence remain unanswered. Drowned in the material world and forgetting that the inner world inside us is far richer, *rajas* people try to evade questions on existence, life, old age, sickness, death, etc. But sooner or later, we all have to face these facts of life. Sometimes a reactionary attitude develops and the balance is shifted to another extreme. It gives rise to the extremes of *sattva* or *tamas.* When the equilibrium shifts to *tamas,* it may give rise to various forms of insanity, depression, disgust, rejection, and so on. This shift can cause serious innate and psychic disorders.

On the other hand, with an extreme wave of *sattva,* people want to reject everything material and spend time in seclusion in search of the "other reality." There are numerous *sādhūs* (holy people) in both India and in the West. These people usually stay idle, and live on others while having the illusion of achieving salvation. They shift between *sattva* and *tamas,* and suffer from imbalance.

Any extreme of the three mind qualities brings mental, physical, and social imbalance. Moderation, an equilibrium between the three qualities will lead us toward a healthy and long life. Without health, all the prosperity in the world is worthless. An unhealthy body and mind cannot lead to salvation. Whatever activity, profession, or aim you choose, it is essential to find a middle ground for the activities of the mind.

Do not get trapped into an extreme *rajas* state. I use the word "trapped" because I see many people around me, both in Europe and in India who live in an illusion of postponing *sattva* and *tamas*. That "later" becomes one day too late, and people are victimized by their unwholesome way of living and get trapped in the cycle shown in figure 58. Always remind yourself that the time to begin a balanced and wholesome way of living is now. Each passing moment is important. An unwholesome way of life leaves marks forever.

A person who wishes to devote his or her time to attain salvation and wants to search for inner light or *sattva* also needs an equilibrium. A middle ground is absolutely essential no matter what our personal goals may be. We have physical needs, and to fulfill them, we must work. When we are not working, and only living for "spirituality," somebody else has to work for our survival–for our food, clothing, and other needs. In the search for truth, some people become lazy and dependent; then they are no more on the path of *sattva* but are moving toward *tamas*.

A particular state of mind, or the domination of one of the three qualities, limits our way of life. A person with a predominance of *rajas* will have a hectic lifestyle. Traveling too much, talking too much, poor posture, eating late or in a hurry are symptoms of *rajas* people. In contrast to this, *tamas* people generally oversleep, and lack of activity may make them fat. They tend to eat *tamas* food which further disturbs the balance in the body. Their laziness and inertia may further increase *tamas* qualities like jealousy, lack of self-control, and listlessness.

On the path of *sattva*, people over-simplify their diets or eat very little, fast too much, or use other means of self-mortification to reach their goal. These methods may lead to an unhealthy body and weak and tired mind. Suffice it to say that whether people are managers or ascetics, they need to adopt a middle way and control mental activity to develop a balance of *sattva, rajas* and *tamas*.

The three *gunas*, or qualities described here, should not be confused with the yin and yang of Chinese tradition. Yin and yang refers to two opposite poles of energies. We call these pairs of opposites–like day and night, sky and earth, cold and hot, soul and non-soul, truth and lie, material and spiritual, etc. The pairs of opposites are easier to understand when we talk about balance and equilibrium. They are like two sides of a balance; neither side should be heavier. However, the three *gunas* denote specifically precise qualities and their three-sided equilibrium. Each is connected to the other and an excess of one imbalances the other two. The three qualities are like three corners of a triangle—interrelated, interconnected, and interdependent.

In the living tradition of Ayurveda, these three qualities have a great importance as they not only apply to the activities of mind, but practically to all other aspects of life. Food, lifestyle, colors, personality, the nature of a person are all described in terms of these qualities. Sometimes, out of ignorance, the deeper philosophical meaning of these three terms is not understood and *tamas* is associated with negative actions and habits, *rajas* with what is royal and luxurious, and *sattva* with spiritual and kind deeds.

Alcohol, meat, onions, strong smelling foods, overcooked or not well-prepared foods are generally referred to as *tamsic* foods. Overeating is a *tamsic* habit. *Rajasic* food is that which is well-prepared; it is moderately spiced, includes delicate food stuffs, appropriate, non-antagonistic Ayurvedic qualities, and is consumed in a medium quantity with a moderate amount of good wine. *Sattvic* food includes all that which is not exciting for the senses and which has a very mild effect on the humors. It is easy to digest and does not make one lazy. Fruits, rice, milk, honey, ghee, vegetables with a mild effect on humors—such as carrots, zucchini, pumpkin, etc., are in this category. *Sattvic* food excludes meat, spices, ginger, garlic, and vegetables that aggravate humors, such as cauliflower, onions, okra, and eggplant. Ascetics generally take only *sattvic* food, and ordinary people observe a *sattvic* regimen once a day, or at certain times of the year for religious, self-control, or health purposes.

What I want to convey with this description of food qualities is that a person—according to his or her nature—dominated by a particular quality will also have the other behavioral tendencies and will pick food of the same nature. Thus, to change the qualities of the activities of mind, one has to also work simultaneously with external factors. For example, if your quality of mind is *tamsic* and you wish to alter it, or lessen it, then change your food habits, wear light colored clothes, get involved in activities and sleep less. External factors are the expression of what is inside and at the same time they affect inner behavior.

THREE KINDS OF TREATMENT–RATIONAL, PSYCHOLOGICAL, AND SPIRITUAL

"There are three types of therapy—spiritual, rational, and psychological. Spiritual therapy consists of the recitation of mantras, wearing roots and gems, auspicious acts, offerings, oblation, following religious precepts, atonement, fasting, invoking blessings, rendering oneself to the gods, pilgrimages, etc. Rational therapy consists of a rational administration of diet and drugs. Psychological therapy is the restraint of mind from unwholesome objects."[5]

We have been largely talking about rational treatment. Now we will discuss all the three types of treatments in relation to each other. Let me make it clear that psychological therapy in this sense is not what is understood by this word in modern medicine. In modern medicine, body and mind are separated, and ailments are divided according to their origin. Rational therapy is separated from psychological therapy, and spiritual therapy does not really exist in modern medicine. However, in Ayurveda, the three types of treatments are interdependent and interrelated, and are therefore inseparable. The same is true for the three kinds of disorders described earlier (see chapter 2). Ayurvedic therapy is three-dimensional. Besides rational therapy which is done with medicine, nutritional care, exercise, and other such external methods, the power of the mind is also used to enhance the process of healing, and that is what is termed psychological therapy. The thought process and the mind is directed toward searching for the cause of the ailment, factors enhancing the ailment, and mental effort and will power are used to eradicate them. If patients are unable to help themselves in this process, the help of a physician or a wise person is provided

---

[5]*Caraka Saṃhitā, Sūtrasthāna,* XI, 54.

to give strength and support. The important factor in this type of therapy is to make patients "know" and "feel" the ailment, to develop a relationship with it, and then to use will power to prevent the causing factors and participate with the healing process.

Before we move on to discuss spiritual therapy, let me give you an example to illustrate the relationship of the two types of therapies described above. Imagine someone suffering from stomach ulcers. This person is given an appropriate medicine, a restricted and specific diet, massage, etc. These are all the methods of rational treatment. But this is only a part of the treatment in Ayurveda. The second part of the therapy is to help the patient realize what the problem is and to teach how the mental energy should be directed to enhance the process of healing to prevent the ailment from reoccurring. The physician searches the causes of the ulcer formation by cross-questioning the patient and then the patient is directed to use his or her power of mind to eradicate the causing factors. Maybe the ulcers were caused because the patient was eating meals when under stress or was worrying too much and it affected his or her generally weak stomach; or the ulcers were caused simply by a mechanical process of retracting the abdominal musculature due to various reasons. Even if the causal factors are none of the above-described ones, and are purely nutritional, the patient's mental participation to understand and visualize the ulcer is considered important to enhance the process of healing. An Ayurvedic physician's role is also to provide needed consolation and courage to the patient along with the rational treatment. If, in the above case, the physician feels that the patient is nervous and agitated, immediate counselling is provided to enhance the cure. In the last chapter of this book, cures for some ailments are described, and these methods of cure are never exclusively rational therapy. People who are used to the allopathic system think that a cure means swallowing medicine. But in Ayurveda, even exclusively rational therapy includes nutritional treatment, exercise, and other such instructions.

The third mode of treatment is spiritual therapy. Whatever methods we may use for the spiritual therapy, the basis is only one—to evoke the power of the self (or the soul), called *ātmaśakti*. Why "evoke" when the soul is the animating principle of the Cosmic Substance and it is energy itself? The answer is that soul, which is the cause of consciousness, is a passive on-looker and does not get involved in the activities of the mind. In this enchanting, fascinating world, we are so enamored that we forget our real self–the power and the light which is within us. We dwell in the ignorance that our material self is our real self. Slowly, there forms a curtain between the outer material self and the inner spiritual self. With constant mental effort, we have to remove the curtain that is covering the inner light. This is what is meant by evoking the inner power. When it is said that our inner power lies dormant, it is, in fact, in the meta-physical sense. When we are able to remove the curtain of ignorance through our *sattvic* efforts, the inner light spreads, and this is the state of enlightenment and awakening. This inner power provides us a capacity to see beyond material reality. An intuitive capacity develops and we are able to foresee and predict. In other words, we develop capabilities beyond what is generally described as normal, and hence the Western term paranormal. In the present context, our purpose is to use our *ātmaśakti* for the purpose of therapy. In the Western world, it is often called "paranormal healing." From the point of view of Ayurveda or Hindu speculative thoughts, these healing capabilities are not considered paranormal, but on the contrary, they are normal and inherent to us. It is only due to our ignorance that they remain suppressed.

We need to make a tremendous effort to develop our inner power. We are all capable of developing this power as we all have the same energy (or essence) within. The two principle factors that lead us to achieve this aim are persistence and a strong will. Various yogic methods of Patañjali described in figure 37 (page 120) lead us to an inner awakening. We have already talked about *yogāsanas* and *prāṇāyāma* which are steps three and four of the eightfold yogic practice. You should follow carefully steps one and two also. The first four steps of the yoga are preparatory for achieving inner stillness. It is very difficult to do as the mind is attracted to this enchanting universe of color, form, smell, touch, and taste. All that is perceived by the senses is cognized by the mind. When the chain of thoughts is broken and the mind is brought to stillness temporarily, that is the state of *sattva* which is the nature of soul. To put it in simple words, we close ourselves off from the outer world and become one with the inner. This is the state of realization of the inner truth or essence which is the cause of being.

With constant effort and practice, we are slowly able to perceive more and more of the inner wealth and enhance *ātmaśakti*. I lay emphasis on constant effort as we required daily practice, especially in the beginning, to achieve even a little success. At least once a day, after *prāṇāyāma* practice, we should try to concentrate for at least five minutes. In the beginning, you should try to get a thought-free mind with the help of *japa* which is done by repeating a single mantra, like OM, or a word again and again to push all thoughts out from the mind. Coordinate the *japa* mantra with *prāṇāyāma* and slowly begin to concentrate on *hṛdya*, the *solar plexus*. The ability to concentrate will increase with time.

When we begin to achieve success and have moments of thought-free mind by breaking the chain of thoughts, we reach a state of realization of the true self and the inner light. We should not limit ourselves to only sitting sessions of concentration practice. We should try to find this moment of stillness during other times of the day as well. At a crowded, noisy place, anywhere, try to retract the senses from the surroundings and momentarily concentrate on the inner light. With this practice, the control of mind over senses will increase and we will be able to prolong the moment of stillness gradually.

The inner light invades the whole body although its principal location is *hṛdya*. To heal a particular part of the body, we concentrate on it and bring the mind to stillness. In the beginning, we concentrate on a particular part of the body. But later, during the process of concentration, the identity of the part should be lost and we should be able to reach a complete thought-free state.

In addition to healing, this practice can be used as a preventive and to promote health. As a daily preventive practice, concentrate on all parts of the body, approaching each part with the thoughts. Finally bring the thoughts to *hṛdya* and concentrate on the inner light. See the spread of this light in all directions and let it form a protective envelope. After reaching this state, try to achieve stillness of mind.

This healing practice can be used to heal others but special care should be taken for that. First of all, do not try to heal others until you feel confident in achieving the state of complete stillness and have really evoked *ātmaśakti*. When the mind acquires a state of complete *sattva* and becomes one with the nature of the soul, then you awaken your inner power. If you have not achieved this state and try to heal others, you will exhaust your bodily energy. The energy of the soul is infinite whereas the energy of the body is limited. You cannot give to others what you do not have. It will take you several years of persistent practice to become capable of healing others.

Until now we were discussing one very technical and secular method of spiritual healing. There are various kinds of spiritual therapies—like wearing roots and gems, auspicious acts, offerings, oblations, following religious precepts, fasting, rendering oneself to the gods, making pilgrimages, etc. Before I proceed further with the explanation of these therapeutic methods—which are not exclusive of rational and psychological Ayurvedic therapies—I want to explain why such methods do not form a part of therapy in modern medicine and are regarded as mere superstition. We have already discussed that the fundamental approach of modern medicine is reductionist and the body is treated like a machine which can be analyzed in terms of its parts. An illness is viewed as a malfunctioning of its parts. In Ayurveda, which has a holistic approach, an individual is considered as a nondivisible unity which cannot be reduced in terms of its parts. Nor can the individual be separated from his or her social, cultural and spiritual environment and cosmic link. An illness is viewed as the consequence of a disharmony with the cosmic order. Thus, ailments are treated in the context of the individual's social, cultural, and spiritual environment. Body, mind, and soul are considered as an integral unity.

I have been talking about mantras in this book, and I think this word deserves an explanation because there are many misconceptions about it. It is generally considered that mantras are mystical formulas or sounds for incantation and invocation. You may say that a mantra is a sound, or a set of words, or a certain formulation for providing support for concentration. Concentration is primarily used here for the purpose of diverting the mind from the outer to the inner, as described earlier. The mantras are used for *japa*, a repetitive pronouncement to get a thought-free mind. Secondly, mantras are used for invoking certain powers. When you concentrate on the "self" or the soul, you form a link with the limitless cosmic energy. You may direct this energy to heal, to sleep, to relax, or to any desired direction. The choice of directing this energy depends upon your power of discretion or *buddhi*. I do not want to go into an elaborate discussion of the mantras here; this explanation is sufficient for our present purpose.

Other methods of spiritual therapy in Ayurveda are as follows. Auspicious acts, offerings, donations, oblations, and other deeds used for spiritual therapy are understood in the context of *karma* theory. We have already discussed that suffering and happiness are due to good or bad karma. When people suffer from an ailment, with the wish to recover, they perform the above mentioned deeds, or pledge to do such a deed after recovery. It is not that good *karma* done can immediately cancel bad *karma* that one is suffering from, but it is believed that the blessings one gets by helping really needy persons can lessen the effect of bad deeds and provide some relief from suffering.

Roots, seeds, gems, or other objects are used for spiritual therapy because some of them contain specific cosmic energy. To carry them on the body influences the body's subtle energy. We have already talked about color in relation to humors. Similarly, gems have an effect on the three qualities of the mind. Gems are very ancient and each is created under specific circumstances, conditions, and time. Each has a specific energy that can in turn influence our bodily energy. For example, for *kapha/tamas* disorders, gems of bright colors resembling the color of fire are prescribed. On the contrary, for *vata-pitta/rajas* disorders, light-colored gems, like pearls, gems of light-blue color or of the color of the earth (grays, blacks, etc.) are prescribed. This therapy is based on Hindu astrology.

Holy places and centers play a great role in spiritual therapy all over the world. Prayers and following religious precepts are other methods of spiritual therapy. Healing ceremonies, along with some special observances like fasting and self-restraint, are effective spiritual therapies, not only in Ayurveda, but also in other ancient disciplines of medicine. In my opinion, the rational basis of these therapies is the same as for concentration practices. Through our power of mind, and with the help of certain action and ceremonies, we are able to go beyond the power of the mind, that is, to the power of the soul.

Nature worship was an important part of the religious and healing ceremonies in all ancient civilizations. This was a way to live with nature, to be a part of it, to show our gratitude to it, and to recognize our cosmic link. We have often discussed in the course of this book that our modern, technologically advanced civilization has alienated us from our surroundings. You have learned that in Ayurveda, the same principles are applied to health which govern the entire cosmos. Humors are derived from the basic elements which form the material reality of the cosmos. The functions of the five elements in us are the same as their functions in nature. They form our physical self and sustain life. In relation to the three qualities of mind, air, and ether are *rajas*, fire (sun) is *sattva*, and water and earth are *tamas*. The five elements are personified in the form of the various Hindu gods and are worshipped for healing and otherwise. For example, the god Hanumān is the son of the wind, and symbolizes *vāta* and *rajas*. He is worshipped for courage, bravery, and curing *vāta*-related disorders. *Pitta/sattva* comes from the sun. It is worshipped for attaining *sattvic* qualities, curing weakness of vision, enhancing mental capacity and intellect. The worship of water and earth is done all over India. The rivers are holy, earth is worshipped before crops, after crops, before building a house, and in millions of other such ceremonies. *Peepal* and some other trees are worshipped in the context of spiritual therapy. A sick person makes a pledge to grow a certain number of holy trees, especially *peepal*. These holy trees have multiple pharmaceutical properties and their products are used in many medicines. Perhaps these are the reasons for their being holy. In other words, it is like showing our gratitude to nature's kindness to us. Similarly special ceremonies are performed on the banks of the rivers for making a wish to get cured from an ailment or fulfilling a pledge made during ailment. The *Ṛg Veda* and *Atharva Veda* contain many hymns for praying to the five elements and seeking blessing for good health. Similarly, other cosmic changes, like the increasing and decreasing of the moon, eclipses and the positions of stars play a great role in the observance of certain precepts for healing therapy.

9

AYURVEDIC REMEDIES AND THE PREVENTION OF AILMENTS

W E HAVE ALREADY discussed various preventive and curative methods. Different recipes have also been mentioned in the chapter on hygiene and care. This chapter
includes remedies for some commonly occurring ailments. For
this, you need a fundamental knowledge about the properties of
the natural substances, the Ayurvedic preparation of drugs, and
some simple equipment. But before discussing remedies and
cures, let us first consider the management of an ailment in general, your attitude toward your sickness, and the characteristics
of a good physician if you need one or you are one yourself.

The first and foremost consideration in Ayurveda is to lead
a healthy and harmonious life which will keep diseases away. As
you must have realized, this needs to be learned, for you must
develop consciousness of your being, learn to listen to the needs
of your body, and make an effort to follow the Ayurvedic way of
life. All this helps you detect any illness before it manifests.
However, despite the successful management of your health,
you may become prey to certain ailments. Sometimes it happens that, due to unavoidable circumstances, you are tired or
under stress, exposed to bad weather, or just so fatigued that
you are vulnerable to an ailment. In addition, depending upon
the *dhatus*, you may have a weak constitution and suffer from
various ailments. You may also become sick due to unusual circumstances, like traveling, a sudden change in climate, etc.,
which may revive a past or chronic ailment, or bring one to the
fore. Therefore, it is essential to learn to manage the most commonly occurring ailments. I have chosen to discuss ailments
that are common and in addition, their successful management
is not known in modern medicine. People tend to suffer a lot

from them and for long periods. Some examples are hay fever, piles, chronic pains, stomach ulcers, etc. However, with the wholesome lifestyle which Ayurveda teaches us, with extra care, and some mild medicine, it is possible to handle these ailments and get a cure in the due course of time.

I have frequently noticed that when people are sick, even with a mild and common ailment like a cough, cold, or a minor fever, they panic and run to a doctor. Many of them go through a standard treatment of antibiotics, analgesics, etc., and they get cured in one week instead of seven days. The key to the self-management of an ailment is not to panic, to be tolerant and not to loose your concentration power with fear. If you become restless, fearful, and are too involved with your ailment, then you will be unable to manage it, and this panic will make you worse. You will not be able to use your discretion to have an appropriate therapy. It is also important to learn that when you are sick, your body is fighting to recover from the ailment, and the purpose of the medicine is to enhance the process of healing and to lessen your suffering. You should do everything that enhances healing. The two important factors are appropriate sleep and rest and right nutrition.

Some people think that medicines are meant to "repair" them immediately so that they can run their "body-machine" once again. They take strong medicines which generally suppress symptoms of the ailment, but that does not mean that they are cured. By using strong medicines, the ailment either lasts for a long time or it may become chronic. Strong medicines, like allopathic drugs which give quick relief, also give a series of side-effects about which even the physician does not know, let alone the patient. I do not mean to say that there are no strong drugs in Ayurveda. But in Ayurvedic ancient literature, warnings about side-effects and specific nutrition to counteract these side-effects are prescribed. For example, if a drug is strong and increases *pitta*, a *pitta*-decreasing diet is prescribed with it. In fact, medicines in Ayurveda are generally meant to be taken with something specific like yogurt, buttermilk, ghee, honey, etc.

If you are unable to manage your sickness and cure yourself, you certainly need the help of a physician. The choice of a physician is very important. According to Ayurveda, "It is better to self-immolate than to be treated by an ignorant physician."[1] A physician should possess the following qualities: "Excellence in theoretical knowledge, extensive practical experience, dexterity, and cleanliness. The physician who possesses the knowledge of the four aspects—cause, symptom, cure, and prevention of disease—is the best. Further, it is said that a physician should be "friendly and compassionate toward the sick and should not be greedy."[2]

In addition to the qualities of a physician, there are other important aspects for appropriate treatment—qualities of the patient and of the drug. "Memory, obedience, fearlessness, and providing all information about the disorder should be the qualities of a patient. Abundance, effectivity, various pharmaceutical forms and an appropriate composition are the four qualities of the drug."[3]

Beware of quacks and do not change your doctor too often. However, do not continue the treatment of a physician who is impatient, impolite, and who is not compassionate. Before visiting a physician, you must speculate on your ailment and all the allied problems, the factors which enhance or lessen your trouble, and your food habits. It is better to classify all this data and write it down so that you are able to tell your physician the precise details. Do not be afraid to talk about your problems, even if you think that perhaps they are not objective or directly related to your ailment. It is also important to follow the advice of the physician and take any prescribed drugs in a timely fashion. If you feel any adverse symptoms, you should inform your physician immediately. Similarly, if you feel that the drug is not effecting you and does not lessen your troubles, then also you should immediately inform your physician.

We are all aware that it is difficult to find a good physician, and this problem is common nearly everywhere in the world. Moreover, physicians with holistic views are rare. Therefore, self-help is absolutely essential and you should be able to enhance the process of your cure even if you are unable to treat yourself entirely and need the help of a physician. You should carefully

---

[1] *Caraka Saṃhitā, Sūtrasthāna,* IX, 15.
[2] *Caraka Saṃhitā, Sūtrasthāna,* IX, 6, 19, 26.
[3] *Caraka Saṃhitā, Sūtrasthāna,* IX, 9.

follow nutritional therapy, various cleaning therapies, and other external health care methods, like oil massages, warm treatments, fortifying herbal remedies, etc.

PHARMACEUTICAL PROPERTIES OF NATURAL SUBSTANCES

Natural substances can be broadly divided into two main categories—food and drugs. (See figure 59). Food substances like rice, wheat, and vegetables nourish the body and help its growth. They affect the humors and their related properties in a subtle and mild way. Drugs do not sustain or nourish the body, but they alter the humors of the body more strongly. Their use is specific and they are given in prescribed quantities to cure ailments. Drugs are divided into three categories—mild, medium, and strong, according to the degree of their effect on the body.

Certain medicinal substances are used in small quantity, and in an infrequent way, as food. They are specifically used to balance the diet. In larger quantities they are used as medicine. Some examples are garlic, ginger, lemon, anise, or cumin. For example, when you add a spoon of anise and cumin seeds to your pot of vegetables, they enhance the taste and flavor. However, they may also be used in a higher quantity for a specific cure. A spoon of crushed cumin with warm water is prescribed against weakness and fatigue. A spoon of anise, kept overnight in water (*fant*) is given to stop diarrhea. This dose is repeated three to four times a day.

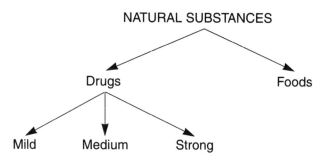

Figure 59. Classification of the natural substances.

Substances in the drug category are mild, medium, or strong. The intensity is a decisive factor for the dosage. There are several detailed classification methods that are used to understand pharmaceutical properties in Ayurveda; however, here we will use the most important and practical aspect, that is the division of drugs according to their taste. In Ayurvedic language, this classification is based upon *rasa* differentiation. It is not possible to translate the word *rasa*. *Rasa* is much more than mere taste; it is a complete sensual experience. For example, if you eat something sour, you know it is sour because of a particular sensation on your tongue. Tongue qualifies the taste; it does not mean that the effect of the sour you are consuming is limited to your tongue. Tongue is the identifier of "sour," but its effect is felt in your whole body. It has an immediate effect on *pitta*, it is like fuel and increases *agni* in the body.

Perhaps it is easy to understand the concept of *rasa* by taking examples from other senses. With our eyes we see the blue sky, a white cow, a green tree, or a beautiful elephant. This perception is not limited to our eyes, or to the mind's identification of a particular color or object. It creates an emotion (good, bad, pleasant, unpleasant) which is the effect of that identification. If we see a wounded person, this sight will not merely register the color of blood or the ripped skin, but will evoke an emotion of horror, pity, or repulsion. Further, this emotion may make you help the wounded person, or may make you cry, sick, or giddy. Similarly, the effect of a particular substance and its characteristic qualities takes place in the whole body. Taste, detected by the tongue, helps to classify the characteristic qualities of a substance and its pharmaceutical effect.

In the chapter on the three humors, you learned that various substances of different tastes can vitiate or cure a vitiated humor. It is very important to learn to know the pharmaceutical properties of substances according to their *rasa*. This knowledge will enable you to make your own Ayurvedic medicines according to time and place. It is not a particular drug that is important but to learn to find the drugs to cure minor ailments according to circumstances and place.

Classification of pharmaceutical properties is done according to six major *rasas* which in turn are derived from the five elements (Table 3). Let us study some details of the *rasa* and their effect on us.

1) Sweet is derived from earth and water. Because of the cold character of these elements, sweet substances are cold in nature and decrease *pitta*. Because of the heavy character of the elements forming the sweet *rasa*, the sweet substances also decrease *vāta*. As earth and water are the formative elements of *kapha*, they will obviously increase *kapha* and vitiate it if taken in excessive quantity.

2) Sour is derived from water and fire. Because of the fire element, they are hot in nature and thus increase *pitta*. Because of the water element, the sour substances also increase *kapha* but decrease *vāta*.

3) Saline or salty substances are derived from earth and fire, and like the sour, they increase *pitta* and *kapha* but decrease *vāta*.

4) Pungent or *katu rasa* is derived from the elements air and fire. In this category are the substances like pepper, ginger, garlic, cardamom, bay leaves, basilica. Since this *rasa* is derived from air and fire, it increases *vāta* and *pitta*, and decreases *kapha*.

5) Bitter *rasa* is derived from the elements air and ether. This *rasa* comprises substances like curcuma, *neem*, or other bitter substances. Since *vāta* is derived from these two fundamental elements, the bitter *rasa* increases this humor and decreases *pitta* and *kapha*.

6) Astringent *rasa* is derived from air and earth. Some common examples of this *rasa* are spinach, jamun, and dates. The astringent decreases *pitta* and *kapha* because of the extremely dry nature of the air, but it increases *vāta*.

From the above description of *rasas*, we can conclude that some *rasas* increase the humors whereas others decrease them. This is summarized in Table 4.

Two important points to remember after having understood the correlation of the five elements to *rasas* and to the humors. First, there are exceptions to the above classification. For example, sweet generally increases *kapha* with the exceptions of honey, crystal candy, wild meat, old rice, barley, wheat, and mung beans.

Table 3.   Relationship of *rasas* to elements and humors.

Rasa	Elements	Vata	Pitta	Kapha
1. Sweet	Earth + Water	–	–	+
2. Sour	Fire + Water	–	+	+
3. Saline	Fire + Earth	–	+	+
4. Pungent	Fire + Air	+	+	–
5. Bitter	Ether + Air	+	–	–
6. Astringent	Earth + Fire	+	–	–

Table 4.   Humor-increasing and decreasing *rasas*.

HUMOR-INCREASING RASAS		
Vata	**Pitta**	**Kapha**
Pungent	Sour	Sweet
Bitter	Salty	Sour
Astringent	Pungent	Salty
HUMOR-DECREASING RASAS		
Vata	**Pitta**	**Kapha**
Sweet	Sweet	Pungent
Sour	Bitter	Bitter
Saline	Astringent	Astringent

Similarly, sour increases *pitta*, except for *amla* and pomegranate. Salty substances increase *pitta* and are harmful for the eyes, with the exception of rock salt. Pungent increases *vāta* and destroys sexual secretions and power of fertility, with the exception of ginger, garlic, and long pepper (*Piper longum*). Bitter also has effects like pungent, with the exception of pointed gourd (which is used as a vegetable in India called *parval*, or *patol* in North India), *Tinospora cordifolia*, called *gilloy* in Hindi. Astringent has an exception of *Terminalia chibula* (*Harad* in Hindi) which does not increase *vāta* nor does it decrease *pitta* or *kapha*.

One must remember that natural substances always have more than one *rasa*, and therefore they have several composite pharmaceutical qualities. However, in some substances, a specific *rasa* is dominating considerably, and this determines their pharmaceutical effect. For example, lime is sour, and also has some negligible contents of sugar. Therefore, lime effects directly on *pitta* and is hot in its pharmaceutical effect. It increases *pitta* and decreases *vāta* and *kapha*. Food is a combination of all *rasas* and the skill of a balanced Ayurvedic diet lies in making a combination where all the *rasas* are in harmony. A meal with an extreme sour, salty, or any other *rasa* will obviously create an imbalance of humors. Such meals, taken over a long period of time, will lead to ill health. On the contrary, you can cure minor ailments by not eating substances that may increase an already vitiated humor and taking specific foods that appease a vitiated humor.

For example, if you have vitiated *vāta* and its allied ailments, you should avoid substances that are pungent, bitter, astringent. You should take sweet and sour food so that *vāta* is subsided and attains an equilibrium with *pitta* and *kapha*. I will give you an example from my personal experience. During a visit to Paris, the first few days of my diet were predominantly French cheese which one does not get elsewhere. This sudden change in diet, and an excessive quantity of cheese, caused some bristles in my mouth. I immediately stopped eating cheese, took plenty of sweet yogurt and cold milk, and this helped cool down the vitiated *pitta* and soon the bristles disappeared. However, if one does not take care at an early stage, and continues to eat an imbalanced diet, small problems become large, and it is too late to use these basic home remedies that relate to nutrition.

The details about *rasas* is provided so you can select a balanced diet, as well as cure minor ailments, and learn to detect pharmacological substances in nature. If the plants described in Ayurveda are not available in your surroundings, you may use the local herbs already being used in your area. Use local drugs in the Ayurvedic way, with reference to their pharmaceutical qualities, and according to *rasas* and the humors. Do not use herbal teas or other medicinal plants on hearsay. Let us consider some examples of famous herbal teas mostly available in the West. Verbena has a sweet *rasa* and will be good for *vāta*- and *pitta*-dominating people, but it would not be good for *kapha*-dominating persons. Thyme tea has an astringent taste and pacifies increased *pitta* and *kapha*. For example, it will cure the negative effects of alcohol by decreasing and pacifying the *agni* (excessive fire) produced by alcohol. Mint tea has a bitter *rasa* and it also decreases *pitta* and *kapha*. Persons suffering from less fire will need drugs with pungent, sour, and saline *rasas*. For example, ginger with lemon juice and salt will immediately cure loss of appetite. It should be taken half an hour before meals. Sour teas, like various fruit teas, rosehips, etc., will increase fire and bring back the normal appetite. A person with vitiated *kapha* should take substances with pungent *rasa* like pepper, garlic, and ginger. Bitter and astringent teas are also helpful to cure vitiated *kapha*.

PREPARATION METHODS

It is essential to learn some simple preparation methods for everyday use as preventive therapy. The methods of preparation are always related to the properties of the drugs (or herbs) so that you don't destroy or make ineffective the active compounds in the substances. I will only mention procedures that can be easily used for home remedies.

Decoctions, Extracts, and Juices

These are the most common forms of preparation for home remedies used in Ayurveda and in ethnic medicine all over the world. In Ayurveda, there are some specific rules for the preparation of decoctions according to their physical nature (hard, soft, etc.) and pharmaceutical nature (*rasa*) of the drugs. The quantity of water and cooking time, according to the physical nature of the substance, is summed up in Table 5 (page 194). Substances should be crushed if so required, as is the case of roots and certain seeds, before making a decoction. They should be cooked at a low fire and should be kept half-covered or covered with a lid that has holes in it during the cooking process.

Simple extracts or *fants* are of two kinds in Ayurveda—hot and cold. Hot extracts are prepared by pouring boiling water on the substance and steeping it for about 15 minutes. Certain aromatic drugs which are also used popularly as herbal teas—mint,

Table 5.   Preparation of decoctions.

Soft Substances	Medium Hard Substances	Hard Substances
Add 1 part substance to 4 parts water and reduce to ¼.	Add 1 part substance to 8 parts water and reduce to ½.	Add 1 part substance to 16 parts water and reduce to ½.
Note: Cook always at low fire half-covered, or with a porous lid. After cooking, drugs are passed through a strainer or thin muslin cloth, and are taken according to specific instruction—hot, cold, with sugar, or honey, etc.		

thyme, verbena, black tea, linden—are prepared this way. Once the medicine is prepared, it can be used cold or hot, with or without sugar as the case may be, depending upon the properties of the medicine, as well as nature of the ailment. For example, NOW's Liver-Revitalizing Tea should be prepared with boiling water, but should be preferably consumed when it is at room temperature. This tea revitalizes liver functions and removes excessive fire from the body. Therefore, it is recommended to use cold, and several doses can be prepared at once. This tea is bitter and some people find it difficult to consume. Therefore, sugar may be added as it does not do anything to change the basic qualities of the drug. You may remember that sweet cures vitiated *vāta* and *pitta,* and in the present case we are dealing with *pitta.* However, if you are taking a drug to cure vitiated *kapha,* then the addition of sugar is not recommended as sweet increases *kapha* and diminishes the effect of the drug.

Cold extracts or *fants* are made of those drugs which are sensitive to heat. They are made by simply putting the drug in water and leaving it overnight. The partly crushed or powdered substance is mixed with six times its quantity of water and kept still for 6 to 10 hours or overnight. Before using, it is stirred and the water is drunk after filtering. If the drug is kept for a longer period in the water, normally it does not do any harm, but in a hot and humid climate it may get infected with some bacteria or fungus.

Examples of drugs prepared using this method are anise and brahmi. Anise is widely used in Europe, especially to help babies stop mild diarrhea. Usually it is prepared either by pouring boiling water on it or by making a decoction which makes this

Figure 60. Rubbing an herb between two stones.

drug partly lose its effect. Do not buy already powdered or industrially treated plants. Crush them yourself just before making *fants*. In some industrially developed countries, they sell you instant mixtures of plants in which you need to add only warm water. There are certain other drugs which need to be given fresh in the form of juice. This, however, depends largely on the availability of the fresh substances. Leaves or the other prescribed parts of the plants are crushed in a stone grinder and the juice is extracted. For example basilica should be used in this manner.

In case fresh plants are not available and one is forced to use the dried, then the following should be done. The powdered dried plant should be mixed with four times the quantity of water. Let it soak for 24 hours so the drug is mixed properly. If such a drug needs to be used immediately, then rub the dried herb between two stones (figure 60) and add a little water. This will leave you with a paste from which juice can be extracted. The herbs should be rubbed for a long time so that the paste becomes very fine and the active component from the drug can be extracted.

SOME METHODS OF PRESERVING REMEDIES

Extracts with oils or ghee are made by cooking the decoctions of the drugs in either of these substances until all the water evaporates. Then the oil is filtered and stored in tightly closed bottles and can be preserved for a long time. This method is already mentioned for the preparation of hair oil. Massage oils can also be made in this manner.

Extracts using sugar and honey are made by mixing decoctions with thick sugar syrup, or honey, or a combination of both. The decoction should be cooked in the sugar until it becomes a thick syrup. Honey is added only after the whole mixture has cooled down. In case the use of pure honey is required, the decoction is cooled and mixed thoroughly with honey by stirring well. These preparations are called *avleha* in Ayurveda, and can be preserved for a long time.

Powders or *churans* are a simple and quick way of taking medicines especially when using dried seeds. Some *churans* or powdered remedies can be preserved up to one year, but it is always more effective to freshly grind the herb you use. *Churans* are mostly consumed with hot water or hot milk.

Sugar syrups or *sharvats* are preparations made by cooking herbs with water and sugar to make a thin syrup. This syrup is consumed with cold water. This preparation is generally used for preparing health-promoting tonics and anti-heat remedies to be consumed only during the summer months. Their use is forbidden during the cold and humid season.

There are many other methods of preparation of medicines in Ayurveda but readers should find professionals to do this. *Aristas*, or *asvas* are alcoholic preparations, *ksaras* are dried extracts, and *bhasmas* are the ashes of a substance. These preparations involve complicated pharmaceutical procedures.

Grinding Equipment

During the course of this book, I have spoken about crushing and powdering drugs. There are several types of grinding equipment, like stone, steel, or clay, and they should be used appropriately. Some very hard drugs (seeds) need steel grinders, whereas soft leaves should be crushed well between two stones. Some drugs need very fine pulverization or the body cannot absorb them. Some examples are medicines for the eyes, healing ointments, and tooth powders. I suggest that you use a clay or stone grinder. To suit the needs of modern living, a small electric grinder like a spice or coffee grinder will be very helpful. This latter is very useful for making *churans* and crushing certain hard drugs before making a decoction. Electric grinders should be used carefully. Stop during the grinding process so that you don't raise the temperature of the drug due to the heat of the motor in the grinder.

Making Fine Powders

For certain prescriptions, you need a very fine powder. For example, if your tooth powder is not fine enough, the particles will get caught in the spaces between your teeth and between the teeth and gums. To obtain a fine powder, you need to pass the powder through a fine cotton cloth after you have ground it. If you need an extremely fine powder, use a thick cloth. If the degree of fineness is not so critical, you may use a piece of muslin. Stretch the piece of cloth either by fixing it on one side and holding the other, or it can be held by two people. Put small quantities of the powder in the cloth and stir it slowly with a spoon (figure 61). Keep a clean container underneath the cloth to collect the fine powder.

Figure 61. Making a powder of an herb.

Making Ghee

I have talked often about the use of ghee during the course of this book. Ghee may not be available outside of India except in grocery stores that cater to the needs of Indians residing abroad. Therefore, it is important to explain what ghee is and how you can make it. Ghee is simply clarified butter. Butter does not contain one hundred percent fat and cannot be preserved for very long. Ghee, however, can be stored for several years. In some countries, butter fat is available but it is not ghee. It is processed differently and contains preservatives. Do not use it to replace ghee.

For making ghee, you need unsalted fresh butter. Put the butter in a pan and heat it on a very low fire. Let it reach the boiling point. You will see that it will slowly acquire a transparent look and a whitish foam will be formed on the top. After it has reached this state, you need to cook it at least 15 minutes more so that all the water contents are completely evaporated and any solid components in addition to the fat are also completely separated. Take care that the ghee remains transparent and clear and does not turn brown. Fifteen minutes are usually enough for cooking after it has reached the boiling point. This time may be variable according to the thickness of the container and the strength of the fire. Therefore, watch it carefully the first few times and you will develop a feeling for making it. Filter it through a muslin cloth when it has cooled. On being cooled down, ghee becomes semisolid. If you forget to filter it at the appropriate time, reheat it and then filter it. Store it in clean glass jars which can be closed firmly. Ghee can be preserved for a long time at room temperature. In summer months, it melts and looks like oil but the melted state does not make any alterations in it.

PREVENTION AND CURE OF
SOME COMMON AILMENTS

I have chosen to discuss a few ailments based on the fact that many people suffer and live with these nagging disorders. It is important to manage minor disorders or they may lead to serious health problems. Besides, discomforts are a hindrance to the activities of life and makes people dissatisfied and irritated. As you learned in the preceding chapter, a disturbed mental state gives rise to innate disorders. Therefore, put your effort and energy into curing yourself immediately. Do not delay, do not postpone, do not take any risk with your health and life.

Fatigue

A prolonged state of decreased efficiency and increased discomfort is usually called fatigue. Fatigue is not an ailment by itself, but if not taken care of, it can give rise to various serious health problems like different aches and pains, headaches, migraines, and backaches. A persistent state of fatigue increases your vulnerability to external infections and makes it difficult for the body to heal itself or recover from ailments. In addition, fatigue leads to anger and irritation which causes unpleasantness in your social environment and ailments like stomach ulcers, stiffness in certain parts of the body, or other innate disorders. Fatigue leads to a lack of coordination between the senses, giving rise to accidents. This can start a never-ending cycle.

Some people stay in a perpetual state of fatigue. Their problems are related mainly to fatigue, and they are unable to deal with its fundamental causes or cure themselves. They keep taking medicines for all the symptomatic ailments created from fatigue and they ignore the simple remedy—rest. I will soon explain what I mean by "rest."

In big cities all over the world fatigue is a very usual complaint and people feel quite helpless about it. They do not know where to place this nagging feeling of discomfort and exhaustion because it is not exactly an ailment and does not have objective symptoms. Therefore, they refrain from seeking medical help. The purpose of this section is to define factors that cause fatigue so we can take the necessary measures to cure the condition.

We have already discussed, during the course of this book, fatigue caused by vitiated *kapha*. In the present context, we are dealing with fatigue caused by the hectic pace of life, pollution, noisy environments, or due to other internal imbalances. In Ayurveda, this fatigue will be classified as *vāta* fatigue. We are not talking about a temporary phase of fatigue caused by a nonspecific ailment or an external attack. We are talking about general, non-specific fatigue signified by constant discomfort and a lack of energy.

The principal cause of fatigue is the lack of appropriate and timely rest. In our modern technologically developed civilization, there is no true leisure. People are always doing something, even during their free time. There is no concept of complete relaxation in a silent environment which our physical being periodically requires. An appropriate rest means to get rid of the idea of doing something, to be free from the tension of what was and what could be, and to have some moments of silence and quietness in a completely tension-free state. It is to be with oneself. All this requires your considerable mental effort. Breathing exercises, *japa* and concentration practices are helpful to leave behind routine worries and forget everything for a while in order to relax completely.

Timely rest is also important to avoid fatigue. For example, if you have had a cough or cold or other such minor ailment, but you have to work during this time, then compensate yourself with extra sleep and rest in the evenings. Lying down in a horizontal position is very important. Similarly, if you feel tired after late evenings, or heavy meals, or drinking, then do not postpone resting and do not drag your fatigue. This is how the fatigue begins to accumulate. Minor fatigue is easy to manage and get rid of. It needs one or two days of rest, a massage, a bath, a light nourishing diet, hot ginger tea, hot milk, and some fortifying decoctions or drugs. But once the fatigue is accumulated, you need more rest and some medical help, as on your own you may feel too weak and confused to even make an effort to get rid of the fatigue.

If you follow the Ayurvedic way of life, you will not suffer from fatigue as you will be periodically cleaning your body and mind. Also you will become conscious of your being and develop an extraordinary sensitivity to your body. We suffer from fatigue because we mistreat ourselves.

We can also suffer from fatigue due to emotional reasons. As I have said before, appropriate rest brings stillness of mind. The subject of controlling the mind has been discussed in previous chapters.

There is another category of fatigue due to a very subtle reason—ego. Some people think that they are irreplaceable, others need them badly and if they did not do all that work they are doing, there would be a catastrophe. In this process, they over-work and exhaust themselves. Apparently, these people are very good and have a great sense of sacrifice. But in the process, they sacrifice their health. In this context, I would like to draw the at-tention of many mothers and housewives who tire themselves like this over the years, and by the end of their 40s, they really find themselves in ill health due to overwork, accumulated fa-tigue, and neglect.

Managers, executives, and other people in important posi-tions are also people who fatigue themselves limitlessly. Added to that, these people lead hectic and irregular lives and finally become prey to many innate disorders. Usually, they have aw-fully busy schedules and they are unable to have a real rest. People of this category have very special health-related prob-lems.

In brief, if you always live according to your basic consti-tution and capacity, and if you need more sleep than others, or you feel easily tired, or going out in the evenings fatigues you, learn to accept this and lead a lifestyle according to your needs. Do not compare yourself to others. I understand that you cannot be selfish and pamper yourselves all the time. Re-alize the limitations of your physical stamina. Fatigue may not have many open symptoms, but over the years, it may turn into a disease. Fatigue enhances *vāta*, and with accumulated fatigue, you will become prone to *vāta*-related disorders. Fatigue is not only bad for your health but it is also bad for the health of those around you as it is not pleasant for them to interact with a person who is not efficient and who gets easily angry and ir-ritated.

In classical Ayurvedic literature, there are descriptions of many medical formulations to be taken in addition to complete rest. These medicines may not be available everywhere and medicines prepared on a commercial scale may not be that ef-fective. Therefore, I will describe nutritional therapy and some simple homemade preparations that you can try.

The following are anti-fatigue foods—hot milk, black tea with ginger, cardamom, cloves, hot vegetable or chicken soup, wheat porridge, ghee, nuts, honey, crystal sugar, apples, fresh fruit juices.

Anti-fatigue Preparations

There are simple formulations you can prepare and take daily in small doses to get more energy.

Almonds	100 gms (about ½ cup)
Cashew nuts	100 gms (about ½ cup)
Crystal sugar	100 gms (about ½ cup)
Anise seeds	50 gms (about ¼ cup)
Black pepper	20 grains

Powder all these things separately. Pass the powdered anise through a thin muslin cloth. Then mix all the ingredients together thoroughly. Store this mixture in a clean and dry container which can be tightly closed. Take a tablespoon full with hot milk daily or when you are tired. This preparation is not only anti-fatigue but is also good for promoting vision.

> Powder ½ teaspoon of cumin along with some crystal sugar and take this preparation with hot water as a daily dose to get over fatigue or whenever you are tired.

This preparation can also be taken as a general tonic from time to time. Use only freshly ground cumin. Do not use carvi instead of cumin. Carvi is darker in color and has slightly rounded edges. See the next chapter for identification. *Caution*: Cumin increases *pitta* and therefore should not be taken over a long period of time or in very hot weather. Cumin has a smell which comes out from the body through the sweat.

Carrots	1 kgm (4 cups)
Apples	1 kgm (4 cups)
Sugar	1 kgm (4 cups)
Cumin	40 gms (3 tablespoons)
Anise	40 gms (3 tablespoons)
Pepper	50 grains (pinch)
Cardamom	25 gms (2 tablespoons)
Clove	25 gms (2 tablespoons)
Cinnamon	25 gms (2 tablespoons)
Basil (*Ocimum sanctum*)	25 gms (2 tablespoons)

Ginger	25 gms (2 tablespoons)
Laurel leaves	25 gms (2 tablespoons)
Ajwain or thyme seeds	25 gms (2 tablespoons)

Wash, peal, and cut carrots and apples into small pieces. Cook them covered in a little water on a slow fire. When they are well cooked and look like a puree, add sugar and cook until it looks like a thick paste. The mixture should be cooked covered on a slow fire and stirred from time to time. Grind the rest of the ingredients into a fine powder and add this powder into the cooked fruits when they are cold. Mix all the ingredients thoroughly by stirring well. Store it in dry, clean, tightly closed containers. Take 2 teaspoons every day with hot milk or otherwise. You may also use it as fruit jam. This preparation alleviates fatigue, restores stamina, and cures loss of appetite.

In the above preparation, you may also add Triphala, the Three-Fruit Combination (a product of great value in Ayurveda). The fruits are dried, powdered, and mixed in equal quantities. These three fruits grow in the Himalayan mountains and have a rejuvenating effect. Their names are amla (*Emblica officinalis*), harad (*Terminalia chebula*) and baheda (*Terminalia bellirica*). Triphala is now available in Ayurvedic shops in the West. Daily intake of this fruit powder in small doses brings the humors into equilibrium, alleviates fatigue, and enhances strength. The addition of 200 gm (1½ cups) of this powder in the above preparation will enhance its qualities and make it a highly beneficial anti-fatigue and rejuvenating product. However, if you add Triphala, its taste will turn slightly medicinal. Triphala may also be used independently to get rid of fatigue and to promote health. Take half to one teaspoon daily, either mixed with honey or by soaking it in a glass of water overnight and then drinking that water.

If you are suffering from fatigue, and you are not doing anything about it, remind yourself: "It is time now to have a break, to slip into inactivity, to rest, to take it easy, to transcend into restfulness and tranquillity."

Caution: You must learn to distinguish between general non-specific fatigue and the fatigue that announces the onset of an ailment. In the latter case, treatment should be given after carefully observing the symptoms. If you are tired in general, also do the diagnostic examination described in chapter 3.

Pain

The domain of pain is vast and we will deal with only a few aspects of it here. First of all, let us see what pain is. In a relatively healthy person, pain is an open demonstration of the disharmony and imbalance prevailing in the body and mind. Pain may also be a demonstration of weakness and vulnerability of a particular body part. In such cases, pain is chronic, that is, reoccurring every now and then. Pain may also be due to degeneration, inflammation, or due to injury. We will deal here with the first two categories of pain, as the third category needs more complex medical care and in most cases the irreversible degeneration has already occurred.

Headaches and Migraines

It seems that headaches are the most commonly occurring pain of our times. There is hardly anybody who has not experienced this ache. I am not referring to headaches allied to other ailments like fever, the common cold, influenza, etc.; I mean the plain headaches that people tend to suffer every now and then. They usually get rid of this ache by swallowing an analgesic.

A healthy person should never have such aches. To cure various kinds of headaches, let us first look into some principal reasons that cause them. One must learn, first of all, to differentiate one type of headache from the other and then cure accordingly.

Headaches may be caused due to vitiation of any of the three humors or due to constipation, stress, nervousness, overactivity, extreme hot and cold weather, or a noisy, polluted environment. *Vāta* vitiation causes constipation and constipation further enhances *vāta*. A mild constipation gives rise to heaviness in the head, but when the accumulated *mala* stays inside the body for a long time, a persistent headache is caused. If this cause of the headache is also accompanied by other factors, like stress and a noisy environment, it escalates quickly and causes a lot of suffering. However, it is easy to treat these headaches by ensuring a regular evacuation accompanied by an enema or purgation therapy done from time to time. If there is no proper evacuation one day, the next day you may feel a heaviness in the head which slowly converts into pain. A hard and black stool, and insufficient excretion is not considered a proper evacuation. In such cases, an immediate enema will be very helpful and remove the headache immediately.

The second type of headache is of a nervous origin, and caused by noisy environments, a hectic lifestyle, over-activity and worries. People who try to do more than their capacity become victims to this type of headache. If headaches of nervous origin are not cured by removing their causes, their symptoms are usually suppressed by taking painkillers. They slowly become chronic and give rise to migraines. Therefore, think twice before taking a painkiller to remove your headache. It only postpones the timely help to cure the ailment.

For curing this type of headache, try to be as calm as possible. Do not speak loudly or shout. If you have an excessive work load or a hectic atmosphere at work, try to compensate it with calm and rest after work. Do not accumulate fatigue. It can cause chronic ailments or a disease and can lead to serious accidents. Do not postpone the need for real rest.

To get rid of the suffering, apply external remedies like balms, mixtures of various herbal oils, or etheric oils. You may also make your own mixture by combining the following:

> five parts of eucalyptus oil
> one part anise oil
> one part menthol crystals
> one part camphor

This external treatment is only for quick relief. The cause of the ailment should be removed.

Migraines are periodic attacks of extreme temporal pain which are usually accompanied by nausea, vomiting, irritability, and photophobia (cannot tolerate light). An attack of migraine may also be only in half the head, around the eye, jaw, or ear, and it is often confused with the troubles in these organs. This extreme pain brings a throbbing sensation and forces one to take bed rest. People who suffer from migraines are generally made to believe that they have to live with this ailment and that there is no real cure for it. Actually, the situation is not hopeless and it is possible to cure migraines with Ayurvedic methods. The real cure of migraine is its prevention.

In case of migraine or other chronic pain, like sciatica, shoulder pain, etc., there are always some pre-attack symptoms that are usually ignored. You should observe these symptoms thoroughly and do everything to prevent the attack. Chronic ailments occur with cumulative physical fatigue, mental stress and/or with vitiation of the humors. For example, you are suffering from slight indigestion but do not take proper care, go to parties, have drinks, late night dinners, and perhaps heavy meals. This will obviously enhance the already-present indigestion and make you fatigued, but you continue with a busy day's routine and doing something in the evenings. Thus, you do not take care, rest, eat boiled food or take appropriate medication to cure yourself. In between, something unexpected and urgent comes up—a visitor, some late night work, or a mentally upsetting incident. This exhausts you even more and your reservoir of energy diminishes. Your *pitta*, perhaps also *vāta*, vitiate more and more because of your stomach problems. With this ongoing struggle, each day your vulnerability increases and your body will protest in the end. If you get chronic migraines or sciatica or any other allied pain, that is your weak point and a protest from the body is manifested in the form of an attack of pain.

If you wish to cure your chronic migraine (also applicable to other recurring pains), then learn to avoid the pain not yet come. Take the following precautions for that.

1) Observe the circumstances when you get an attack of your recurring pain. There are certain minor and subtle pre-symptoms which warn you about the onset of pain. Take as much rest as possible and avoid everything that brings you toward this pain. When you are reading this, your first reaction may be of confusion, as you may not be aware of the pre-symptoms I am talking about because you never paid attention. An attack of migraine may occur because of a combination of fear and stress, a feeling of helplessness, or aimlessness accompanied by excessive physi-

cal exertion. Physical exertion may be of any kind—speaking too much or too loud, dwelling in noisy environments, walking in the hot sun, doing too many things at a time, insufficient rest and sleep, too much walking and standing, etc. It is up to you to avoid those factors which slowly drag you toward the suffering due to migraine. Rest when you are exhausted. Remember the basic Ayurvedic principle that the first priority of life is maintaining good health. Therefore, the time to act is NOW.

2) Do not do your routine yogic exercises or other physical exertion when you are tired and feel you are heading toward an attack of migraine.

3) Drink plenty of water, take light nourishing food—specially vegetable or chicken soups. Avoid fatty, heavy, fried food, and eat salads and fresh fruits. Ensure proper evacuation. Practice *jaldhauti* (described in chapter 4).

4) A massage followed by a bath that includes a few drops of sandalwood oil will be very helpful in relaxing, removing *mala* from the outer skin, and opening channels.

5) Do *japa* and *prāṇāyāma* and tell yourself repeatedly that all else in the world is unimportant for you at this particular moment, and the most important thing is to save yourself from the piercing, terrible pain which makes you suffer.

6) Make for yourself small healing prayers which repeat your determination not to host the pain and to be free of these nagging attacks of migraines forever. You may address these prayers to the Sun, Earth, or a special tree, place, temple, or anything in your surroundings. If you do not want to do so, concentrate on your inner energy, which is the cause of your being, and repeat your determination of not getting this pain.

If you are determined and you make every effort to study the pre-symptoms of pain and take all possible precautions to avoid pain, you will be able to cure your migraine in due course of time.

Migraine patients should be very particular about diet, should not have long intervals without food, and should not eat excessively. Drinking too much or drinking bad quality alcohol is equally harmful. Dry sour wine, new wine, and strong drinks like whisky or liquors make grounds for an attack of migraine. Migraine is an inborn disorder and therefore the internal purification practices described earlier will help eradicate this pain.

Sciatica

It is a sudden attack of pain in the leg beginning at the back and upper part of the thigh. Like migraine, sciatica is related to blood vessels and nerves. The most important remedy for sciatica is the four yogic practices called *uttanpadāsana*.[4] These āsanas slowly strengthen the legs by enhancing blood circulation and activating the peripheral nerves. A sciatica patient should do these exercises regularly in order to avert the attack.

The second way to ward off this pain is to avoid exposure to cold or draft. A mixture of fatigue and exposure triggers this pain. As for the pre-symptoms and the precautionary measures taken at that stage, they are the same as described for migraines. In case of the slightest feeling of discomfort in the lower back region or legs, sciatica patients should immediately take rest, keep warm, use some pain-relieving oils or ointments and apply heat with a hot water bottle or other available measures.

Massage and a hot bath will also be helpful to avert pain, as these therapies will alleviate *vāta*. If you are a sciatica patient or have frequent pains in other parts of your body, remember that you should take *vāta*-alleviating nutrition. A regular use of ginger, garlic, pepper, and other spices will be helpful. Strictly avoid *basa* food and other *vāta*-increasing products like potatoes, cauliflower, and rice. Never use preserved food in any form including pre-cooked frozen foods. Do not drink preserved fruit or vegetable juices. They increase *vāta* tremendously. Only freshly pressed juices should be used.

It is not really necessary to take specific medicines for sciatica, as it can be cured with precautionary measures. However, I will prescribe the daily use of a mixture of cloves and garlic. Crush two cloves with two cloves of garlic and take it once a day. If you find it hard to digest garlic, take only half a dose. That means one clove crushed with a clove of garlic. Although the ad-

---

[4]See *Yoga for Internal Health* (New Delhi: Hind Pocket Books, 1991).

dition of cloves into garlic decreases its *pitta* effect, you should drink plenty of water to counteract any *pitta* effect from garlic. If you are troubled by the offensive smell of garlic, chew a few cardamoms.

Note: In case of chronic pain, apply some pain-relieving ointment every day, or especially when one is tired. One should not wait until the pain is actually there. Precautionary measures should be taken as a daily routine to get rid of the pain completely.

Arthritic Pain

I will speak here only of preventive measures, as once arthritis is there, it requires very complicated Ayurvedic medicines, treatment, and therapy which require the services of a physician.

Arthritic pains are initially caused by *vāta-kapha* vitiation. As you know, there are many ailments caused by the vitiation of humors, especially when they are not attended to over a number of years. Vitiation of each humor gives rise to many ailments, but which of these ailments one becomes prey to depends upon the individual constitution and other circumstances. The aim here is to eradicate those factors that lead directly or indirectly to an ailment.

For the prevention of arthritic pain, you should take the general precautions described previously for prevention of *vāta* vitiation. You should do yogic exercises regularly, involving all your body parts so that *kapha* does not accumulate anywhere, and there is a free flow of energy. You should particularly pay attention to those parts used for performing specific functions, like fingers in the case of typewriter/computer users, the back in the case of office workers, feet in the case of people who walk a lot, and so on. Various specific exercises as preventive measures have been described previously.

Exposure to cold, humidity, drafts, sudden changes from hot to cold, a sedentary life, heavy fried foods, overweight, over-exertion and over-use of a particular part of the body, accumulation of stress, accumulation of *mala*, are some of the principal factors besides the *vāta-kapha* vitiation which pave the way to arthritic problems. Some precautionary measures are suggested below.

1) Never bathe or shower immediately after coming out from bed.

2) Never bathe immediately after doing physical exercise, exertion, or when you are sweating.

3) Have a bath with moderately hot water, neither too hot nor too cold.

4) Do not expose yourself to a draft after having a bath, even during the summer months.

5) Do not put your hands or feet in hot and then immediately in cold water.

6) Pay attention to the smallest pains or stiffness in the body and make every effort to cure them. Do not postpone the cure. Keep warm, apply ointments, get massages and use pain-relieving oils. If you feel stiff when you wake up, or feel stiffness in a particular part of your body, immediately take measures to cure *vāta*.

7) You should do internal purification regularly so that *mala* does not accumulate in your body.

8) Excess weight makes grounds for all ailments, including arthritic pains. Shed extra weight.

Backache, Neck Pain and Other Non-specific Pains

Many people suffer from backaches, neck pains, shoulder, arm or wrist pains, etc., which are caused for diverse reasons. Posture defects, stress, overwork, worries, feelings of helplessness, are some of the major causes of these pains. Many people live in an illusion of curing these pains by taking painkillers.

I have discussed elsewhere in detail the yogic therapy for curing pains related to the spine. For curing shoulder, wrist and ankle pains, observe the factors or circumstances which cause the particular pain. For example, sometimes people stiffen a particular part of the body during certain stress situations. Some people wear tight or high-heeled shoes that cause pain in the ankle, knee or feet. It has been observed that wrist and shoulder pain is caused in many cases as a sign of rebellion to undesired circumstances. For example, some people do not like their jobs, or they are in an unhappy marital situation, or feel juxtaposed in some other circumstances in life and begin to get such pains. In any case, one should deal with the factors causing the pain to get rid of it.

Remember that when you get pain in a particular part of your body, it is due to accumulation of *kapha* which also blocks the passage of *vāta* in that region. *Kapha* may accumulate due to an injury, displacement, physical shock, bad posture, or mental tension. Therefore, if you have a pain, do not stop moving the ailing part as a measure of cure. By doing so, you may feel temporary relief, but it is not a cure, as it will worsen the situation with the accumulation of more *kapha*. You need specific movements to get rid of *kapha* accumulation. Even if the cause of your pain may be overwork, you need physical exercise to get rid of your pain. For example, if you have a pain in your shoulder because of too much writing, to cure it, you need to do exercises involving hands, fingers, shoulders, and arms by making slow and round movements. These movements should be done in both the directions—clockwise and counterclockwise.

In brief, for any pain, besides working with exercise, ointments, massage, applying heat, etc., one should discover the factors causing it and try to eradicate them. Otherwise, it will be only a symptomatic cure and the pain will come again.

Pain-Relieving Oil

There are many herbal pain-relieving oils or ointments available. We make one which has an immediate effect to relieve pain. But the process of making it is complicated and long and should be handled only by specialists. Nearly everywhere in the world, the Chinese pain-relieving balms are available. Some mixtures of etheric oils remove pain, but a single oil, like lavender, or eucalyptus, or citronella, are not all that effective. That is why it is more wise to buy a mixture or an ointment.

Sleep and Its Disorders

"When the mind is exhausted and the exhausted sense organs retract from their objects, a person sleeps. . . . Dependent on sleep are happiness and misery, corpulence and leanness, strength and weakness, potency and impotency, intellect and non-intellect, life and death. An untimely, excessive and bad sleep takes away happiness and life like a nightmare. The same, if properly observed, provides happiness and longevity, just like a flash of true knowledge provides accomplishment to a yogi. . . . As wholesome diet is needed for maintaining body, similarly one requires a wholesome sleep. Obesity and leanness are particularly caused by sleep and diet."[5]

Sleep is a periodic rest when senses and mind withdraw from activities and the mind is closed to any new knowledge. Sleep is associated with the falling of the night and is therefore *tamas* in nature. However, during sleep, the *rajas* quality of the mind (activity) does not alter, it is only closed to new knowledge which the mind constantly obtains through the senses during wakeful state. "During sleep, the mind is subjected to pre-existing pleasant or unpleasant subjects either from this life or from previous lives through the *rajas* quality of the mind."[6]

A wholesome sleep is sound, undisturbed, sufficient in quantity, and synchronized with time. For example, day sleep is unwholesome, whereas night sleep is wholesome. Ayurveda forbids day sleep except in the summer months. Similarly, a wholesome sleep is synchronized with long and short nights in winter and summer respectively. A wholesome sleep is neither too much nor too little, and is according to age and circumstances.

The process of sleep is an automatic phenomenon that occurs when body and mind are fatigued. The quantity of sleep required depends on age, the type of work one does and other circumstances. When a baby is born, he or she comes out of *tamas* (the mother's womb) and slowly adapts to *rajas*. Therefore babies require tremendous amounts of sleep (15–16 hours) while going through this transitional period. Growing children need 9–10 hours of sleep, whereas adults need between 6–8 hours, depending on their constitution and the type of work they do. Those doing physical labor need less sleep than those who do intellectual work. Old people (above 60 according to Ayurveda) require relatively less sleep, but this depends on their physical condition. During sickness, convalescence, and wound-healing, one requires more sleep. Sleep enhances the process of healing and recovery.

---

[5] *Caraka Saṃhitā, Sūtrasthāna*, XXI, 35–38, 51.
[6] *Suśruta Saṃhitā, Śarīrasthānam*, IV, 36.

There are three principal kinds of sleep disorders: 1) deficient sleep due to an inability to sleep, or insomnia; 2) disturbed sleep; 3) excessive sleep. Chronic insomnia is usually caused by vitiated *vāta* or heightened *rajas*. I used the word chronic, as insomnia may be caused temporarily due to another ailment—pain, indigestion, etc. Disturbed sleep may be caused by multiple reasons—gastrointestinal problems, excessive or lack of sexual activity, *vāta-pitta*-related disorders, psychic disorders etc. Excessive sleep is caused by a vitiated *kapha*. Let us discuss the factors causing these disorders and their cure in detail.

Insomnia

This is a widespread problem in technologically advanced societies. Many people cannot sleep without the help of drugs and these sleeping drugs have long-lasting harmful effects. Insomnia can be easily cured by understanding the specific problems that cause it, and then taking the appropriate Ayurvedic measures to remove the cause. I suggest some simple methods and precautions to cure and prevent insomnia.

1. If you are suffering from insomnia, first make sure you get rid of vitiated *vāta*. Take a *vāta*-decreasing and *kapha*-increasing diet. Minimize the consumption of black tea, coffee, or caffeine-containing cold drinks. Do not take any of these after 5 in the evening. Although the effect of these substances may vary in certain exceptional cases, in general they keep you awake. Tea has a prolonged effect and if taken late at night, it may not affect sleep during the early part of night but may wake you up later.

2. Hot, sweetened milk, bananas, some herbal teas (like linden tea) are sleep-inducing and should be taken before going to bed.

3. To get proper sleep it is important to create a sleep environment which slowly induces you to sleep. Remember that you are not like your bed lamp which can be switched on and off. Many people have a hectic routine at work and in the evening they have a family and social life which is often loud. People keep working mentally to solve professional problems, family disputes, emotions of love, hatred, ambivalence, and the mind is over-active at bedtime. They switch off the light and want to

sleep. Since they cannot sleep with this active mind, this makes
them tense and increases mental activity. This is a vicious cycle.
Sleeplessness increases *vāta* and *vāta* increases sleeplessness.

Do not talk for at least 15 minutes before going to bed and
do not stay in a noisy atmosphere (no television, radio, etc.). Try
to read something light before going to bed. Before sleeping, do
your yogic breathing exercises for a minute at least. Also do
śavāsana or the dead body posture to completely relax your
body and mind. Concentrate on the darkness of night and pray
that it showers upon you a profound refreshing sleep.

Remember that night is meant for rest. It is not the time to
solve office problems or disputes, neither will it offer you a solution to other problems which hinder your sleep. Many people
brood in bed. Do not waste your breath on the worthless. I understand that the subjects you keep brooding over during the
silent night hours are very important for you, but remember that
the first priority of life is life itself. When that is lost, all is lost
and there are no more problems to be solved! The state of sleep
is a slow transformation of *rajas* to *tamas* and similarly the
process of waking up is reverse. Normally, this transition is natural and linked to the cycle of day and night. In the case of derangement, you should participate in harmonizing this rhythm
once again by your own mental effort.

Do some *japa* (repetition of a mantra) before going to bed,
in dim light or in the dark. This will bring you from *rajas* to *sattva*
and give you tranquillity. When your mind becomes tranquil and
your eyelids begin to get heavy, then say the following prayer:

> Oh night's energy, bless me with a tranquil, unbroken sleep until to-
> morrow morning. Bless me so that I wake up refreshed and full of
> energy after a deep and undisturbed sleep. Oh night's energy, let
> my senses be closed to their objects.[7] Oh night's energy, may my

---

[7]The objects of the senses are their cause of functioning. For example, the object
of the sense of sight is appearance, the sense of hearing is sound, the sense of
smell is odor, the sense of taste is flavor, and the sense of feeling is touch. During sleep, the senses are not responsive to their objects, and therefore the mind
is closed to new knowledge. Even if there is light, one does not perceive it during sleep. The same is true for the other senses in relation to their objects. When
one perceives objects, or one hears or smells something, one is no longer asleep.

mind be still. I bow to you oh night's energy, bless me with peace. It is you who renew my energy by blessing me with periodic rest. You provide me with comfort and beauty. I am grateful to you for this periodic rest which keeps me healthy. I bow to you and seek your blessings oh night's energy. Bless me with tranquil unbroken sleep until tomorrow morning.

4. As I said earlier, insomnia is a *vāta* ailment. Take an enema and a massage from time to time. Both are helpful for curing insomnia and other sleep disorders, for they regulate the vitiated *vāta*. An enema immediately pacifies the excess of *vāta* in the body, purifies the blood, and gives a feeling of tranquility.

Regular meals and a balanced diet keep *vāta* in equilibrium. On the contrary, untimely meals, especially late night dinners, heavy fatty food, the suppression of the non-suppressible urges, and a hectic lifestyle contribute further to vitiation of *vāta*, giving rise to restlessness and sleep disorders.

5. The inhalation of certain mixtures of etheric oils are sleep-inducing. There are many kinds of Thai or Chinese balms available which can be rubbed around the nose while going to bed. If you find them too strong, you may put a little bit of balm on a wet, hot towel and put it close to your nose. Such balms and mixtures are usually sold to cure common colds and coughs. While traveling in Thailand, I realized that the use of such balms is very common before going to sleep. I cannot explain scientifically how the etheric oils work to induce sleep, but I can say from personal experience that such inhalations have very tranquilizing and lulling effects.

Do not expect these methods to work instantaneously like a sleeping pill. They are not meant to put your restless, hyperactive self into an artificially created lull. Rather, with your own efforts and by using these methods, you bring your whole being to a natural way of life. As I said before, sleep is a natural phenomenon and the above-described methods are meant to bring you back to the ways of nature. Have a look at a sleeping baby or a child. They fall asleep anywhere and enjoy profound sleep. You did the same when you were a little boy or girl. What happened to all that later? Our aim here is to bring back that spontaneity and let the natural phenomenon take its own course.

Some people may suffer from insomnia due to psychic disorders. As you may recall, according to Ayurveda, psychic disorders are caused by the nonfulfillment of desires or facing the undesired. It is up to you to control your mind and not to desire the inaccessible. By talking to people who suffer from insomnia, I realized that the people of the "worrying" category indulge in self-pity and suffering. Happiness is a mental state which you can learn. Worldly pleasures—wealth, children, wife, husband—none can make you happy if you do not make an effort for your own happiness. Ups and downs are a part of life. We all have our past *karma* to which we are answerable, but we also have the freedom to experience our present *karma*. By grumbling over what we do not have, we also ruin our present *karma*.

In Ayurveda, the following foods are recommended for inducing sleep:

◊ A round variety of rice that has a natural white color is recommended. The rice should be boiled and then eaten with hot, sweetened milk.

◊ Wheat porridge or soups made using wheat.

◊ In general, a sweet and unctuous diet is sleep-inducing. Salty, rough, and dry foods should be avoided.

In my opinion, one should use all possible preventive measures; nutritional therapy, mild sleep-inducing teas, breathing exercises, a head massage with herbal oils, pressing massage, hand or foot massage, are sensible sleep-inducing techniques.

Disturbed Sleep

Many people do not suffer from deficient sleep but they cannot sleep through the night. They wake up many times. Some are frightened; sleep disturbances may also be due to blocked nasal and pharyngeal passages. This latter also leads to snoring. Suppressed or excessive sexuality also gives rise to sleep disorders.

You should carefully observe the cause of the sleep disturbance and should make every effort to remove the cause. For example, if nasal and pharyngeal passages are blocked, you should regularly do yogic practices like *jalneti* and *jaldhauti.* In case you wake up with fear, or have bad dreams, you should recite the sleep prayers before going to bed or if you wake up during the night. *Japa* and other concentration practices are also recommended.

Some people do not drink sufficient fluid and they experience a loss of water from the body during the night. They wake up with a throbbing heart or numbness in some body parts. The cure is very simple. Take more fluids, include soups in your diet, and eat plenty of salads and fruits. You may also drink a few glasses of water during the evening.

Some sleep disorders are caused by heavy, undigested food and gastrointestinal problems. Gastrointestinal problems may also lead to a fearful state or bad dreams. Constipation may have the same effect. In such cases, the causes can be removed by altering your diet.

Excess Sleep

We have already discussed that vitiated *kapha* makes one lazy and gives rise to excessive sleep. Despite lots of sleep, these people are tired. Their yawns are accompanied by watery eyes. They feel drowsy during the day and get sudden fits of fatigue, as if their senses want to shut down to the external world. These symptoms are opposite to the excessive *vāta* symptoms of hyperactivity.

We have already discussed the remedies for excessive *kapha.* Cure the vitiated *kapha* and that will cure the allied sleep disorders. Do not submit to laziness, use rough and hot measures, eat spicy food, and do physical exercise.

In certain cases, sleep problems are merely due to a disturbed sleep routine. Staying up late, long distance air traveling or other reasons may disturb the normal sleep rhythm. You may be unable to sleep at night whereas during the day or during early hours of the morning, you feel drowsy. To cure this disorder, keep to your usual sleep routine and try to bring back sleep by using nutritional therapy, sleep-inducing herbal teas, or massage. Do not submit to untimely sleep as this will go on making the sleep cycle worse.

Eyes and Vision

The humor responsible for vision is *pitta*. When *pitta* is vitiated, vision is weakened. An excess of *kapha* also has a negative effect on vision as it suppresses *pitta*. I have already talked about red eyes caused by an excess of *pitta*, or weakness of vision due to sinusitis. If you feel that your eyes get a burning sensation and redness, try to cure your *pitta*.

1) A decoction of coriander seeds is very beneficial for curing a burning sensation in the eyes and redness due to an excess of *pitta*. Besides washing your eyes two or three times a day with this decoction, you may also drink a small cup of it once or twice a day to decrease *pitta*.

2) Put sandalwood paste on your eyelids and forehead and leave it for some time. It has a very cooling effect and removes an excess of *pitta*. Sandalwood paste is made by rubbing a piece of sandalwood on a stone with a little water.

3) A decoction of liquorice is also helpful to cure burning red eyes. Wash the eyes with it two or three times a day.

Pain around the eyes and minor problems in vision may occur after a cold. Use various methods like *jalneti, jaldhauti* and eye exercises to take out the accumulated *kapha* from inside.

I have already talked about a vision-promoting recipe in the section on fatigue. There are other methods that can be used for promoting vision and the ingredients are available almost anywhere in the world.

1) Liquorice is a very effective medicine for promoting vision. It helps cure problems of vitiated *pitta* and *kapha*. A daily dose of liquorice root is about three grams. It can be either taken by chewing the root, or in powder form with water, or by making a decoction. It is highly recommended to take it as a preventive measure after age 35 as many people tend to get problems with

their vision around that age. Besides being vision-promoting, liquorice is also intellect-promoting.

2) Take a small amount of garlic (1–2 cloves) every day. This therapy is very effective if vision is deteriorating due to excess of *kapha*. This is particularly beneficial for children as you know that childhood is *kapha*-dominating and many children get vision problems related to *kapha*.

3) In ethnic medicine, it is recommended to massage one's toes with ghee everyday before bathing and for promoting vision.

4) Grate 2 medium-sized tender carrots and cook them in milk for about fifteen minutes on a low fire. Powder 5 almonds and 1 cardamom, and add to this mixture while it is cooking. You may add sugar according to taste. Eat this preparation daily or often during carrot season. This preparation is not only vision-promoting, but it also gives strength and removes fatigue. Carrots are a very good food from the Ayurvedic point of view as they bring the humors in equilibrium. I especially recommend this preparation as a breakfast for children.

Bad Throat, Colds, and Coughs

These are minor and very common troubles which exist all over the world. They are especially more frequent in areas with air pollution. To get rid of a bad throat, or as a preventive measure against it, I have already discussed some throat and nose-cleaning practices in chapter 4 and 5. Since the throat and nose are connected, and an infection in the throat immediately spreads in the region, the cleaning of the nose with *jalneti* is essential to cure a bad throat. When the infection attacks the nose, one suffers from an excretion of mucus generally termed as "cold." These infections are usually caused by a large variety of viruses and also by bacteria in certain cases. They may or may not be accompanied by fever.

As is true for many ailments, if one reacts in time, the suffering from colds and the coughs which usually follow a bad throat can be avoided. Gargling is very important at the initial stages of the attack. Some of the plants for gargling have been already mentioned in chapter 4. Besides gargling, get enough rest to accumulate energy for fighting the external attack and do psychological and spiritual therapy (see chapter 8) at this initial stage of infection to avert the ailment. Concentrate on the affected part and tell this external infection that you do not want it and you do not accept it.

Drink plenty of liquids, like hot tea, freshly pressed orange juice, hot water with lemon, etc. Coffee and black tea are good analgesics but do not take them too much as they keep you awake and will upset your stomach.

The following preparations work very well to cure minor throat and cold infections and/or fever.

1) Take 11 leaves of fresh basil (*Ocimum sanctum*) or a teaspoon if you are using dried leaves, 2 grams (½ tsp.) fresh ginger (¼ teaspoon if you are using dried, powdered ginger) and 5 black pepper grains. Crush all these together and put them in about 200 ml (1 cup) boiling water and let it cook covered on a low fire. Either you can drink this preparation after filtering and adding some sugar in it, or you may make black tea out of it. For the latter, add ½ teaspoon of small leaf black tea, some milk, and sugar, and boil together for half a minute. Filter it and drink it while it is hot. After drinking it, lie down and cover yourself well so that you can sweat. Depending upon the gravity of your trouble, take two or three times a day. If you have a sensitive stomach, use only 2 grains of pepper.

2) This preparation is made from gram flour (chickpea flour) or from wheat husk if the former is not available. Fry 1½ soupspoons of this flour with 1 teaspoon of ghee on a very low fire. When it is a little cooked, add a glass of water to it while stirring constantly. Add 2 to 3 teaspoons sugar and keep stirring. Let it come to a boil and cook for another half a minute and it is ready. It looks like a thick soup. Lie down after drinking it and cover yourself well so you can sweat. Like the above preparation, take it two or three times a day.

3) This is a recipe for preparing lozenges for curing bad throats and calming down coughs.

> Cardamom, 5 gms (1 tsp.)
> Laurel leaves, 5 gms (1 tsp.)

Cinnamon, 5 gms (1 tsp.)
Black pepper, 15 grains (pinch)
Dates (dried), 25 gms (2 tbl.)
Raisins (dried), 25 gms (2 tbl.)
Liquorice, 25 gms (2 tbl.)

Powder all except dates and raisins, and pass through a cloth to make a fine powder (see page 197). Crush dates and raisins and mix with the powder into a fine paste. Add some honey in order to obtain a thick paste. You may either store this paste as such or make lozenges the size of a pepper by rolling on your palm. Spread these on a plate and let them dry in the shade. Then they can be stored in a bottle.

An attack of bad throat and cold may be followed by a cough. These lozenges should be taken to calm down the cough and clear the voice. In addition, take a liquorice decoction twice a day.

4) Another simple method to cure a cough is to take 1 teaspoon fresh ginger juice along with three semi-crushed black pepper grains in 2 teaspoons honey. Mix together to make one dose. Take it twice a day. It is especially beneficial to take at night before going to bed.

Inhalation with mixtures of etheric oils or balms is very helpful for curing colds and coughs. Etheric oils are described in the section on headaches (page 204). Apply the same or a similar commercial product on your chest, back, and throat before going to bed. Do some inhalations from this mixture either directly or by adding a few drops of it to hot water. It will be very helpful to open the blocked nose. Another recipe for an inhalation oil is described in the section on sinusitis (see page 223).

Chronic Cough and Asthma

Until now, we were talking about coughs accompanied by a cold, which are usually cured in the due course of time. But coughs may also be caused due to some other infection or allergies. It may become bronchial and even spread deeper. In many cases, it becomes chronic. In asthma, there is a spasmodic contraction of bronchi either due to an infection or due to an allergic reaction. There is a panting for breath. For curing these two ailments, you will have to follow a strict regimen along with regular exercise.

1) Do the two *yogāsanas* regularly twice a day, in the morning and in the evening before going to bed. These are *bhujangāsana* (the serpent posture) and *paschimottanāsana* (the forward-stretching posture). These asanas have been described in detail previously. Follow the instructions carefully and devote at least half an hour daily to them, that is, fifteen minutes in the morning and fifteen minutes in the evening. Remember that you are doing these yogic postures to cure a serious ailment. It is a part of your therapy to do them regularly.

2) Do the *prāṇāyāma* exercises described in chapter 5. In the beginning, you may have problems, but do them according to your capacity. With improvement, your capacity to inhale and exhale and its time period will increase. It will also indicate to you your state of recovery.

3) Do *jaldhauti* regularly as described in chapter 5. You will observe that phlegm will come out and you will have a feeling of well-being after vomiting. You may do this therapy during the day, also to get rid of discomfort and cough. Babies often vomit when they are suffering from severe cough and they feel better afterward.

4) Do not eat nuts, dried foods like biscuits, bread, bananas, cold milk preparations, or ice creams. Do not drink any cold drinks. Always drink warm drinks and also drink warm water with food or otherwise.

5) Your diet should consist of very light liquids and vegetable soups, gruels, well-cooked rice mixed with soups, and other foods. Avoid all that increases *kapha.*

6) Drink astringent herbal teas like thyme, *ajwain* or any others native to your particular geographical location.

7) Follow the other instructions described for colds and coughs.

8) If your cough or asthma are due to some allergic reactions, you are advised to take curcuma therapy. You should take $1/2$ teaspoon of curcuma every day for a year. According to Ayurveda, it slowly purifies the blood and makes one free from allergic reactions and skin problems. Half a teaspoon of curcuma added to a spoon of ghee should be fried on a low fire while stirring. After frying a little, add 1–2 teaspoons sugar and stir again. Then add 1 cup milk and stir constantly. Let the whole preparation come to a boil. Drink it hot.

In the case of a chronic cough or asthma, the healing process is very long because coughing causes wounds and inflammation. Make every effort to cure yourself and heal these wounds. Once you are cured, take every precaution so you do not get an attack again. As has been already said in the context of chronic pain, the ailing part is a weak point in your body. Take precautions to avoid the ailment from recurring. Follow the above-described instructions even when you feel you are nearly cured. Save yourself from exposure to colds, apply ointments on your chest, back, and neck regularly, and do inhalations.

Always insure proper evacuation and apply purification therapies regularly. Any stress or tension enhances the ailment and hinders the process of healing. Try to keep yourself free of stress.

Ayruveda has contributed a great medicine to the world for curing asthma. This preparation comes from a plant called *Somalata* (*Ephedra gerardiana*) which grows high in the Himalayan mountains. The active compound in the plant is ephedrine. You should look for a commercial preparation which contains ephedrine as it is not possible to get this plant everywhere in the world.

Sinusitis

In the cranium (the bones of the upper part of the head), there are many cavities which are called sinuses. When any of these cavities get inflamed and infected, it is considered sinusitis. Sinusitis is painful, causes discomfort, and hinders the passage of *vāta*. It may become chronic and may lead to weakness of vision, headaches, and gray hair. Sinusitis may last briefly after a cold or it may become chronic. Chronic sinusitis may recur even after a surgical intervention. It is a nagging ailment and may also become the cause of frequent attacks of coughs and colds. The methods described below will cure minor cases of sinusitis, but for old and more serious cases, you may have to take precautions all your life.

1) There is no better method to cure and prevent sinusitis than to do *jalneti* (see chapter 5) daily. This practice slowly opens the blocked passages and reduces pain due to *kapha* in the sinus. Use warm water for *jalneti*. It helps melt[8] cumulative *kapha* and brings it out. Although the *neti* water does not go to different parts of the sinus, when *kapha* from the nasal passage comes out, it frees the passage for *vāta* and helps soften the accumulated *kapha* in the inner parts, like around the eyes and in the upper parts of the cheeks. You will observe that when you are doing *jalneti* regularly, for the first several days old, dark-colored phlegm will come out when blowing your nose after the practice. However, after several days, only a fluid will come out, and the pain will disappear.

Some people with vitiated *vāta-kapha* may feel dryness in their nostrils, and warm water *neti* may hurt them. They should apply some ghee in the nostrils prior to *neti* and should also do *neti* with milk from time to time.

2) The second part of the cure for sinusitis is the inhalation of a mixture of etheric oils combined with special breathing exercises. Either use a commercial mixture of these oils or add a little bit of pain-relieving balm in boiling hot water. You may also make your own mixture for inhalation. Take Eucalyptus oil, citronella and menthol crystals (five parts each), anise oil and camphor (two parts each), and one part lavender oil. Mix them together and let the mixture stand for at least a week before use. This mixture can be preserved for years if kept in a tightly closed bottle. Never use plastic bottles to keep these oils. Always re-

---

[8]It is believed that the vitiated *kapha* at a particular place almost solidifies there and one needs treatment and medication to make it fluid again so that it can be thrown out. In English I have used the word "melt" which expresses this idea better than the word "liquifies."

place the lid immediately otherwise they evaporate. Take some from the stock for everyday use.

During an attack of sinusitis, you should do inhalations by adding a few drops of the above mixture in boiling hot water. Either use commercially available apparatus for this purpose or put a piece of cardboard around the container to direct the vapors toward your nose. Begin inhalation by simply breathing in these vapors and let them go inside whatever way possible– nose or mouth. This will give an initial help to open the passage. Imagine that your nasal passage is blocked. Take a deep breath from the vapors through your mouth and try to exhale through your nose. In this process, slowly, the nasal passage will be freed from phlegm. Now do the inhalation rhythmically through your mouth and exhale through your nose. Then inhale through your nose and exhale through your mouth. In this process, you might have to stop in between to blow your nose and spit out excessive saliva. This inhalation activates the salivary glands. Blow your nose with force so that the old stuck phlegm is blown out. After this, inhale from one nostril while the other is kept closed (as you did for *prāṇāyāma*). Keep the vapors inside by closing both nostrils. Then exhale from the other nostril and inhale from the same. Repeat this a few times so that the passage between your two nostrils gets free, and by closing both nostrils, the vapors are forced to go to the other parts of the sinus.

The next step is to inhale to your full capacity through nostrils or mouth and then hold the nostrils and shut the mouth and try to push the air out with pressure. Since mouth and nostrils are kept closed, the vapors will be forced to go to the other parts because of the force you are applying. You may feel some sensation in your ears by doing so. These vapors you are inhaling are full of etheric oils with a high penetration capacity. They will melt the blocked *kapha* in the sinus passages and take it out. They will also cure the infection by making an extremely disagreeable environment for the virus. These etheric oils have anti-viral, anti-fungus and antibiotic qualities. However, to get rid of the infection completely, you will have to do this practice regularly because these viruses and bacteria multiply very quickly.

At the time of the sinusitis attack, do not hesitate to do the inhalation several times a day. After the inhalation, lie down for some time and keep yourself warm.

As a preventive measure, you need not take these inhalations every day. You may do *jalneti* regularly, inhale the above oil directly from the bottle and do the *prāṇāyāma* practices described earlier. Before going to bed, put a few drops of this oil on a wet hot towel and inhale. The *kapha* is related to *tamas* and it is at night that *kapha* accumulates. Therefore, inhalation before going to bed is preventive in this disorder. The other precautions which have been described in the case of coughs and colds should also be observed in case of sinusitis.

Hay Fever

The term Hay Fever includes a variety of seasonal allergic reactions due to pollen or some other substances in the air, marked by conjunctivitis, swelling of nasal mucosa, tears in the eyes, itching, sneezing, etc. It seems that there is no cure for it in modern medicine and some people suffer throughout their lives from this seasonal ailment. However, Ayurvedic and Homeopathic methods have successfully cured this ailment.

According to Ayurveda, an allergic reaction is caused by impurities in the blood. There are many blood-purifying medicines in Ayurveda. The simplest one is the curcuma therapy which has been already described. It is a very slow acting therapy and you will have to do it continuously for a year. In fact, this therapy is suggested for curing any allergy. Those who have access to Indian Ayurvedic products may also alternatively take *Mahāmanjiṣṭhā*, a classical Ayurvedic preparation for purifying blood.

Besides the blood-purifying therapy, you should also do inhalations with etheric oils every day as has been described previously. Do not begin treating hay fever when the attack has already started. Treatment that leads to a cure of this malady should be taken throughout the year. This way, you will be able to develop a resistance and tolerance to those particular elements in the air which cause you this trouble. You have to strengthen the weak parts of your body, whether it is nasal mucosa or your throat and eyes which react adversely to some particles in the air. A regular inhalation has given very positive results in this direction.

A daily practice of *jalneti* is recommended which strengthens the secretory cells of the nasal passage. A passage of hot water through nostrils which are meant for air creates a "challenge situation" for the inner lining of the cells (epithelial cells) and makes them active to face any outer attack. To further strengthen these cells, you should do *jalneti* with slightly salted water, and also with milk from time to time.

Do various practices of *prāṇāyāma* daily, especially before going to bed. Make a mixture of the etheric oils described previously. For curing hay fever, you should mix 10 ml (2 tsp.) of this oil with 5 gms (½ tsp.) of menthol crystals. You should do your *prāṇāyāma* practices by inhaling from this bottle. This is another way to activate the mucous-secreting cells. Before the suspected period of attack and during the season of the attack, keep the above mixture always with you and do inhalations from it (directly from the bottle) three to four times a day.

Do not hope to cure yourself with these practices if they are not done regularly throughout the year. The idea of curing yourself only at the onset of your seasonal trouble is equivalent to casting weapons when the war has already begun. If you are to successfully fight against these unknown elements in the air which bring you annual suffering, you will have to prepare yourself well in advance.

Problems of Digestive Tract

Digestion and assimilation are the source of *agni* or bodily fire. As has already been said, this denotes the production of the body's energy at the physiological level. Any problem with this system will lead to the vitiation of *pitta* followed by the vitiation of *vāta*. Digestive problems lead to fatigue and a lack of energy almost immediately. Therefore, one should carefully examine oneself daily with the previously described diagnostic methods and attend to the problems of digestion immediately.

Digestive problems are very varied and may occur at any step of digestion—stomach, liver, intestines, rectum, etc. We will deal only with some commonly occurring complaints and their remedies will be described.

Lack of Appetite or Excessive Appetite

Appetite is a desire for food linked to hunger. One may feel hungry but not have a desire to eat. When food is eaten without appetite, it may cause gastric problems. Not eating will lead to weakness and fatigue. Similarly, some people suffer from an excessive desire to eat which is equally a disorder. It leads to indiscriminant eating and thus, gives rise to digestive disorders and obesity. Both these disorders should not be ignored.

First of all, let us see what causes a deranged appetite. Both the above-described problems may be caused by *pitta* vitiation. Therefore, you should check by various diagnostic methods if your *pitta* is in equilibrium. If the lack of appetite is due to *pitta* vitiation, you have no desire to eat and there is also a lack of hunger. If the excessive desire to eat is due to vitiated *pitta*, you feel constantly hungry and the food gets digested very quickly. If these symptoms accompany an excessive or diminished appetite, take measures to appease the vitiated *pitta* and the disorder will be cured.

Now we come to the problem of deranged appetite which is not associated with *pitta* vitiation. A desire to reject food is not independent of the rest of your life. It represents a desire to withdraw or escape from problems, people, things, or other environmental factors. Try to diagnose the problems that cause the apparent symptom. You need consolation and assurance. In the face of problems which make you withdraw like this, try to tell yourself that it is not the end of the world and that nothing stays forever—neither the good times nor the bad times. Food is vitality, if it is rejected, it poses a threat to life. To solve your problems and get out of a difficult situation, you need more vitality and vigor. Therefore do not reject food. Remind yourself that the first priority is to safeguard life.

As we discussed earlier, problems often originate because we take things too seriously and make ourselves indispensable. We forget that life on earth will go on even when we are not here. Therefore, learn to take it easy, do not reject; accept, face, and think about the positive aspects of even a rough experience.

Besides working with yourself and sorting out problems, take the following measures to increase appetite: Half an hour before every meal, eat some fresh ginger (1 to 2 gms, or 1 tsp.)

with lemon and salt. If you do not want to chew ginger as it is too strong, then take 1 teaspoon ginger juice with $\frac{1}{2}$ teaspoon lemon juice, and a grain of salt. You may take this in some water if you like.

Some people suffer from an excess of appetite due to depression, aimlessness, helplessness, or a feeling of being worthless or unwanted. People suffering from this ailment are strongly driven by a desire to eat without even being hungry. They walk to their kitchens, open the refrigerator, sometimes without even thinking about their actions.

The purpose of the Ayurvedic way of life is self-awareness and self-realization. Thus, if you suffer from this ailment, search for the underlying cause and deal with it bravely. Take up some hobbies or creative activities which really interest you. They will divert your mind from eating and at least you will be saved from obesity. However, a real solution is to find the underlying cause and deal with it.

Stomach Acidity and Ulcers

The stomach is a very interesting organ. Inside it, nutrients are broken into smaller units for the purpose of assimilation. It can digest things similar to its own structure and composition—like a piece of meat. But then how come the stomach doesn't digest itself? The process of digestion takes place because of many different gastric secretions which are all highly acidic. What prevents the stomach from digesting itself are the cells which form its inner lining. These cells have a special permeability barrier which does not let anything permeate. These guardian cells of the stomach are constantly renewed. This permeability barrier is challenged with certain foods like too much tea, coffee, or alcohol, or chemical drugs, especially some pain-relieving and anti-arthritic drugs. When the permeability barrier is weakened or damaged, the highly acidic medium which prevails in the stomach traverses the stomach cell lining and reaches inside the stomach wall, thus, causing pain and discomfort. If the acid permeability barrier is repeatedly challenged, it can slowly harm the cells, can cause inflammation and hence degeneration (gastritis). It may even give rise to ulcers. Ulcers are wounds inside the stomach. If these recurring problems are not cured in time, they may lead to stomach cancer.

Stomach acidity, which occurs from time to time, is due to an improper regimen, and can be easily cured by the following simple methods:

1) A glass of cold, sweetened milk helps cure the acidity. If you have a sensitive stomach and you are prone to stomach acidity, drink cold sweetened milk every night before going to bed.

2) After every meal, chew a clove. Do not chew it too rapidly. Let it be in your mouth and eat it slowly.

3) Avoid everything that causes acidity in your particular case. Whenever you drink alcohol or other things your stomach is sensitive to, take precautionary measures before the onset of the trouble. Some people are sensitive to certain varieties of wines. With a careful observation, they should find out exactly the wines that give them trouble so they can avoid them.

4) *Pitta*-dominating people are particularly sensitive, and they get acidity very easily. First of all, they should eat a *pitta*-decreasing diet. They should avoid eating sour and spicy foods. If they wish to take sour fruits like grapefruit, orange, or plum, they should eat them with salt or sugar to lessen the *pitta* effect on the body.

5) A regular practice of *jaldhauti* saves one from the problems of acidity, helps relax the stomach, and keeps it clean. This practice is good for everybody as a preventive practice.

You should be aware that many stomach problems are caused by stress. To get rid of them, one needs to remove the underlying causes besides using the above-described curative methods. Do not store stress in the stomach. Many people get stomach ulcers when they have problems with the boss, wife, husband, or other similar situations. In Ayurvedic terminology, facing the undesired causes these situations, and they translate into one malady or another. When people have stress, ulcers, for example, ailment makes them all the more nervous from their already "unhappy situation." They take strong medications to cure themselves, but somehow the process of healing is delayed because of stress.

You must know that stomach ulcers are like the wounds on your outer skin which should be healed by your body in a brief period. Normally, you do not require special medicines to heal these wounds. You need to create a congenial climate to help the stomach heal itself. For that, you need a strict diet. Imagine a wound on your finger. What will you do to heal it? First of all, you will make every effort to keep it clean. You will protect it from strong and irritants like soap, salt, vinegar, etc. You will try, perhaps, to put an antiseptic cream on it in order to protect it from external attacks of bacteria, fungus, virus, to enhance the process of healing. As you know, within a few days, this wound will be healed and you will forget about it. Treat the wound in your stomach in the same manner and do not panic. Unlike the wound on your finger, you cannot see the one in your stomach, but you can try to feel it and feel for it.

As I have told you, the stomach cells are constantly renewed. If the ulcer is not very old, it is quite easily healed. However, when the stomach suffers for a long time, the inflammation of the cells leads to dysfunction and unhealthy new cells. To cure stomach ulcers, you should do everything to enhance the process of healing and foremost is a strict regimen. Here are some suggestions for diet.

1) Do not eat any spicy, sour, or pungent foods. Eat very simple foods with a predominatingly sweet *rasa*. Well-cooked small, round rice, along with freshly prepared yogurt is highly recommended.

The following recipes will help you nourish yourself adequately.

Preparation of Curd-rice: Take a measured quantity of white, round variety of rice (like south Indian, Chinese, or Japanese rice). Wash well and let it soak in water for five minutes. Boil double the amount of water than the rice in a pot and add some anise seeds along with the rice in the boiling water. Cook covered, on a very low fire. When all the water is evaporated, remove from the fire and let the rice stay like this, well-covered with lid, another five minutes. This preparation is called boiled rice.

Take freshly prepared curd (yogurt) which is not sour. Stir it well with a spoon, add a pinch of salt. Now add an equal quantity of the rice you have already prepared. Do not add very hot rice into the yogurt. It should be just warm. Eat this in a small quantity. It is better to eat several times a day in small quantities than in large quantities at once.

Preparation of vegetables: You should carefully choose vegetables with sweet *rasa*, like carrots, various varieties of zucchini, turnips, potatoes, pumpkin, etc. Always make a mixed vegetable preparation. Cut the vegetables into small pieces after washing and peeling. Cook covered with a little water on a low fire. Add some anise seeds along with the vegetables. Cook until the water evaporates and vegetables are well-cooked. You may eat these vegetables with boiled rice, or, alternatively, you may add some washed and soaked rice to be cooked along with the vegetables. Do not add too much rice. The quantity of vegetables should be in equal proportion to the rice. You may add some ghee to this preparation. It depends on the degree of your ailment and your power of digestion at the time. You must make this judgment yourself. Add a small quantity of ghee in the beginning and observe carefully whether it is well-digested. Eat fresh preparations. Do not keep them more than five to six hours. Never eat food prepared a day in advance.

2) For breakfast, you may eat boiled rice (described above) with some cold milk and sugar. Alternatively, a preparation from wheat is suggested. Soak the wheat grains for about 24 hours. They become very soft. Then crush them in a mixer or in a stone grinder. After partially crushing these grains, cook them in water for about 10 minutes. Then pass them through a fine strainer to extract the wheat milk. The wheat milk may be taken after adding some sugar in it, or it can be cooked another few minutes with the same quantity of cow's milk. In some advanced cases of ulceration, the patient cannot even digest milk. In that case, one has to leave the milk out.

3) You may also eat hot rice with some sugar and ghee for breakfast, but the rice should always be cooked as stated above. If the rice is not well-cooked, it becomes difficult to digest.

Try to obtain fresh milk which is not homogenized and with no preservatives. Methods of making fresh yogurt in a simple way has been described elsewhere.[9]

4) You may also take vegetable, chicken, wheat, rice, or barley gruels. Use very little or no salt and the things you eat should never be sour.

5) Among the fruits, papaya, *bilva* (*Aegle marmelos*), and banana may be eaten.

During the healing process, you should only eat the minimum quantity of food you require for survival.

Besides all this, you should massage your abdomen gently twice a day before your bath and before going to bed. Also apply pain-relieving oil or ointment every night before going to bed. It helps relax the stiffened and ailing stomach musculature.

Do not get desperate about your ailment. Keep courage and be confident that you will be better soon. You should be able to manage your ailment. Your ailment should not manage you and make you a nervous, frightened person. In such circumstances, the healing process is delayed and your nervousness gives rise to fresh troubles.

Do healing practices. Personify your stomach and talk to it. Give it courage. Tell it to be brave. Tell it to get rid of the sickness soon and be in harmony with the rest of the body. "Oh stomach! You are indispensable for my survival. It is you who provide energy for my activities by assimilating nutrients. You are very powerful. Even the toughest things you break into small pieces for the purpose of digestion and nourishing my body. I regret not taking care of you earlier. I request you to excuse me and I beg to you to get well again. Oh stomach! be healthy again to harmonize with the rhythm of my body."

During the healing process, relax as much as possible. Do not do stressful jobs and physical exercise. Stop doing yogic pos-

---

[9]See *Ayurvedic Instructions on Nutrition, Healing and Sexual Energy.* This book has been published in German by Aurum Verlag (1991), but is not available in English yet.

tures also. Concentrate all your energy on healing the wounds and the inflammation in your stomach.

Other Gastric Troubles

Some people suffer from gas. A regular evacuation, timely enema therapy and appropriate food will cure this trouble. This is a *vāta* ailment and immediate measures should be taken to pacify *vāta*. Foods made with heavy-to-digest grains or fats, the intake of too many products with yeast, eating *basa* and eating too frequently cause this trouble. In addition, late night heavy dinners, excessively spicy and salty meals, or extremely sour foods enhance the problem of fermentation. Avoid the *vāta*-promoting foods or make sure they are prepared with *vāta*-decreasing spices.

Drink warm water with some lemon juice in it or take some *ajwāin* with warm water, or drink thyme tea if *ajwāin* is not available. If you have nothing else available, drink some hot water. The regular use of garlic is a preventive measure for this ailment. Take two small garlic cloves, peal them and crush them with 5-6 large dried raisins and eat them. This immediately calms down troubles caused by fermentation and gas in the digestive tract. Seeds of garden cress (*Lepidium sativum*) are another effective medicine to cure a gas problem. Crush about ⅓ teaspoon of seeds and take them with warm water. Like garlic, cress also promotes *pitta*, so be careful with its use, especially if you are a *pitta*-dominating person. Take appropriate *pitta*-reducing measures.

Constipation

I have discussed this problem in various contexts during the course of this book. As you know, constipation is dangerous for health and becomes the cause of hundreds of other ailments. According to Ayurveda, the accumulation of *mala* causes impurities in the blood. Once the blood is polluted, it shows its ill-effect all over the body. Impure blood causes various skin ailments, allergies, boils and pimples, and makes one weak and unable to fight external attacks. It is commonly observed that a person suffering from constipation gets frequent colds, coughs, and other minor ailments. As you know, an accumulation of "minor" leads to "major" and therefore one should be cautious when there is still time. I am writing this repeatedly because most people ignore constipation and do not think it is an ailment, or that it causes a serious threat to health. Besides the above-said problems, constipation increases *vāta* and leads to all *vāta*-related disorders. I have often observed that people try to treat rough skin and drab looks with various cosmetics. Sometimes it is simply constipation which is responsible for all these. Therefore learn to go deeper into the causes of the problems.

Following are some simple methods to cure constipation:

1) The most simple and effective method to cure constipation is drinking water in the morning. Keep a pint of water in a covered clean container overnight and drink it the next morning on waking up. Do not lie down after drinking the water. Move around and do some exercise. You will have the urge to evacuate after about ten minutes. If this method does not work, then drink warm water. But the quantity of water should be about a pint. If you are drinking bottled mineral water, then you need not keep it overnight. Drink only plain water.

2) Appropriate nutrition is important for proper evacuation. Do not eat too many dry foods like bread or cheese. Your meals, especially dinner, should include vegetables and salads. Vegetable soup is good. Drink a hot cup of milk before going to bed as it helps cure constipation in some cases. Do not eat *vāta*-increasing foods like preserved juices and *basa* foods. Make it a habit to eat fruit after your meals rather than cakes and other bakery products as desserts. Do not eat things made of white flour. Do not eat too many potatoes, or eat them in combination with green vegetables. For example, a meal of meat and potatoes without a salad or vegetable soup is unwholesome and may cause constipation. *Vāta*-dominating people are more susceptible to this ailment and therefore should be careful to avoid *vāta*-increasing substances.

3) One or two teaspoons of rose marmalade with a cup of hot milk taken every night before going to bed ensures proper evacuation. For preparing rose marmalade, take equal amounts of fresh rose petals and sugar and cook them covered for an hour at least. Add some water if needed. Stir from time to time while cooking so it does not stick to the pot.

If the problem of constipation persists, take a non-unctuous enema followed by an unctuous enema. The best cure to eradicate constipation is through nutrition suited to your humoral nature.

Lastly, I want to add that too much sitting, inactivity, and stress may also cause constipation. You should carefully study your particular case. During stress situations, various people react differently and make certain parts of their bodies tense. For example, some stiffen their shoulders or neck region, others retract their abdomen and some make rectal muscles tense. Constipation may also be caused due to a subtle feeling of insecurity attached to fear and anxiety. This constipation problem is coupled with a lack of self-expression and withdrawn behavior. Oil massage is very helpful in such cases. In any case, work on yourself to get rid of fundamental problems that cause constipation. Consult a physician or wise person if you are unable to locate the cause of your constipation yourself.

Liver Problems

Many people suffer from the sluggish function of the liver. This makes them look pale, decreases their digestive power (*agni*) and increases vulnerability to external infections. In Ayurveda, liver functions are given great importance for the general strength of the body. I am not talking about the cure of liver dysfunctions as this needs long term and complicated treatment. I will discuss various ways to keep the liver in good condition so its functions do not become sluggish and one is able to prevent a number of other ailments.

Let us see why liver functions are important for good general health. The liver is the principal site of *agni* (the bodily fire) which provides energy for all other functions of the body. Besides secreting bile which helps digestion, most of the nutrients (products of digestion) are passed to the liver after assimilation and from there, they are transferred to the blood for storage and circulation. The liver is interposed between the intestinal tract and blood circulation. The liver does the storage and filtrating for the blood. Lastly, the liver may also receive toxic substances from the blood and is capable of detoxifying them. Therefore, take care of your liver. Following are suggestions to keep your liver in order and to give you a youthful look.

1) Do not drink too much alcohol, and especially not when you are hungry. Bad quality wines harm the liver and stomach. Wine taken with food, as the French drink, does less harm than any alcoholic beverage taken before food. Do not drink strong alcohols without diluting them, especially when you drink them before meals or several hours after a meal. As all of you are aware, a large intake of alcohol over a long period of time causes serious liver damage and is life-threatening. In Ayurveda, a mild quantity of good wine is recommended with food. In Ayurvedic literature, it seems that in ancient times, people had an elaborate wine culture[10] which did not survive to modern times.

2) Do not drink too much tea or coffee. Do not take these drinks on an empty stomach, unless you add milk. These beverages should never be made too strong.

3) Do not fast too much. Avoid long intervals without food. It is better to eat small quantities 3 - 4 times a day than two excessively elaborate meals.

4) Fried foods, oil used for frying several times, hydrogenated oils (like margarine or artificial ghees), or rapeseed oil are heavy on the liver and make its functions sluggish. Therefore, these products should be avoided.

5) As you all know, too much food or eating an excessively fat-containing diet tells upon the liver. We have already discussed the quantity and quality of food from the Ayurvedic point of view in chapter 6.

I will mention some products that promote liver functions. Their use will be helpful as preventive medicine and curatives when you have minor problems with the liver due to an excess of drinking or eating.

1) Some food products described in Ayurvedic literature promote liver functions and are available everywhere. These are: cumin, caraway (or carvi), lemon, pomegranate, ginger, laurel leaves, plums and figs. A regular use of these products is highly

---

[10] *Caraka Saṃhitā, Sūtrasthāna*, XXVII, 178–195.

recommended. The addition of pepper, cumin, and ginger as spices in different food preparations is beneficial.

2) Two products used as medicines to promote the functions of a sluggish liver are: 1: long pepper (*Piper longum*), daily dose $\frac{1}{2}$ gram ($\frac{1}{8}$ tsp.); and 2: picrorhiza, daily dose $\frac{1}{2}$ gram ($\frac{1}{8}$ tsp.). There are four kinds of rock salts described in Ayurveda, and among them is "black salt" which is natural ammonium chloride mixed with other salts. This salt can be mixed with four times its quantity of *ajwāin* (*Trachyspermum ammi*) and lemon juice (enough to make it wet). Then this mixture is dried in the shade and stored. It is very good to cure a malaise after a heavy meal, the ill effect of alcohol, and other minor liver disorders due to diverse reasons. Take $\frac{1}{2}$-1 teaspoon of this mixture with warm water. *Ajwāin* may be replaced with thyme seeds if it is not available, but the latter is less effective. Thyme tea may be taken from time to time as a preventive measure to promote *agni* and the liver function.

I would like to add that the sensitivity of your liver to alcohol and other harmful products depends upon your basic constitution. The *pitta*-dominating people are generally more tolerant to improper regimen in this respect than the others. Therefore, you should not compare yourself to others. Many people have weak livers due to the use of chemical drugs. They should be more careful and regularly take something to revitalize the liver.

Hemorrhoids (Piles)

The last part of the intestinal tract before it terminates into the anus opening is prone to a number of ailments—the most common being hemorrhoids. This is another ailment of modern civilization caused by a sedentary life, especially due to too much sitting. This ailment is due to the dilation of a vein in the hemorrhoidal plexus. It causes pain and/or bleeding due to hemorrhage in this region. This trouble is very persistent, and in modern medicine there is no cure for it except surgery. Even after surgery, the vein may dilate again. In Ayurveda, there are medicines which really cure hemorrhoids. However, the medicine is very complicated to make and it is not possible to describe it here. We make it at NOW and it takes fifteen days to prepare one of the several ingredients for it. I will explain some other methods helpful in curing minor cases and subsiding even advanced cases. However, for a complete eradication, six months to one year of treatment with the medication from my center is required.

1) Do not let yourself accumulate *mala* and save yourself from constipation. You should make sure that you pass stools at least once a day and the stool should not be hard. I will strongly suggest morning water-drinking therapy as described previously to ensure a complete excretion of the intestinal *mala*. Passing hard stools and an accumulation of stools inside aggravate this trouble, and may give rise to other serious ailments.

2) Sitting for long periods at a time, especially in chairs, is one of the major causes of this ailment. As said earlier, we all have various modes of making one or the other part of the body stiff while sitting and working in a posture for a long time. Like the neck, shoulders, wrists, lower back, or stomach, the terminal part of the digestive tract is another vulnerable part affected easily by stress and bad posture. Therefore, always try to check your sitting style. Do not keep your legs in the same place for a long time. It is useful to have a footrest. It lessens the pressure on the rectum and allied muscles. Break long sitting sessions by walking from time to time, or stretching your legs apart and making round movements with them.

According to Ayurvedic wisdom, sitting in chairs with your legs down is not a very healthy sitting posture for the body. In the ancient times, people sat either cross-legged on mats and carpets, or on low sofas and divans. In fact, these folded-leg postures are better for the abdomen and rectum. They are also good for blood circulation and save the blood vessels from excessive pressure. Obviously, in an office or in public places, you cannot sit cross-legged, but at home when you are relaxing, sit either cross-legged or with leg rests, or with stretched legs. I have described elsewhere the two yogic postures which are particularly beneficial for people suffering from hemorrhoids. These are the rock posture and forward-stretching posture. You should make these postures every day for 10 to 15 minutes. You may sit in the rock posture any time while you work or relax. However, it takes time to master this posture.

3) Some women suffer from hemorrhoids after childbirth. In fact, their bodies are too stiff and during delivery, the vein in the hemorrhoidal plexus is dilated. It is advised to do preparatory yogic exercises before deciding to have a baby as described in chapter 5.

4) Always drink plenty of liquids, and eat fresh fruits and vegetables. Do not eat fried, hard, or dried foods. Eat soups, salads, fresh juices, and rice rather than bread, cheese, or fried meats, and potatoes. Take plenty of *lassi*, which is made by beating yogurt and mixing it with water. One may add sugar or salt to it.

5) Radish is a beneficial food to cure hemorrhoids. Use the big white radish because it is more beneficial than small round radishes. In ethnic medicine, they suggest drinking radish juice every day for curing hemorrhoids.

Following are recipes suggested to cure hemorrhoids. These are mostly easy to make, and the ingredients are available everywhere.

1) Black sesame seeds should be taken in a daily dose of 3–4 gms (1 tsp.). Crush them and drink in hot water. They increase *pitta*, therefore, their use in summer should be accompanied by *pitta*-decreasing measures.

2) A decoction of the bark of the banyan tree or country fig or sacred fig (*peeple*) should be taken daily. The daily dose is 100 to 500 ml (½ to 2 cups).

3) Eat one or two figs daily.

4) Powdered dill seeds (daily dose 1 to 3 gms or ½ tsp.), bring relief to dried piles. You may also take 1 to 3 drops dill oil.

5) Powdered Java long peppers (*Piper retrofractum*), 1 to 2 gms (½ tsp.) daily, is beneficial in the case of dried piles.

6) Another home remedy is to take either fresh ginger juice (5–10 ml, ½ tsp.) or 1 to 2 gms (½ tsp.) of dried ginger daily.

At the initial stages of the ailment, you can easily cure piles with the above-said precautions and home remedies. Therefore, try your best to cure yourself at the beginning of the ailment. Otherwise you will have to take long term medication as well as follow instructions for nutrition and exercise.

Female Problems

It seems that women are the silent sufferers for many problems are associated with menstruation, the uterus, and the vagina. Most of the world's physicians and research scientists have been men who remain alien to the subtleties of women's problems. Although in pregnancy and childbirth there has been tremendous progress, the problems related to menstruation, infections, and general health conditions linked to these problems are not well looked after and their cure remains very primitive. Let us see what Ayurveda offers us in this direction.

Menstrual Pain and Allied Problems

Many women suffer from pain during menstruation as well as allied digestive problems. They cope with nausea, vomiting, stomach upsets, gas, constipation, etc. Some also get an attack of hemorrhoids shortly before menstruation. To get rid of these problems women need to change their lifestyle. Here are some effective suggestions to this effect.

1) Constipation before menstruation can lead to pain, an attack of hemorrhoids, and stomach problems. The pre-menstruation period is a *vāta* period, but shortly before menstruation (1–2 days) *kapha* dominates. Drink your morning warm water regularly for ten days before menstruation to ensure proper evacuation and to suppress *vāta*. Do not eat fried, dried, or fatty foods, particularly about ten days before menstruation. During this time, eat plenty of vegetables, soups, salads, and other liquids.

2) Do yogāsanas regularly. *Sūrya namaskāra*, done 12 times daily, is very helpful. In chapter 5, I have also described some specific yogāsanas for the reproductive organs. Yogic practice will slowly establish a hormonal balance by revitalizing the internal organs.

3) An abdominal massage done once a week is also very helpful. It releases tension from this area and relaxes the internal organs.

4) For relief of menstrual pain, eat 8 to 10 almonds every day after soaking them in water overnight and then peeling them. Do this either throughout the month or at least 15 days before menstruation. Remember that you are taking these almonds as medicine and not food. Therefore, chew them well and eat them before breakfast.

5) For curing menstrual pain, take ½ teaspoon *kalongī* (*Nigella sativa*) twice a day during menstruation. For identification and availability of *kalongī*, see the next chapter. Powder these seeds and take them with warm water. If you are suffering from menstrual pain, then begin this therapy 3 to 4 days before menstruation and continue until the end of menstruation.

6) The application of pain-relieving oils or ointments on the abdomen and back give relief to these pains. Application of dry heat is another effective measure to get rid of pain.

7) The following recipe for a tea helps get rid of menstrual pain and tension. Crush 2–3 gms (1 tsp.) ginger, 4 black peppercorns, and a big cardamom. Put them in boiling water. Add black tea, milk, and sugar. Bring to a boil and drink it hot.

8) Half a teaspoon of garden cress (*Lepidium sativum*), crushed and taken daily with warm water about 3–4 days before menstruation, and during menstruation, helps release menstrual tension, pain, and cures related digestive problems. Cress decreases *vāta* and *kapha* both, but it increases *pitta*. Therefore, be careful with its use and take a smaller dose if you are a *pitta* person or take other *pitta*-decreasing measures.

Irregular Menstruation

This problem has two aspects: delayed menstruation with scanty blood or early menstruation with excessive blood. A regular menstruation may also have scanty or excessive bleeding. In case of scanty bleeding, you will require things which increase *pitta* and suppress *vāta*. In case of excessive bleeding, you require just the contrary, that is, the drugs which suppress excessive *pitta* and establish equilibrium in your body.

In the case of excessive bleeding and early menstruation, take one of the following measures.

1) Take a decoction of coriander everyday. Take a daily dose of $1\frac{1}{2}$ teaspoons coriander, crush it and make a decoction as has been described earlier.

2) Radish seeds are very beneficial to regulate excessive and untimely bleeding. Take $\frac{1}{2}$ teaspoon of these seeds, crush them and drink them with warm water. Take this every other day for one month.

In case of delayed menstruation, take one of the following measures.

1) Make a decoction of rose petals and anise seeds. Make sure that you take petals from the red rose (with perfume). Do not take cross-breeds of the rose. Take 3 tablespoons petals and 1 teaspoon anise seed and make a decoction. Take this once or twice a day. This decoction is also helpful to terminate an early pregnancy (only a few days). Perhaps it hinders the fertilized egg from implantation.

2) A decoction of sesame seed (daily dose 3–4 gms, 1 tsp.) is also taken in cases of delayed menstruation.

Leukorrhea

An abnormal, viscous discharge from the vagina and uterine cavity is called leukorrhea. In Ayurveda, the following four kinds of leukorrhea are described.

1) *Vāta* leukorrhea is marked by a foamy, slightly pinkish discharge without smell.

2) *Pitta* leukorrhea has a bluish, reddish secretion with traces of blood.

3) *Kapha* leukorrhea has a discharge which is white, thick, and sometimes slightly yellowish.

4) *Tridoṣa* leukorrhea is due to an imbalance of all three humors. It has a very viscous secretion (like honey) and has a bad smell.

You should make your diagnosis carefully and begin the first step of treatment by curing the vitiated humor or humors. In Ayurveda, the most effective medicine for leukorrhea and for many other related problems of women is a bark from a tree called *Aśoka* (*Saraca asoca*). The daily dose is 50 ml (½ cup) decoction from this bark. One can also make a preparation with ghee from this bark with the method described earlier. The famous Ayurvedic preparation from this bark is called *Aśokāriṣṭa* and it is an alcoholic preparation.

A home remedy for leukorrhea is the following. Make a paste by stone-crushing bamboo leaves and banana leaves in equal quantities and mix this paste with one fourth of its quantity of honey. Take a teaspoon of it twice a day.

Both the above-described medicines are not available everywhere in the world. In folklore medicine, it is suggested to use a ripe banana, mash it and mix with honey, and eat this mixture every day to cure leukorrhea.

Neem (Margosa tree, or *Azadirichta indica*) is a very effective plant to cure leucorrhea. Crush 8 to 10 leaves of *neem* with ½ teaspoon cumin for making one dose. Since *neem* is bitter, you may add sugar or honey to it. Take this with water once or twice a day, depending upon the intensity of your ailment. Keep taking the medicine until you get completely cured.

Minor Vaginal Infections

Many women get various vaginal infections, like fungus, caused by bacteria. This may be due to a lack of hygiene or disturbance in normal fauna of the vagina or the mouth of the uterus. We have already discussed hygiene in chapter 4, and now let us see how the normal fauna protect us from infections.

In normal healthy conditions, we have a bacteria called *Doderline* which keeps the vaginal medium acidic by converting glycogen (a kind of sugar secreted by vaginal cells) into lactic acid. The acidic vaginal medium is a kind of defense mechanism which makes unfavorable conditions for the growth of various pathological agents. But if the *Doderline* are dead, this defense against the infection is gone and the vagina, which is warm and humid, forms a good terrain for the bacteria, fungus, or other unicellular parasites. They multiply very fast and cause various troubles like irritation, inflammation, wounds, and so forth.

By the intake of antibiotics which people generally take to get rid of pathological bacterial infections, the useful bacteria in the body in the mouth, digestive tract, or vagina, are also destroyed, harming the natural defenses of the body. Those of you who take antibiotics from time to time must have realized that you get a bad taste in your mouth after this treatment. It happens because the useful bacteria residing in the buccal cavity are killed with antibiotics and the mouth gets various fungal infections. Therefore, avoid taking antibiotics as much as possible, and if you really have to, then eat plenty of yogurt during the time of medication. You may also smear some yogurt in and around the vagina or simply wear a sanitary towel with a little yogurt on it. Make sure that the yogurt you use has living bacteria, as in the West many commercial yogurts are sold with already dead bacteria, caused by the preservatives in the yogurt. It is better if you use homemade yogurt.

Following are some other methods of treatment against minor vaginal infections.

1) A very effective method to get rid of vaginal infections at initial stages is to wash the vagina with fresh cow's milk. Milk used for this purpose should not be subjected to any treatment like boiling, or any other method of preservation. The fresh cow's milk has an active fauna which reforms the original fauna of the vagina and helps to fight the pathological bacteria by creating a competitive environment for the enemy—the parasite.

2) Soak some cotton in honey or ghee and place it in the vaginal cavity. If this treatment makes you feel better, repeat it a few times.

3) Extract the juice of *neem* and paste your vaginal wall with it with your finger. When fresh fruits are not available, make an extract from the dried fruit as has been described earlier in this chapter. You may also use the juice of *neem* leaves. This treatment is, however, restricted to the geographical locations where *neem* is available.

4) In case of dryness or slight irritations caused by infection, use mustard or coconut oil. Apply the oil either with your finger or put inside a little cotton soaked with one of these oils. Mustard oil is very strong. Therefore, be careful with its use. Its application may hurt a little bit on the already dried parts.

5) Make a very fine paste of caster seeds and mustard oil by grinding the two together. Use it as an ointment on the vaginal wall. You may also make a paste with cress seeds and coconut oil, but it is very strong. Apply very little at first to make sure you don't get an allergic reaction to it. You are more prone to get a reaction if you are a *pitta* person.

6) Make a paste with a fine powder of liquorice and ghee. Apply this paste on the vaginal walls and around it. This is particularly useful to get rid of wounds caused by parasites.

After you make a treatment to get rid of a vaginal infection, make sure that it is followed by a treatment which helps develop the natural fauna. This treatment is done with yogurt and/or milk as described above.

Pregnancy

The subject of women's health care is vast and requires perhaps a separate book. However, here I will just mention some Ayurvedic instructions for pregnant women.

1) Pregnant women should not use alcohol, tobacco, *bhang* (*Cannabis sativa*) or drugs which contain opium or its products. Follow nutritional therapy to cure minor ailments during pregnancy and do not take chemical drugs or other strong drugs.

2) Do not eat *pitta*-promoting things during early pregnancy. However, during the last two weeks of pregnancy, you should eat *pitta*-promoting nutrition because it will help facilitate delivery.

3) Take every care to avoid constipation during pregnancy. It is uncomfortable and troublesome for you, and bad for the baby's health. Some women suffer from anemia during pregnancy and they are given iron tablets. Iron tablets increase *vāta* in the body and cause constipation which leads to other troubles. Therefore,

cure your anemia by eating apples, *amla*, spinach, and tomatoes, rather than taking iron tablets.

4) Always eat a light, fluid diet that is nourishing. Take plenty of fresh fruits and salads. Do not eat preserved food. Avoid anything that increases *vāta* in your body. It will trouble you and your baby both. Make every effort to maintain your humoral balance, which may get easily disturbed during pregnancy.

Following are some remedies to cure sickness during pregnancy.

1) Make a syrup with crystal candy as has been described earlier. Add two powdered cloves in a few spoons of this syrup and mix well. Add cold water and drink when you feel sick.

2) Freshly squeezed juice from small, sweet oranges or other citrus fruits helps stop sickness. Make sure that this juice is not too sour, otherwise it will increase *pitta*. You can always add some crystal candy syrup into it.

3) Use crystal candy to sweeten your foods rather than normal sugar. If you may recall from the description of *rasas*, the crystal candy does not increase *kapha* as the sugar does.

4) Soak some cumin in lemon juice for a few hours and then let the juice dry in shade. When you feel sick, put a few seeds in your mouth.

5) Chewing cardamom is very beneficial to get rid of sickness.

Falling and Graying Hair

We have already discussed this subject in chapter 4. Here, I want to add that this problem has quite similar causes to those described for vision. The *pitta* and *kapha* vitiation leads to graying and falling hair. A dry and rough appearance to the hair is usually caused by *vāta* vitiation.

Baldness in men is another frequently occurring problem. You can take appropriate measures to prevent it. These precautions should be taken when you feel that you are losing more hair than getting new growth. Actually, hair falling is a normal phenomenon as new hair growth replaces the old. However, when this balance is disturbed and the lost hairs are not re-placed, you are heading toward baldness. The loss and growth of hair is variable during different seasons. In cold northern cli-mates where winters are very cold, people lose plenty of hair during the autumn and winter. In normal conditions, this loss should be compensated in spring and summer. However, when the humoral balance is disturbed, you slowly lose more than the new growth and ultimately there is less hair over a period of time.

From the Ayurvedic point of view, good hair growth is not only for beauty and appearance, for the density of the hair is in-dicative of general health conditions and the mental state. No-tice carefully that when you feel good and are cheerful, your hair has also a lively look, and when you are depressed and feel pes-simistic, your hair acquires a fallen and "lifeless" look. When you have problems with your hair, in one way or the other, they in-dicate your humoral imbalance, as well as a disequilibrium of the activities of your mind. Of course, I do not deny that some peo-ple may have problems with their hair at a very superficial level as they may be washing with strong shampoos or drying the hair with too much hot air from hair dryers. Besides, in the West, people (particularly women) tend to use industrial chemicals for dying and styling their hair which slowly ruin the hair. In my opinion, when people feel the need to dye their hair, it is indica-tive of anguish and frustration. You have already learned in chapter 7 and 8 that you must make an effort to face life situa-tions.

Worrying excessively, or psychological shocks also give rise to various problems with the hair. With profound grief and pain, some people turn gray within a few weeks. Indeed, to live in pain and grief is a lack of wisdom. As I have said earlier, you have to prepare yourself for death, sickness, or loss, and should not let yourself be destroyed by the happenings in life. You must always derive inspiration from others who have lost every-thing due to a war, or an earthquake, or any other catastrophe, but with courage and wisdom, have rebuilt and found reasons to live happily. Do not give up in life and do not let life situa-tions manipulate you and destroy you. Learn to live well in har-mony with this ever-changing, beautiful cosmos, and appreciate each day.

Following are some more suggestions for the care of your hair and for prevention of hair loss and graying.

1) Do not let *kapha* accumulate in your head. There are people who suffer perpetually from cold. These people get gray hair at an early age. Do not take a persisting common cold lightly. Get rid of it. The instructions to this effect have been given earlier in this chapter.

2) Sinusitis has adverse effects on hair and vision. Therefore, this problem should not be neglected and appropriate measures should be taken immediately.

3) Do the yogic practice of *jaldhauti* regularly so you do not accumulate *kapha* and the energy channels in the head can remain open. You should do purification practices from time to time and follow the other instructions to keep a humoral equilibrium.

4) Do regularly those āsanas recommended for preventing hair from falling and graying (see the section on yoga).

5) Make sure that your digestion functions well, your liver is healthy, and that you do not suffer from other gastric troubles. A sluggish liver and other digestive troubles promote hair loss and turn hair gray.

6) Regular care and Ayurvedic massage of the head is absolutely essential to revitalize the scalp.

10

SELECTION AND IDENTIFICATION OF MEDICINAL PLANTS

Y OU MAY RECALL that in chapter 2, I cited Caraka in reference to environmental pollution and its effect on the
properties of medicinal plants. This concept should be considered seriously in our times because our environmental pollution
has reached such catastrophic levels. Everything is grown everywhere by creating artificial climatic conditions. In India, elderly
people are constantly saying that food has lost its taste. Similarly,
medicinal plants also lose their properties with the changing environment so you need to be careful when you select a medicine.
Ask the shopkeeper about the origin of the substances you buy.
Do not buy plants grown near big cities or in other polluted
areas, or plants not grown in their original climatic conditions.

Climatic conditions play an extremely important role in de-
termining the properties of medicines. It is possible to grow plants
out of their natural environment, but due to the change in climate,
they may lose their pharmaceutical effect. To illustrate this, I will
give you an example of a plant used as food in addition to being
considered a mild drug. That is black tea. You may grow this plant
anywhere, but the original taste and flavor will be lost. Darjeeling
tea may be grown in the mountains in Turkey, but it cannot match
the taste, flavor and strength of the Himalayan tea. Several people
in Northern Europe have succeeded in growing the forbidden
plants of *bhang* (*cannabis sativa*) but much to their distress, they realized that the drug they grew had little or no narcotic effect. The
reason for this is that with the change of climate, the humoral
qualities of the plants are altered and they change the *rasa* of these
substances. In other words, due to a lack or an excess of sun, rain,
humidity, etc., chemical processes are hindered. Maybe some of
you have experienced herbs like thyme, dill, laurel leaves, etc., that

came from your home towns. They are distinctly moderate in their perfumes as compared to the same plants brought from Turkey, Greece, or southern European countries.

The second thing to consider is that medicinal substances should not be stored for a long time. With aromatic plants, you should crush some on your palm and check the aroma. Generally, aromatic plants should be dried in the shade. There is also a specific season for plucking them. For example, in certain cases, the new plants of the season are stronger pharamaceutically than old ones, whereas this may be just the reverse in other cases. This knowledge is very complicated, and I do not mean to say that you should collect herbs yourself. What I wish to convey is that you should carefully choose your place of purchase. Do not buy medicinal plants in tea bags. Keep the drugs in tightly closed boxes after drying them properly and store them in a cool place. Do not buy too much in quantity as time will make them ineffective. However, after preserving the medicines in certain preparations—like oil, or ghee, or syrup form—you may store them for a very long time. It is important to buy the right medicine. Don't get confused with various names. When you learn about a new medicine, ask for its name and its identification, which part of the plant should be used, its color, smell, etc., so you can correctly identify it. Always look at herbs and other plant materials carefully to register their shape, form, and color. Make it a habit to crush dried plants on your palm and observe the color and the smell.

Know your medicinal plants from their pharmaceutical properties, that is, from their *rasas* in the present context. Do not take drugs upon hearsay even when they are mild. Always consider your humoral nature before using any drug. The *rasas* of the drug should coordinate with your humors or you should take other precautionary measures so that the medicine does not disturb your humoral equilibrium.

For readers who are unfamiliar with Indian culture and Ayurveda, some descriptions of common medicines are included here. Pharmaceutical properties are also given. These herbs and medicines are generally used in Indian cuisine, but they are available all over the world where people from the Indian continent reside. These communities usually have their own shops where you can buy anise, *ajwāin, kalongī*, ginger, coriander, etc. You must call them by the original Indian names which I mention below, and identify them with the help of these pictures. If there is no such shop around where you live, try Chinese, Turkish, or other exotic shops. However, in these shops, the shopkeepers may not be able to help you much. Some of these medicines are available in the spice and herb sections of big European stores but they are usually old. The reason for this is that they do not sell much, and the herbs lose their pharmaceutical properties.

I mention the Hindi names of the medicines along with Latin and common English names. With the Hindi names provided here, you may not be able to get these drugs in south India, but in Indian shops in foreign countries these names are written on the packets. Some pharmaceutical properties are described but I do not want to get into complicated details of Ayurvedic pharmacology here. The purpose of these descriptions is to teach you to identify substances so can buy them anywhere in the world and use them. Besides *rasa*, I have also mentioned the *virya* of the remedies. The substances are classified in two principal categories—hot and cold. Hot are *pitta*-promoting, whereas cold are *pitta*-decreasing. This classification is helpful to determine their use according to the hot and cold seasons, and clarifies the precautionary measures you should take when you have to use hot remedies in the hot season and cold in winter.

Anise Seeds (*Saunf, Funiculum vulgare*)

As is clear from the name, the parts used are the seeds. Anise oil is used for relieving pain and perfuming other etheric oil mixtures. Anise seeds are light green in color and sweet in taste. They promote digestion and that is why in India they are generally eaten after meals. They have a strong perfume and help overcome the strong smell of garlic, onions, and other spices that are part of the Indian diet. Several medicinal qualities and the appropriate recipes have been already mentioned. Daily dose of seeds is 3 to 6 grams (½ tsp.) and oil is 5 to 10 drops.

Humors: Cures vitiated *vāta* and *pitta*.
Rasa: sweet, pungent, bitter.
Virya: Cold.

Lesser Cardamom (*choṭī Ilāyachī*, *Elettaria cardamomum*)

It is generally called the small or lesser cardamom as compared to the big one mentioned below. You should not confuse the similar names as the pharmaceutical properties are very different. Usually, this one is simply known as cardamom, as the bigger seed is little known and its use is limited to medicines only. In this book, I have used "lesser cardamon" as cardamom.

The seeds of this plant are used. They are in light green pods. Inside, the seeds range from light-brown to dark-brown-blackish. The darker seeds are better and have more perfume. The lighter ones are dried and not fully developed seeds. Therefore choose nice blackish seeds. There is also another variety of this cardamom available in the West which has a white pod. It is different in taste and properties and you should not buy it.

Cardamom is versatile and has good perfume to flavor both sweet and salty foods. It promotes digestion and cleans the mouth. It is very good for the care of your teeth. I recommend eating a cardamom after meals for digestion. If you find it too strong, eat it with some crystal candy. This does not take care of only your teeth. Cardamom cures sickness from indigestion, traveling or malaise due to any other reason. Keep it with you while traveling. Its regular use strengthens the heart. It is given to cure sore throats. It improves the voice and is highly recommended for singers. It should be kept in the mouth and slowly chewed. Keep cardamom with you and make it a habit to eat them from time to time. Daily dose is ½ to 1 gram.

Do not buy powered cardamom. Peal the pods just before use and crush them if needed.

> Humors: Cardamom is good for all the three humors and cures them if they are vitiated.
> *Rasa*: Pungent, sweet.
> *Virya*: Cold.

Greater Cardamom (*badī Ilāyachī*, *Amomum subulatum*)

This form of cardamom is also in pods. The pods are brown and the seeds inside are darker than the pods. As said above, peel the pods and crush the seeds just before use. The greater cardamom alleviates fatigue and cures low blood pressure. Do not use it if you are suffering from high blood pressure. It is good for curing coughs and is used in many cough syrups. It is very good to cure pain or fever originating from cold weather. Daily dose is 1 to 3 grams.

Humors: Increases *pitta*, but cures vitiated *kapha* and *vāta*.
Rasa: Bitter, pungent.
Virya: Hot.

Cinnamon (*Dālchīnī*, *Cinnamomum zeylanicum*)

The part used is bark. Its use is very common in Western cuisine now. However, people generally buy it powdered and therefore they are familiar with its taste and smell, but not its form. Its oil has pain-relieving qualities and its tea, along with the bigger cardamom, alleviates fatigue, fever, and pain. In headaches due to fatigue or cold, this tea is very helpful. Cinnamon increases *ojas* and purifies the blood. It has anti-fungal, antiviral and antibiotic qualities. Daily dose for the seeds is 1 to 3 grams (½ tsp.); the oil is 2 to 5 drops.

Humors: Increases *pitta*, but cures vitiated *kapha* and *vāta*.
Rasa: Sweet, bitter, pungent.
Virya: Hot.

Liquorice (*mulathī*, *Glycyrrhiza glabra*)

The part of the plant used is the root. As already stated, liquorice is fifty times sweeter than sugar. It is chewed directly, or its powder is taken to prevent bad throats and coughs. It is vision-promoting, nerve strengthening and memory-promoting. Its powder has excellent healing qualities. It may be applied on wounds as an ointment made by mixing its fine powder with ghee. Daily dose is 3 to 5 grams (½ tsp.).

Humors: Liquorice cures vitiated *vāta* and *pitta*.
Rasa: Sweet.
Virya: Cold.

Cumin Seeds (*Jīra*, *Cuminum cyminum*)

Cumin seeds resemble anise seeds but are light brown and slightly smaller in size. They are not sweet like anise seeds. They are rather pungent in taste. They increase the digestive power and therefore are frequently used in cooking. They also purify blood. Daily dose is 3 to 6 grams (½ tsp.).

Cumin seeds should not be confused with carvi or caraway (*Carum carvi*). The latter is darker in color, smaller in size, and slightly turned at the edges. There is also another variety of caraway (*Carum bulbocastanum*) in which the edges are not turned and it is darker in color and stronger in taste. Sometimes in Europe carvi is sold for cumin. As you have read in the last chapter, these two plants have different medicinal properties.

> Humors: Cures vitiated *kapha* and *vāta*, but increases *pitta*.
> *Rasa*: Pungent.
> *Virya*: Hot.

Ajwāin (*Trachyspermum ammi*)

I have mentioned *ajwāin* (there is no English equivalent) for curing different ailments during the course of this book. The seeds are used and they are very tiny, light brown in color, nearly heartshaped and have lines on their surface. *Ajwāin* has a strong smell which resembles thyme. You will get it only at Indian shops abroad. It is a very important medicine so try to get it. It very rapidly cures any malaise caused by indigestion. You should mix it with some salt and take it with warm water. You can also make a preparation of *ajwāin* by soaking it in some lemon juice mixed with salt and then drying it in shade. *Ajwāin* promotes the liver function and is especially beneficial for those who take alcohol often. It is also helpful for gastric troubles and cures lack of appetite. *Ajwāin* oil may also be used. A daily dose for the seeds is 1 to 3 grams (½ tsp.); oil is 1 to 3 drops.

> Humors: *Ajwāin* increases *pitta* and cures vitiated *kapha* and *vāta*.
> *Rasa:* Pungent, bitter.
> *Virya*: Hot.

Coriander (*Dhaniā, Coriandur sativum*)

Coriander seeds and leaves are used. Seeds are round and yellow. Both leaves and seeds are highly aromatic and are used in cooking. Coriander is useful for curing fevers caused by excessive heat. It is nerve and brain strengthening. It is used to cure the ill effects of an excessive intake of garlic. Daily dose is 3 to 6 grams (1/2 tsp.).

> Humors: Coriander is good to cure vitiated humors as it brings all the three humors in equilibrium.
> *Rosa*: Sweet, bitter, astringent, pungent.
> *Virya*: Cold.

Fenugreek (*Methī*, *Trigonella foenumgraecum*)

The seeds are used as medicine and the leaves are used as a vegetable or salad. The seeds are dull yellow and nearly rectangular in shape. It is available at health food stores in the West. Fenugreek is particularly good for curing vitiated *vāta* and related disorders. It is used to cure weak nerves. It is also given as a general tonic and is particularly good when one feels weak or has pain in the whole body. After childbirth, women are given fenugreek in sweet preparations made of flour and ghee. It enlarges the breasts and promotes milk. Daily dose of powdered seeds is 1 to 3 grams (½ tsp.).

It is suggested that you include fenugreek in your food as a spice to get rid of the *vāta* effect of many substances. In winter, you may germinate it and eat it as salad. In India, it is an important winter vegetable.

> Humors: It is particularly good for curing excessive *vāta* and related disorders.
> *Rasa*: Pungent.
> *Virya*: Hot.

Dill (*Soyā*, *Anethum sowa*)

This plant does not need much explanation or identification as it is available everywhere in the West. It is used often in European cuisine. The fruit and oil of this plant are also used as medicine. Dill promotes digestion. It cures minor fevers, lack of appetite, sickness and stomachache. It also cures painful menstruation. The daily dose of fruit powder is 1 to 3 grams (½ tsp);

oil is 1 to 3 drops. Dill water may also be used. The dose for it is 20 to 40 ml ($\frac{1}{8}$–$\frac{1}{4}$ cup).

> Humors: It cures vitiated *kapha* and *vāta*.
> *Rasa*: Pungent, bitter.
> *Virya*: Hot.

Kalongī (Nigella sativa)

Kalongī seeds are easy to recognize because of their black color. They are tiny seeds with one side round and the other conical. As is already mentioned, *kalongī* is very good for curing menstrual pains. It is a good medicine to cure *vāta*. *Kalongī* is good for promoting milk in lactating mothers and it is given to clean the uterus after childbirth.[1] Daily dose is 1 to 3 grams ($\frac{1}{2}$ tsp.).

> Humors: *Kalongī* cures vitiated *vāta* and *kapha*, but promotes *pitta*.
> *Rasa*: Bitter and pungent.
> *Virya*: Hot.

Clove (Long, Syzygium aromaticum)

The buds of this plant are used. It is easy to recognize them as they are brown and retain their form of a little bud with a tiny stalk. The cloves are hard and highly aromatic. Clove oil can be used to relieve toothaches by keeping the oil-soaked cotton at the place of pain. Clove has antibiotic, anti-viral and anti-fungal qualities. It is used in Ayurvedic tooth powders and is chewed after meals to promote digestion, for the care of the teeth, and to get rid of bad breath. It removes *kapha* and is very beneficial to chew for coughs and other respiratory troubles. Clove oil, along

---

[1] In Ayurveda, several substances are used to clean or purify the uterus and breasts. It is considered important to do this therapy after childbirth and generally from time to time. In Ayurvedic terminology, this reestablishes the humoral balance once again to ensure proper functioning after they have undergone tremendous physiological changes during pregnancy, childbirth and lactation. The physiological changes also occur with age, and therefore it is important to purify the uterus and breasts.

with other etheric oils, is used for pain relieving, inhalations, and to cure fungus infection on the skin. It increases blood pressure and removes blood impurities. People with high blood pressure should not take it too much. On the contrary, it should be used to cure low blood pressure by mixing it with big cardamom and cinnamon. These latter two have hot *virya* and clove has cold, and therefore a balance is created by the combination of these three. A daily dose is ½ to 1 gram (¼ tsp.) for the cloves and 1 to 3 drops oil.

Humors: Cloves cure vitiated *kapha* and *pitta*.
Rasa: Pungent, bitter.
Virya: Cold.

Cress (*Chansur* or *Halim, Lepidium sativum*)

Seeds of this plant are used as medicine and leaves are used as food. Generally a salad is made from the leaves. Cress is a blood purifier. Its paste with ghee is also used to cure skin infections. It is given after delivery as a general tonic, to promote milk and to clean the uterus. Cress seeds are easily available in health food stores. The seeds may be germinated in winter for making a salad. Daily dose of the seeds is 1 to 2 grams (½ tsp.).

Humors: Cress seeds are vitiated *kapha* and *vāta*.
Rasa: Pungent.
Virya: Hot.

Holy Basil (*Tulsī, Ocimum sanctum*)

I have mentioned basil often in various recipes during the course of this book. It is a home plant in India and is worshipped. In Hindu homes, a little lamp is lit in front of this small plant every evening. Its leaves are used to cure many minor ailments. This plant is also common in Southern Europe; however, it loses its pharmaceutical properties when grown in the colder climate of Northern Europe. The seeds of this plant may also be used. A daily dose of crushed seeds is 3 to 5 grams (½ tsp.).

The juice of the leaves (1 teaspoon) along with ½ teaspoon ginger juice and three grains black pepper should be given to cure minor fevers, coughs, colds and indigestion. For babies, one may give exclusively ½ teaspoon juice from fresh basil leaves, or alternatively, an extract prepared from dried leaves or powdered seeds. About 6 basil leaves with 3 black pepper grains taken everyday are a preventive against malaria, and are vision-promoting. Basil leaves should be dried in the shade and cannot be kept for very long. They lose their pharmaceutical properties. You should check that with the aroma of the plants.

> Humors: Basil cures vitiated *kapha* and *vāta*, and promotes *pitta*.
> *Rasa*: Pungent, bitter.
> *Virya*: Hot.

Turmeric or Curcuma (*Haldi, Curcuma longa*)

The tuber root of this plant is used. It looks like fresh ginger in shape. However, it has a bright yellow color and is easy to recognize. What you get in the market as a spice is the powder from these yellow roots. For medicinal use, curcuma should not be more than a year old. It slowly loses its pharmaceutical properties and becomes less effective. Curcuma is a blood purifier and cures allergies. It is helpful to cure skin problems. Curcuma therapy has been already described. It has antibiotic, anti-inflammatory properties and is used on wounds. Use of curcuma is good for pain and other minor problems in the breasts. Curcuma milk (see recipe in chapter 9) also alleviates fatigue and promotes strength. It is given to alleviate pain from internal injuries due to falls or accidents. I recommend that from time to time you take curcuma milk, especially in winter. Daily dose is 1 to 3 grams (½ tsp.).

> Humors: It cures all three humors if vitiated.
> *Rasa*: Pungent, astringent.
> *Virya*: Hot.

Margosa Tree (*Neem, Azadirachta indica*)

Margosa is a big tree that may grow to a height of 16 meters (50 feet). Flowers, seeds, leaves, and bark are used in various medical preparations. The oil from its seeds is used to cure boils and other skin ailments. Its oil is also used in medicines for curing diabetes. A decoction of *neem* leaves taken regularly saves one from any skin disorder and gives smooth skin, keeping away acne and pimples. In India, little children in the villages always eat *neem* fruits called *nimboli* during monsoons, and this dose saves them from skin disorders throughout the year. In Ayurveda, it is believed that one must eat certain blood purifying substances from time to time. They increase *ojas*, help the liver function, and are good for general health. Juice from *neem* bark mixed with honey is given to cure liver ailments and sluggish functions of the liver. *Neem* seeds are given in case of delayed and painful childbirth as they cause contractions in the uterus. *Neem* is also used to cure fevers. A decoction of leaves and bark is made for this purpose. A daily dose is 10 to 20 ml juice from leaves or fruits, 2 to 4 grams (½ tsp.) powdered bark, or 5 to 10 drops oil.[2]

Humors: *Neem* cures vitiated *pitta* and *kapha*.
Rasa: Bitter, astringent.
Virya: Cold.

Sacred Fig (*Peeple, Ficus religiosa*)

As is clear from the name, this is a sacred tree. Those of you who have visited India or Nepal can recognize it easily as it is always grown around the temples and there are statues of gods or little replicas of temples under the trees, along with various kinds of offerings and oil lamps. The fig is a big tree that spreads around and gives cool shade in summer. It grows nearly everywhere in India. Fruits and the bark of *peeple* are used in various medicinal preparations. Like *neem, peeple* purifies the blood. The powder of its fruits is used to cure coughs and other respiratory ailments. It

---

[2]I am very well aware of the fact that many of the readers of this book will not have access to *neem* products. If I were writing this book twenty-five years ago, you would see few of the above-mentioned plants in the West. With the increasing communication on our globe, I am hopeful that it will be possible to get *neem* products also. Our organization is making an effort in this direction and we invite various European and American importers to contact us concerning this. There is no lack of *neem* in India. It grows nearly everywhere in the country.

is given to facilitate pregnancy as it promotes sexual desire as well as increases the chances of implantation of the fertilized egg. Some other uses have already been described. It is not easily available in the West. Daily dose of its decoction is 50 to 100 ml (¼ to ½ cup).

Humors: *Peeple* cures vitiated *pitta* and *kapha.*
Rasa: Sweet, astringent.
Virya: Cold.

Ginger (*Adrak* [fresh], *Śunṭhī* [dried], *Zingiber officinale*)

The roots are used as both food and medicine. Chinese and Indian peoples have brought fresh ginger to the West. However, the dried ginger you get in the West is not comparable to *śunṭhī*, as in Ayurveda there is a special method for drying it. You may get this from Indian food shops. Do not buy ginger powder as it loses its pharmaceutical properties. You may make the powder yourself from *śunṭhī* whenever you need. I would recommend a regular intake of fresh ginger in your food except when it is very hot. It is good for liver functions and does not let the *vāta* vitiate. Black tea with ginger is a preventive for bad throats and ginger removes the acidity of the tea. Ginger should be given to children in one form or the other as it cures vitiated *kapha* and increases their appetite. Daily dose is 5 to 10 ml for juice and 1 to 2 grams (½ tsp.) of the dried root.

Humors: Ginger cures vitiated *vāta* and *kapha.*
Rasa: Pungent.
Virya: Hot.

Garlic (*Lahsan, Alium sativum*)

A friend from Germany once told me that he had never seen or eaten garlic until he was 18 and had gone to study in Berlin. His family in North Germany, near the Denmark border, still does not use garlic. If I had not had this experience six years ago, I would have left out the description of garlic, thinking everyone knows it. Besides, garlic deserves its Ayurvedic description because its benefits have been much advertised in recent years and sometimes people use it indiscriminately.

These days, there is a large variety of garlic in the market which may not be good for medicinal purposes. Use garlic that is smaller in size and is grown without fertilizers. From the Ayurvedic point of view, only fresh garlic should be taken as medicine. It is not possible to preserve the etheric oils present in garlic and preservation alters its humoral composition.

I will explain why garlic is so important in Ayurveda. It contains all five *rasas* accept sour, and that is the secret of its versatility in medicine. Garlic paste can be applied directly on the skin to get rid of pain. Generally one does not do so because of its strong smell, but you should remember this in an emergency. A regular use of garlic saves you from insect bites, hence it is a preventive against malaria and other ailments spread by insects. It is vision-promoting, and strengthens nerves, brain, blood vessels and the heart. It increases *ojas* and strengthens the general immunity of the body. It is a very good preventive medicine for arthritis because its regular use does not let the *vāta* vitiate. It promotes liver functions and digestion. Considering all this, I highly recommend the use of garlic in a small quantity every day. You may take one to two cloves of garlic every day. If you are a *pitta* person, crush the garlic with some sugar and take it with cold water. If you are a *vāta* person, take it with some ghee. If you are a *kapha* person, take garlic with honey. In case of vitiated *pitta*, do not take garlic. Pregnant women should not take garlic. An excess of garlic gives rise to restlessness and excessive thirst. To get over the ill effects of a high dose, you take a coriander decoction. A daily dose of garlic is 1 to 4 grams (1 clove) and you must find an appropriate dose for yourself according to your humoral nature. However, as a preventive measure, you may take the above-said daily dose. To get over the smell as well as *pitta* effect of garlic, chew anise and cardamom.

Humors: It cures vitiated *vāta* and *kapha*.
Rasa: Sweet, saline, pungent, bitter, astringent.
Virya: Hot.

Asafoetida *(Heeng, Ferula narthex)*

Asafoetida is an oily resin from a small tree which is about six feet high. It has an awful stink and that is why, despite its wonderful properties, I have not described it in the previous editions of this book. It is very difficult to use in most Western homes. You should make sure that you get pure, good quality Asafoetida. The pure substance is water soluble, makes water milky and does not leave any residue. It burns easily and leaves very little ash.

It is very "hot" in its Ayurvedic properties and thus cures vitiation of *vāta* and *kapha*, but enhances *pitta*. Its external application is pain relieving. It is especially good for curing chest pain, old coughs and whooping cough. It cures bladder infections and is also given to clean the uterus after childbirth. It cures delayed menstruation. It has an aphrodisiac effect. It is used externally as well as internally to cure impotency. Because of its *pitta*-promoting qualities, it is advised to use this drug in ghee. Add the required dose in hot ghee and heat another 30 seconds on a low fire. Eat this ghee with a soup or a vegetable preparation. The recommended daily dose is from 0.12 to 0.3 gm ($\frac{1}{8}$ tsp.).

> Humors: It cures vitiated *vāta* and *kapha*, but enhances *pitta*.
> *Rasa*: Pungent.
> *Virya*: Hot.

Nutmeg (*jayaphal, Myristic fragrans*)

Most of you are familiar with nutmeg, as it is commonly used in Western cuisine. Besides the seeds, the outer part of the fruit is also used. This is orange in color and looks like dried flowers. Nutmeg is used to cure vitiation of *vāta* and *kapha*. Its paste is applied externally to relieve pain. The paste is prepared in mustard oil to cure boils. Nutmeg paste is used to induce erections. It is applied to the penis and a betel leaf is wrapped around it.

Nutmeg is sleep-inducing and calms down a hectic state of mind. It is given to cure vomiting and diarrhea. It strengthens the heart. It is used to cure delayed and painful menstruation.

Daily dose of fruit or flower powder is $\frac{1}{2}$ to 1 gm ($\frac{1}{4}$ tsp.) and oil is 1 to 3 drops.

> Humors: It cures vitiated *vāta* and *kapha*.
> *Rasa*: Bitter, pungent.
> *Virya*: Hot.

IN CONCLUSION

Throughout this book, I have been talking about equilibrium, harmony, and balance, and have said that health in the context of Ayurveda is to tune oneself with the cosmic rhythm. We have been learning the equilibrium of the three humors—*vāta, pitta,* and *kapha,* and the three qualities—*sattva, rajas* and *tamas* in body, mind, environment, and cosmos. I have discussed various ailments prevalent in our technologically advanced civilization. The purpose of this book is to promote awareness that health is an individual responsibility, and that each of us should be aware of our food, our activities, our breathing, and all other mental and physiological phenomena. With all this, we can learn to ward off illness before it happens. While making this effort, we should be aware of the fact that environmental pollution, the use of pesticides, chemical fertilizers, and millions of other threats to health, leave us quite helpless. In a dirty environment, all kinds of pathogenic viruses and bacteria flourish. In addition, the fatigue of living in a big metropolis lowers our *ojas*.

In such environments, we all suffer. How are people with the Ayurvedic way of life better than others in face of such circumstances? People who have an equilibrium of the humors and a balance of the three qualities will be less vulnerable to epidemics and other health-damaging factors. People of the Ayurvedic way have shorter periods of illness and faster recoveries. In the long run, these people reduce the possibility of getting diseases when compared to those who do not take care of themselves.

An equilibrium of *guṇas* and the capability of evoking inner energy (*ātmaśakti*) makes us courageous and brave in face of stressful situations. The Ayurvedic way of life teaches us to face life rather than escape it. It teaches us not to accumulate worries, anger, aggressivity, and negative feelings. A slow churning of all this inside us over a long period of time bursts out in one form or another; it either gives rise to mental maladies or the madness of cells at a physiological level—I mean cancer. It is interesting to note that in the Ayurvedic tradition, a great emphasis is laid upon the release of tension and stress. *Vaidyas* (Ayurvedic physicians) and sages believe that worries, shock, stress, feelings of helplessness, fear, etc., may become the cause for serious maladies.

With this logic in mind, a person is forcibly made to cry if he/she does not do so on the death of a dear one. For these reasons, many rituals and ceremonies are performed on death. They help us realize the departure of a dear one and to make us, the remaining living ones, realize that nobody stays here forever. In this holistic way of health care, at other occasions also, the social, religious and spiritual rituals play a very important role in realization of the self and a consciousness of various aspects of our journey on this earth. For example, the beginning of pregnancy is marked by a ceremony which is associated with the commencement of special nutrition for the woman. Childbirth is accompanied by various religious ceremonies which include food and medical preparations to purify the uterus, to promote milk, and to reestablish the lost energy of the woman. Special offerings and ceremonies are made when one has escaped from a major danger. What does it mean? Besides showing one's gratefulness to the cosmic energy for giving life, the ceremonies bring an awareness of the state of shock and the emotions accompanying it. It is only by conscious realization that one is able to bring profound fears to the surface to get rid of them.

Special mantras to bring delayed monsoons, to avert excessive rain, wind, storms, or other catastrophes, worship of the five basic elements in one form or the other, pilgrim centers associated with them—all these ceremonies are meant to bring the consciousness of life, itself, its ever-changing quality, and our interaction with our surroundings. We, as living beings, are a part of the phenomena which make our universe. Worship of water, trees, earth, sky, wind, sun is nothing else but a realization of ourselves on this earth in relation to our environment. When we strain or sever our relationship with our environment, we are alone. The "inner" and "outer" parts of the individual are not in balance anymore.

The fluidity of the great rivers of the world, the stability of the earth, this is the *kapha* within us. There is also a sunshine within us, which is part of the bigger sun that makes life possible. Ether and wind are our movement, our thought process, and the flow of blood in our bodies. Let all these flow smoothly in rhythm with the cosmic orchestra. When too much wind erodes the earth, moves the mountains, when water sources become stagnant and infected, when big rocks block the passage of the wind, when fire becomes angry and converts all into ashes, we call them catastrophes. Let there be no catastrophes within us. For maintaining health, we ward off inner catastrophes by keeping inner harmony, balance, and a rhythm that coordinates with the cosmic order.

Each cell of our body is a world by itself. It can build, construct, ingest, destroy and do much more. Scientists sit in laboratories for many years, long hours each day, to understand receptors, release mechanisms, or communication within the cells. The more we know about cell biology, the more we are ignorant. Each discovery opens up a series of new questions. After a single cell, there is a bigger organization—the group of cells which makes an organism. Some cells die, others replace them, and all the cells in an organism perform a coordinated function, working in harmony with each other for the fulfillment of a goal. All our organs working together in harmony perform all the functions of our living being. Each smaller organization is within another bigger equally perfected organization. Yet, the bigger ones do not enclose the smaller ones (figure 1, page 268). Instead, the bigger emerges out of the smaller or the smaller terminates into the bigger one, forming a spiral (figure 2, page 268). This way, the whole cosmic reality is formed. The smaller, the bigger and the still bigger are connected to each other in continuum in such a way that a disturbance in one causes disturbances in all.

Now, let us see how an ailment is caused in this ordered, harmonized system. The spiral (figure 2) shows a smaller orga-

Figure 1.
The circle.

Figure 2.
The spiral.

Figure 3.
Unbalanced energy.

nization terminating into a bigger organization. In the present context of health, our bodily organization is made by an equilibrium of *vāta, pitta, kapha,* and *sattva, rajas,* and *tamas.* When these humors and qualities are not in balance, this organization is disturbed. *Vāta* moving too much, too fast destroys *kapha* and increases *pitta.* Too much *pitta* makes the nutrition system deranged. Obstruction of *kapha* hinders the passage of *vāta,* which is also the carrier of *pitta.* With this derangement, a disorganization within the system begins to take place. Some parts of this system leave the normal rhythm of the spiral, find their own direction, and become chaotic (figure 3). This newly created chaos, if not taken care of in time, begins to develop and forms an independent subsystem which is not harmonious with the cosmic rhythm. This is what a major disease is. This is how I look at a cancerous growth or a mental disorder. The two are not very different from each other. In a mental disorder, the patient creates his or her own world of reality, thereby making a subsystem within the thinking process. In a cancerous growth, the cells begin to multiply in an abnormal way; they are larger in size, they do not belong to the well-organized cells of the organism they originate from. They are rebel cells who have the capacity to invade other organs. Thus, they are capable of spreading and causing pathological effects in the whole body. They have their own organization and well-defined functions. That is why I call it a subsystem within the bigger order. But this subsystem is not in tune with the rest and thus causes pathological effects.

Balancing the three humors and qualities can be compared to a smooth flow of a river. Too much wind causes a disturbance in this smooth flow and disrupts the well-defined banks of the river. If this smooth flow is obstructed by a landslide or an accumulation of mud or stones etc., there are floods, destruction and the stagnation of water. This is what *kapha* does. Too much heat can dry the river water (*pitta*). What happens is that in a smooth flow of life, the disruptions caused due to imbalance of humors give rise to minor disorders. If these disruptions are not attended to over a long period of time, a disease develops. To put in a very simple words, a tumor will be caused due to accumulation of *kapha* at a specific place. This accumulation is a blockage. It hinders the passage of *vāta* and *vāta* begins to aggravate at that particular place. Since it is *vāta* which distributes nutrients of *pitta* (the fire, the energy), with its vitiation, *pitta* also vitiates at that particular place. With the vitiation of all the humors, that particular place begins to show pathological signs and struggles to survive. The struggle to survive is an innate quality of all living beings, down to the smallest unicellular animals. If it survives in the given abnormal conditions (abnormal proportion of humors), it develops its independent system (figure 3).

In essence, I wish to convey to you that all this fuss and effort to adopt an Ayurvedic way of life, in fact, is a longterm management of one's life, to make the best out of our existence on this planet. We all know that we are not going to stay here forever. All who are born are bound to die. Life is a passage between birth and death. It is not to avoid death that one needs an Ayurvedic way of life. It is to make life pleasant, harmonious, disease-free and long. If you are healthy now, think of maintaining this state of health until your last days. If you are troubled by small ailments, take them as a challenge, cure them, and uproot them with Ayurvedic methods and cures. If you have bigger health problems, struggle to get rid of them. Use the available methods to be healthy and then do everything to maintain that state of health. Remember always this Ayurvedic mantra—THE FIRST PRIORITY OF LIFE IS LIFE ITSELF.

If you recall the quotation from the *Upaniṣad* in chapter 5, comparing the body to a chariot, you should realize that a driver (intellect) will be of no use unless the wagon or chariot (body) is in a good condition. Reins (mind) are not required for a broken chariot. It is only a well-kept, properly functioning, chariot which can lead its owner (the soul or the real self of an individual) toward any desired goal. Whether your goal is to enjoy this life, or the lives after, or to gain immortality by merging into the Universal Soul, for all these, keep your "chariot" in a good condition and do everything you can to make it last a long, long time.

OM SHANTI

INDEX

Dr. Vinod Verma received a Ph.D. in Reproduction Biology from the Punjab University in India and a Ph.D. in Neurobiology from the University of Paris. She went on to do advanced research at the National Institutes of Health in Bethesda, Maryland and the Max-Planck Institute in Freiburg, Germany. At the height of her career as a medical researcher, Dr. Verma came to realize that the modern approach to health care is non-holistic, and that more attention is often directed to curing the disease rather than maintaining proper health. As a response to this lack of attention to the conservation of the health of individuals, Dr. Verma founded NOW, the New Way Health Organization currently housed at the Noida Center near New Delhi, India.

As President and spokesperson of NOW, Dr. Verma travels thoroughout the world offering lectures, conferences, and workshops about holistic living, and training people in alternative and preventative health care practices. She is also engaged in numerous research projects involving finding cures through yoga, nutrition, and herbal and mineral medicines. Among her other accomplishments are the construction of a second NOW center with an Ayurvedic garden in the Himalayas, and the creation of a living museum of herbal medicines with a nursery in the Delhi region, in addition to a center located in Freiburg, Germany.